FALLING
AWAKE

TODD L. BLATTNER

 FriesenPress

Suite 300 - 990 Fort St
Victoria, BC, V8V 3K2
Canada

www.friesenpress.com

ISBN
978-1-4602-0990-5 (Hardcover)
978-1-4602-0988-2 (Paperback)
978-1-4602-0989-9 (eBook)

1. SELF-HELP

Distributed to the trade by The Ingram Book Company

With Gratitude

to Kassia and Ian,

to my parents, Gary and Judy

and to Joy

GARY+JUDY 250 567 4850
TODD 250 944 0861
5 Schools
Chilian
Korean

Table of Contents

Out beyond ideas of rightdoing and wrongdoing, there is a field.
I'll meet you there.

Rumi

P197 – The ground in which
There is no need for action
or intended action in
any direction.
(Here in this place, that is
everywhere or nowhere,)
That contains everything
and also nothing!
that is also beyond mind
and also the source of
mind, in this place
that is not a place, there
is nothing else that needs
doing.
In all cases, in this field, not
beyond wrongdoing and
rightdoing, you are already
home.

199 All of us connected in the Field.
(Entire mass consciousness)

Acknowledgments

The writing of this book happened over a five-year period, but forming the ideas has been a process that has stretched across most of my life. I would like to express my gratitude to my father, therefore, for teaching me to look directly at my fears, tell the truth, grow in integrity, look at things from many perspectives, and extend thoughts to their ultimate conclusion in order to see the ramifications of actions. His unwavering love and support are foundation stones beneath the words on these pages.

To my mother, thank you for your lessons of unconditional love, communion with nature, care for plants and animals, connections with perspectives of energy and healing, making a home that was beautiful and safe, and always believing that it is better to put a net under the tree or a bandage on the knee than to say "no" to an adventure.

Much of what I have written has been shaped by the teachings of Luangpor Phosrisuriya Khemarito, spiritual teacher and founder of the Rombodhidharma Temple in Thailand. His patience, generosity, powerful presence, and "un-teaching" enabled my understanding of "Awakening" to move from something that may happen in a nearly impossible and distant future to something that is always present, already here and only hidden because of our great belief in other things. He changed my path from searching, to finding, and then pointed me to the place where even the path is no longer necessary. For this, no words are enough to express my gratitude.

The concepts in this book have also been shaped by the writings and teachings of many great teachers, including Adyashanti, Gangaji, Mooji, J. Krishnamurti, Nisargadatta Maharaj and Ramana Maharshi, and with deep devotion and gratitude to Jesus, and Siddhartha Gothama Buddha. They are brilliant lights of varying colours and intensities, shining out to all who wish to see. Their words are different, speaking so that different people can hear, but the heart of their teachings is the same. I am deeply grateful to live in a time when their teachings are available to so many, and deeply humbled by the gift of Truth that they offer. My own words are only fingers, pointing to theirs.

Writing a book can be a long and arduous task. I am grateful for the many people who helped and encouraged me along the way, including my parents, my brother Jeremy, Craig Hooper and Grace Hardy Gana. Very special thanks to Matt Shaw for agreeing to the painstaking job of editing the final manuscript and for giving me a push to continue when I really needed it.

Finally, thank you to my wife Joy. Our time together was short, but your gifts of dedication, faith, humility, service, joyfulness, gentleness and love will be with me for the rest of my life. By sharing your light so freely and openly with me, you helped me to see my own. I don't think that a greater gift can be given.

Introduction

The ideas and concepts in this book have been collected and refined from my life experience, which is now passing the fifty year mark, and so I think it is helpful to explain a bit of the context from which the ideas have come. During this life, so far, I have had experiences working in construction, commercial fishing, forestry, ranching, teaching, and counselling. I've been a father and a husband, a divorcee and single dad, a husband again and shortly thereafter a widower. I've traveled in many parts of the world, been a Buddhist monk, lived in a monastic community in Thailand, worked in isolated First Nations communities, organized a powwow, taken part in sweat ceremonies, worked with shamans, studied sciences and religions, and practiced meditation intensely. I've been to leper colonies in India and worked in one of Mother Theresa's homes for the dying, walked in slums and mountains, stayed in five-star hotels, and slept on the ground. I've talked with monks and gurus, beggars and millionaires, children and business people from many cultures and many religions in many countries, and through it all I have looked for the commonalities and deeper truths that seem to lie beneath what we normally perceive.

This book offers a way of seeing our lives that is somewhat different from what is taught to us by our culture. Most of the ideas are not particularly new, but they are not particularly common or well-understood either. A discerning reader may well ask, "Are these ideas just made up, or is there something that supports and validates them?"

In the end, the best validation is your own experience as you use the concepts and discover for yourself whether or not they work for you. In the meantime, however, it is helpful to start somewhere. This book is based on many supporting references, noted throughout the text. However, it is also based on real-life experiences, both personal and professional, a few of which are included here.

I think it is also important to note that there are many levels of understanding represented in what is written here. It is quite possible, and likely, that you will find different meanings and different understandings as you find changes happening in yourself. Something that irritates you or seems unreasonable today may be the point of growth or expansion for tomorrow. Something that you miss entirely in one moment may stand out like a flash of realization in another. It is helpful, therefore, not to treat this book as a novel, to be read quickly from cover to cover, but to use it more like a reference, to return to often, and over a fairly long period of time. If you do, you will find that your reactions to its contents change as you change.

I have found the ideas and practices in this book to be effective and helpful in my own life, and so I also want to communicate them to others—to friends and family who have expressed interest, to my children who are not particularly interested but, I hope, some day will be, and to other friends and like-minded people that I have not yet met. I hope that at least some of the words will be helpful to some people and that this can be a small part of the immense groundswell of change that is happening in the world. One by one, we each make our voices known in whatever way we can, and slowly the world around us begins to change.

I believe that change happens most effectively when it happens first on the inside. Simply by living in and following our own truth, each of us grows and expands and this expansion helps others around us to expand as well. It is my great hope that this book will help you to expand, to feel your own truth more fully, and to express your truth gently, respectfully, and without fear.

There is so much potential in every human being, regardless of what appearances may suggest. May you recognize this in yourself and in those with whom you are in contact. As you choose to see beauty and freedom both in you and around you, may you fall awake into the beauty and freedom that reside in all of us.

Chapter 1
A new worldview

"Any scientific data or personal observations that cannot be explained by the prevailing paradigm must be considered as magic—until an expanded paradigm accepts their lawfulness as an important part of nature's manifest expressions."

William A. Tiller, 2004

There is something both new and old that is happening on this planet right now. It can appear to be a quiet and subtle change. However, it is also a powerful change that will completely alter the way that we perceive ourselves, our world, and each other.

We are living in a time in which a number of factors have come together to cause an acceleration in the speed of growth of the entire race. Computer and information technology, nano-technology and bio-technology are working both separately and together in an accelerating and synergistic way with ramifications that we can't begin to comprehend. In addition, we are threatened with global crises that are threatening the existence of our race. We have become terribly unbalanced with the incredible power of our technology and the equally incredible lack of regard and respect for ourselves and our planet that has come with it. These factors, taken together, have accelerated the rate of change in the physical world around us. In order to survive, we have to change—and change quickly.

In this time of change, there is a strong polarization of intentions. On one pole are people who are afraid of change and are clinging desperately to old ways of seeing the world and themselves. These people are attempting to find a sense of security and stability by maintaining a worldview that no longer functions. They are supported by governments and media that promote state of emergency thinking, violence, and fear of everything from terrorists to criminals to germs and disease. For these people, solutions to problems generally involve a battle or getting rid of something. They also tend to simplify the world in an attempt to make things black and white and easier to understand. A complex world is a frightening world, as is one where the "good guys" and "bad guys" are not clearly defined.

On the other pole are people who see that there is a tremendous amount wrong with the world, and they want to fix it. These people have the very noble intention of righting the wrongs that they see all around them and of creating a better world. They can see so many things that are wrong, so many ways in which we are harming ourselves and bringing about our own destruction. People on this second pole experience a very real anguish and desperation to bring about a more sane kind of human existence. These people are also afraid and are also fighting, though their way of fighting is generally much gentler, or more internalized.

Between these two poles is a middle ground where people are gently beginning to understand that they do not have to fight anymore. By shedding the old perceptual filters and looking through new eyes, people are finding that they can see the world and its issues in a very different way. This new way of seeing represents a transition from one set of assumptions and beliefs about how the world works to another—from one worldview to a new and less limiting worldview.

For purposes of simplicity, this book will use the term objective/material to refer to the basic worldview that most of us were taught in school. In this worldview, matter is considered to be made of atoms that are like little solar systems made of solid and predictable particles,[1] where all particles are ultimately separate and disconnected from each other. Since atoms are made

---

1 This is the model originally hypothesized by Bohr in 1912. Although it does give a simplistic way of visualizing an atom, and explains many observable facts, it is very different from what is now known about the real nature of atoms. This model is still taught in most secondary schools because it is simple—but it does not give an accurate picture of reality.

of solid and predictable particles, the universe is ultimately "knowable", and it operates like clockwork gears, or an automated factory. Everything in it, including a human, is simply a cog in a wheel, a part of the machine—ultimately predictable, ultimately expendable, and ultimately interchangeable.

In addition, in this worldview, the way to know something is to take it apart and look at its pieces. Since the universe is thought to be divisible into tiny individual building blocks and to work like a machine, understanding something simply requires taking it apart. The machine is no more than a sum of its parts.

Darwinian evolution is also a strong cornerstone for the objective/material worldview. Darwin saw that in populations, individuals are relatively unimportant. Survival depends on genetic traits and these traits need to be passed on to future generations. Individuals are important for two reasons only: First for their numbers—more is generally better—and second for their survival capacity. Stronger and fitter is better while the weak are weeded out and left to die. This understanding of nature fits very comfortably into the objective/material worldview. People, like atoms, are understood to be solid, separate, interchangeable, expendable and ultimately predictable.

Though the objective/material worldview tends to be a violent, lonely and impersonal one, it is also a worldview that proffers a possibility of order, stability and predictability. It predicts that the mysteries of the universe are ultimately knowable and that humankind will one day be able to effectively remove all the problems which plague us. It has brought the human race as a whole to a place where many of us live in more comfort and with more power over the environment around us than ever before in human history. It has virtually eradicated many of the diseases that have plagued humankind since the dawn of our race, and it has helped to improve the physical lives of billions of people. It has provided the means to educate the human race, to lift us out of older and more limiting belief systems, and to set us on an accelerating path of growth and change.

For these and many other reasons, the objective/material worldview has been, and continues to be, very valuable. However, it is also limited and we have come to a point where the very worldview that brought us out of the dark ages could possibly plunge us back into an even worse condition.

As we will discuss later, every *truth* has limitations, and every worldview must eventually be transcended. We are currently living in a time where the human race is struggling to step up and out of one worldview and into a more expanded one, rediscovering on a global level what has been known to only a few in the past.

Of course, what we are stepping up and out into is not yet clearly defined. However, it does need to be called something, and so in this book I will refer to the new worldview interchangeably as the *quantum* worldview or *energy* worldview. These are terms that are in reasonably wide usage; they are based both on old spiritual and philosophical ideas and on relatively new scientific findings.

From the quantum perspective, atoms are a very small degree more solid than energy and electrons are clouds of energetic probability, ultimately unpredictable and ephemeral. Sometimes a wave, sometimes a particle, sometimes no more than a probability equation, electrons pop in and out of existence, pass from one place to another without transiting the intervening space, and generally confound the objective/material worldview's orderly way of seeing things.

In this emerging worldview, it is understood that an object is more than the sum of its parts. A leaf, or an insect, or a human, can be reduced to the atoms from which they are made, but the same leaf, insect, or human cannot be rebuilt simply by mixing these atoms back together again. There is something mysteriously *more* about the complexity of parts that make up a life form, and taking them apart will not answer the question of what that *more* is.

As we move away from the simplifying reductionism of the objective/material worldview, it also becomes clearer that even concepts such as evolution tend to lose their meaning if not understood and taken as a whole. Evolution occurs through a variety of complex interconnections of which survival of the fittest is simply the most easily observable. New information about the mechanisms of heredity is reopening the debate about evolution through acquired characteristics first presented by Lamarck in 1801. Epigenetics, the study of one such mechanism, shows that acquired characteristics can be inherited and that chemical, environmental, and behavioural influences on a parent can be passed on to children through many generations.

This kind of inheritance of acquired characteristics was considered to be impossible only a few years ago, so it is not completely illogical to consider that other even more subtle evolutionary mechanisms will be discovered. Evolution is far more complex than simple survival of the fittest and like other aspects of the objective/material worldview, reducing it to a simple formula does not accurately describe the real world.

In the worldview to which we are awakening, the basic structure of the universe is understood not as predictable solid particles, but as a vast informational field, animated by an action potential called *energy*. The idea of a field is not meant to be a closed and definitive description. It is simply a way of conceptualizing, and putting a name to, a vast creative matrix from which all else arises. Perhaps better ways of conceptualization will come along in the future.

Energy is a generalized term that probably includes a variety of different forms of potential for movement, action, or communication. Electricity is one form of energy that is more or less familiar to most people, and the equation $E = mc^2$ is a reasonably familiar reminder of the possibility of reducing any collection of atoms to the energy from which they are formed. Other forms of energy, such as prana, mana, ki (or chi) or life force energy have been known to mystics for millennia but are not yet scientifically accepted. These forms of energy are more subtle and still remain a mystery, though they can often be experienced and sensed by sensitive people.

The *Field* then, is the matrix, context or structural medium in which the universe (or multiverse) rests. It is also the repository of all information. *Energy* refers to that which moves, animates and communicates within the structure of the field and is itself a manifestation of the Field. As humans, we are made from—and animated by—the combination of Field and energy and we are interconnected within it.

In the quantum worldview, humans are not simply cogs in a gear of a machine, but active co-creators in an interconnected and excitingly unpredictable world where there is no end to what we can become. Call it God, call it universal energy, call it love, call it what you like—there is a joining principle and a connected oneness which we can experience. One by one, we are awakening to the *at-one-ment*.

The objective/material worldview is not able to incorporate adequately the advances of science into its framework, and this is one reason that it is beginning to change. We are beginning to understand that the framework for seeing the world that has taken us so far and given us so much is just as incomplete as the worldviews that it replaced—the mythical/magical understanding of the world that belonged to earlier humans, or the rigidly hierarchical and dogmatic worldview of paternalistic religious governments[2]. We are now outgrowing the objective/material worldview and beginning to *awaken* again; we are moving to a new and more powerful base of understanding.

* * *

As you read this book you will be asked to examine your assumptions and to turn inward in order to use your own mind and body as a laboratory. In this laboratory of your own mind/body/spirit system you can experiment with new thought systems, observing carefully how they affect you. You will be offered ideas, questions or experiences that you can try on—and then you can let your own experience be your guide. In this way, you can experiment and then decide for yourself what works for you.

However, as you read and practice, remember that everything discussed is based on a single idea and premise: *The fundamental basis of this universe is a unified field from which arises all objects and phenomena.* This can initially seem to be a kind of "so what?" statement. However, it is a radical idea that completely changes the meaning and purpose of being human.

---

2 According to Beck and Cohen in their excellent book *Spiral Dynamics: Mastering Values Leadership and* Change (1996) there are actually a series of worldviews that have been operative in the human race and which are still operative in individuals and groups. This book is somewhat complex but highly recommended for those interested in the idea of worldviews and their progression in individual development as well as the developmental progression of worldviews for the human race as a whole.

Like most radical ideas, such as "love your neighbor as yourself"[3] for instance, this is a premise which can enter into a person and create profound changes, or it can be filed in the "so what?" box and never be really used. An idea can be believed, considered, argued, intellectualized, but never truly accepted in a way that allows it to be lived.

We are not like the atoms visualized by Bohr. We are not separate. We are not even solid—despite appearances to the contrary. The principle objective of this book is to help you understand that you, and everything that exists, are connected. *You are a being of light and energy, literally made from the dust of stars, which is itself energy and vibration. You are the Field, and it is you.*

How might your concept of yourself and the world change if you fully lived from this perspective?

---

3 Mark 12:31, Holy Bible, New International Version

Chapter 2
A very brief historical perspective

"During the time men live without a common power to keep them all in awe, they are in that condition which is called war; and such a war as is of every man against every man."

Thomas Hobbes, 1651, Leviathan

"Every body continues in its state of rest, or of uniform motion in a right line, unless it is compelled to change that state by forces impressed upon it."

Sir Isaac Newton, 1687—Principia Mathematica

Over the course of the past five hundred years or so the human race as a whole has gone from the idea that the world is flat and the center of a relatively small universe to the realization that the earth is round and a small part of a solar system, which is a tiny part of a galaxy, which is one of trillions of galaxies, all of which could very well reside in a universe which is simply one among an infinite number of others.

This expansion of our viewpoint has corresponded with a paradoxical change of our collective sense of self. When the earth was the center of the universe, humans were important and their choices were important. They believed that there were Gods who listened to what they said and cared about what they did. There was a sense of connection to something greater that could alleviate some of the fear of being small, powerless, and insignificant that seems to be a perennial challenge of being human.

9

With the advent of science, the importance of God has diminished. Rather than putting our faith in a distant and generally unobtainable higher being, we have put our faith in what we can see, hear, touch, taste and smell. We have chosen to remove our belief in anything that cannot be measured or observed in a concrete way and in so doing we have become more powerful than ever before—at least in a material sense. The average human today, especially in the Western world, wields more power over nature than any king of even a century ago could have dreamed of. We have become powerful indeed.

However, the power that we have found has been countered by a growing disconnection from the world around us, disconnection from each other and on a deeper level, disconnection from ourselves. As we grow in power over the material world, we also grow in awareness of our own insignificance. Our world is no longer the center of the universe. In terms of size and relevance, it's no more than a grain of sand somewhere on the bottom of a particularly inaccessible part of a large ocean. All of our great endeavors and mighty achievements become somewhat questionable when seen on this scale.

Moreover, we still die. We still have violence and suffering, disease, hatred, and all of the pestilences that have troubled us for all time. In fact, along with this prosperity and power has come the ability to harm ourselves in more drastic, devastating and permanent ways than have ever existed in the past.

Despite our apparent power over the world around us, our view of who we are has become even smaller and more powerless than it was before. As world population grows, resources diminish, ecological damage expands and the planetary balance that sustains us becomes increasingly threatened, we live in a paradox where we are both the masters of the earth and a pestilence moving across it like a cancer. As our power grows, so too does our awareness that we could be snuffed out rapidly and completely—and no-one may be left to care.

This paradox is a difficult one to manage psychologically. Most of us deny that there is a problem, pushing the awareness into the depths of the subconscious mind where it festers in our dreams and adds to a sense of collective guilt. Some of us wear the guilt on our sleeves and try to "save the earth", but the problem seems so large and it is hard to escape from the systems in which we are trapped. It is hard to be authentic about saving the earth while still being completely dependent for survival on food, water, shelter, transportation, communication and energy that come from the system that is itself the problem.

While we attempt to deny that our growth and use of resources is a problem, we also continue to be ensnared in an economic model that demands continuous growth as a fact of survival. Lack of growth is a disaster, and though we all know that continuous growth in a finite environment is impossible, we cling to the delusion that things will be able to continue as they are. This is another mind-bending paradox—we know that our way of life will eventually kill us, or our children, or perhaps our children's children. However, we need to live now and change is difficult. These two realities are stressful and add to the sense of dis-ease and entrapment that fuels so much anxiety, depression, or anger.

We also live in a system that teaches that we are all equal but fundamentally believes in survival of the fittest. Darwin's observation that the fittest survive has become so much a part of every aspect of our culture that we no longer even question or consider it. The idea that we are individually important, equal, and worthy, but that only those of us who are strong enough, smart enough, pretty enough, or privileged enough will actually *make it* is yet another paradox that bends our minds and makes modern living difficult. This belief adds to our sense of vulnerability, powerlessness, and smallness, while at the same time promoting the idea that we should be able to achieve anything we want.

Those of us who live in democratic countries believe that we have a say in how our government works, but voting apathy speaks loudly of the underlying fear that a vote will really have no meaning. We think that we are free and that we have individual importance, but at a deeper level we believe that our thoughts and actions will have no effect, that we will not be heard, and that our voices ultimately don't matter. Like overindulged and under-loved children, we live in a dream of entitlement, substituting material gain and the search for social power for the connection and love that our armored hearts are aching for.

Ignoring the frightening depths of what it means to *be*, we seek to control the world around us, and for the past five centuries or more we humans have progressively placed our focus on perfecting this external control. We have taken the *outside* apart bit by bit, examined the pieces, and learned how to control them. We have applied the concept of control to our physical world, to each other, and to ourselves. We have learned to look for the cause of our problems outside ourselves and to effectively control or destroy this apparent cause in order to fix the problem.

As this push to control, fix or eradicate has moved forward, it has brought an age of material prosperity and progress. It has also brought an age of paradoxical disconnection, powerlessness, and depression. In an age where communication is instantaneous, ubiquitous, and global, people feel increasingly isolated, lost, and alone.

Although we have progressed incredibly in our search for power over nature, and over each other, the progress toward internal mastery has been much slower. Our ability to shape our own nature in positive and life-affirming directions has changed very little over the course of the centuries. Spiritual teachers have been telling us for thousands of years that we need to love each other. The Bible says that of all Jesus' teachings, the most important is love, and every great religion teaches that love and kindness are necessary for our own happiness, growth, and well-being, as well as our spiritual salvation or enlightenment. However, judging from the news reports that are broadcast at us constantly, we as humans are no closer to understanding or using this simple message than we were two thousand years ago. Like small children who know what they should do but can't seem to actually do it, we continue to act completely against our own best interests, even though we know (and have been told for millennia) what our best interests are.

The objective/material worldview has given us the age of reason, science, industry, medicine, the space age, and miracles of technology that would have been considered magic even a century ago. Unfortunately, it has also separated us from our sense of soul and self, disconnected us from our innate understanding of interconnection with our world, and removed our sense of higher purpose. As in Hobbes' quote from "Leviathan" at the beginning of this chapter, the objective/material worldview has reduced, and in many cases entirely removed, the common power that keeps us all in awe, and the impression we are given from our media is of growing disconnection, war, and fear. As individuals, we have become disenfranchised, disconnected from each other, cogs in the wheels of the machine, pawns and consumers exploited by big business whose only god is the aggregation of wealth and power. Living from the outside in, we have substituted the search for external control for the search for internal mastery, and we have therefore gained the world and lost ourselves.

At this time, however, all around the world, there is a growing awareness that the power and control that science has brought to us in the external world must be balanced, and that this balance will come from looking inward and applying an equally rigorous study to what it means to be human—from the inside out.

From within the objective/material worldview, as we have seen, a human individual is a separate, isolated, powerless and ultimately insignificant collection of inert substances which has somehow become aware of itself. From within this perspective, we have no reason to feel responsibility to anything or anyone. We are weak, puny, ultimately powerless beings who must seek power over others and scramble for whatever comfort or happiness we can find because there is nothing better. From within this perspective, consumerism, violence and competition are really the only options which are consistent with reality. We are simply living in accordance with our assumptions about who we are and this is why it is impossible to change the conditions of the world while still functioning within the current worldview.

To repeat the fundamental premise: *You are a being of light and energy, literally made from the dust of stars, which is itself energy and vibration. You are the field, it is you, and everything is connected.* This is a worldview which fosters internal mastery instead of external mastery, interconnection instead of disconnection, cooperation vs. competition and nobility of spirit vs. denial of spirit.

How might our world change if a majority of us lived this worldview as truth?

Chapter 3
Shifting up or shifting out
and a little leap of faith

The highest heavens belong to the LORD, but the earth he has given to man.

Psalm 115:16 (New International Version)

It is not contrary to reason to prefer the destruction of the
whole world to the scratching of my (own) finger.

David Hume, 1739—A Treatise upon Human Nature

It has been said that any behaviour is logical if you understand the assumptions which underlie it. In order to change the behaviour, the assumptions must first be known and then altered. When this happens, the behaviour will change itself. As mentioned previously, it is quite logical that there is widespread violence, anger, depression, disconnection, abuse of drugs and other forms of disrespect of self, other, and planet. The belief system on which Western culture is now founded, and to which much of the rest of the world aspires, is based on the premise that we are powerless, insignificant and ultimately purposeless beings. This is glossed over with delusions of power and grandeur in our control of the external world. However, deep inside we cannot quite hide from the knowledge that we will die and that none of this control or grandeur will go with us. Moreover, we cannot completely hide from the fact that we are killing our world, that our own death is hastened by our actions, and that there is no escape. How can this not result in the anger of powerlessness and helplessness?

A very large and growing number of people have lost their ability to believe in traditional religion but have not found something with which to replace it. Even those who still believe in a spiritual tradition often find their beliefs to be seriously challenged and threatened by the objective/material worldview. The current growth-based economy and political and business worldview based largely on the idea of survival of the fittest is hard to escape. Add to this the underlying belief that we are the result of random evolutionary mutations, programmed by natural selection to compete, reproduce, and die, and one is left with a certain amount of bleakness in outlook—as well as with very little space in which to place spirit. For most believers, spirit happens only in the cracks and spaces that are left over when everything else is done.

Without an acceptable substitute for the structure and purpose that is provided by religion, we are left with little to help us find a sense of comfort or stability and even less to determine how we should act. I have met many people who think of themselves as "recovering Catholics" or who have given up one religion or another but are still haunted by fears that their choice may be wrong. Moreover, they are confounded by a lack of something new or better with which to replace their faith. This often causes a sense of tension and unsettled searching. The religion that they came from has ceased to explain adequately their own experience in the world, but there is nothing better to turn to. The secular world (and science) provides many answers and explanations, but these explanations are lifeless, empty, and unsatisfying. There is enough *truth* in scientific answers to point out the inadequacy of religion, but there is not enough *life* in them to give us comfort.

An example of this is the theory of evolution, which has been reduced to survival of the fittest by Western culture and embraced wholeheartedly as a doctrine for control, competition, and domination. Despite its obvious scientific usefulness, evolution has had dire social and spiritual consequences. Along with Newton's idea of the clockwork universe, Darwin's survival of the fittest observations have propelled us into a profound state of disconnected limbo[4], where the only identifiable purpose for life is to get as much as we can while we have the chance, pass on our genes to the next generation, and out-compete everyone we can. The world of business has very happily adopted these values and is in the process of expanding them to the fullest extent possible. Unfortunately, the result of this is corporate actions that tend to fit criteria for antisocial personality disorder[5] and a social value system that responds to profit and loss statements rather than considering what is good for humans.

It should be noted, however, that spiritual traditions have also helped to create the present situation. The idea of survival of the fittest, as well as the control of the external world, would not have been so wholeheartedly adopted had not the Bible proclaimed, in the following passage, among several others:

> "Be fruitful and increase in number; fill the earth and *subdue* it. Rule over the fish in the sea and the birds in the air and over every living creature that moves on the ground."[6]

This we have done, with such amazing success that we are now on the brink of destroying ourselves and that over which we "rule". In our quest to rule and subdue we have driven thousands of species to extinction and are working very hard at depleting the ocean's ability to sustain life, changing our climate, and paving over our sustaining ecosystems. We have also expended incredible amounts of energy on attempting to rule and subdue each other, inflicting unimaginable suffering on each other in the name of faith and of the particular version of God in which we believe.

---

4 This is not to blame it all on Newton and Darwin. Their ideas have been immensely positive and useful and certainly were not intended as foundations for a global neurosis. In addition, Newton and Darwin are by far not the only thinkers to have contributed to the current dominant worldview. However, their ideas are extremely prominent and fundamental to this worldview and so they have been singled out here as a way of symbolizing all of the rest.

5 This disorder is characterized by persistent disregard for, and violation of, the rights of others and includes deceitfulness, aggressiveness, and lack of remorse for one's actions.

6 Genesis 1:28 (Holy Bible, New International Version). Emphasis on the word "subdue" added by the author.

There is a story that is often told of an old man living in China with his family many years ago. The old man and his family were poor farmers, living a life of meager subsistence from what they could grow on their small farm. They had few animals, and the work was very hard.

One day, a horse came wandering into their farm from somewhere beyond the mountains. All the family rejoiced at their good fortune, knowing how much help the horse could be in their lives and how much it could help with their work. However, the old man did not rejoice along with the rest. He just sat and watched and said "Could be good, could be bad—who knows."

A few days later one of the old man's grandsons was trying to break the horse for riding. He was bucked off and broke a leg. Now the family members were all in despair, crying and wailing because of the great bad fortune. This was a strong young man and now he would be unable to help in the fields. However, the old man did not join in with the crying and despair. He just sat and watched and said, "Could be good, could be bad—who knows?"

Not long after that an envoy from the Emperor came with soldiers to the farm looking for young men for the army. The young man who had broken his leg was of fighting age, but he was passed over because of his broken leg. Once more the family rejoiced at their good fortune and gave thanks for all of the circumstances that had saved the young man from service in the army. Once more, however, the old man simply said, "Could be good, could be bad, who knows?"

For better or for worse, both religion and science have worked together to create the world situation in which we now find ourselves. Together they have formed the belief systems and worldviews that have created the results that we now see and the conditions in which we now live. Both good and bad has come of this, as well as both peril and opportunity.

However, it seems to be increasingly clear that the worldview that we have been using is no longer working well and that the solutions that it offers are no longer adequate for the complexity of the problems that we face. Now we are faced with the choice to either shift up— to a new way of seeing the world and how we fit into it, or to eventually be forced to shift out—to the logical conclusion of our present path which has every indication of being death and whatever may or may not lie beyond.

Unfortunately, perhaps, the first steps of change require a small act of faith. Shifting *up* requires letting go of the familiar and habitual beliefs with which we have been raised and starting the process of rebuilding the way that we understand ourselves and the world around us. Shifting *out* is simpler—it requires nothing more than continuing to do what we have always done. However, when you do what you've always done, you get what you've always gotten. The world appears to be on the brink of not being able to handle getting what it's always gotten for much longer. A new perspective is badly needed.

The most fundamental shift between the worldview of the new awakening and that of the objective/material perspective is the idea of *energy,* in the quantum sense, as the fundamental building substance of all things, rather than *particles* and it is this fundamental shift that requires a modicum of faith—or trust, whichever word you prefer.

The energy perspective is supported by science—but only at the quantum level. There is as yet little scientific evidence that quantum level effects and processes have any measureable effect at the macroscopic level of humans, animals, and observable physical life. This disconnection between the world of the very small—which is our most fundamental reality—and the reality that can be perceived by our five senses, is what causes the difficulties. In order to begin to experience energy we first have to be able to learn to experience very subtle sensations and to use neglected parts of our minds. This requires having a small amount of trust—trust in our ability to try new things, to let go of old assumptions, and to believe that we can experience the world in a new way.

Among the many arguments that can come up when making this shift, and arguing against this small bit of trust, are the simple questions "So what? So the universe is based on energy. I can't feel it and it doesn't affect me. Why should I care?" These are valid questions and can only be answered by taking a step of trust and by having a willingness to experiment. A blind man can't know if a room is lighted or not and can't understand how helpful the light is unless he learns to see. If he trusts a doctor, has an operation and can then see, the helpfulness of light will be obvious. In exactly this way, as the depth and meaning of the energy paradigm begins to be felt, it is easier to understand its power to have a positive effect on everything we perceive, choose, and do.

The idea that all matter (including the matter that makes up people) is based on energy has been around as a scientific fact for more than a century. It has also been around as philosophical teaching in many traditions including Taoism, Buddhism, Hinduism, Sufism, Cabalism, and the mystical branches of Christianity for centuries—and in some cases millennia. Manna, Chi, Ki, prana, vital force, bio-energy, orgone, Ruach (Hebrew), Baraka (Islamic tradition), Holy Ghost—there are many names, but most ancient societies had a concept for a kind of energy or force that animates life and that lies at the base of what we think of as being solid and real.

The choice to *believe* in energy is an important one. The experience of energy is subtle and subject to interference from the mind. Since everything we can experience is ultimately filtered through the mind and the beliefs that it has learned to cling to, disbelief in something can effectively filter it out of our awareness. This is especially true for faint and subtle phenomena, and the experience of energy is initially very subtle. You can turn off your ability to feel it or experience it simply by believing that it doesn't exist or by believing that even if it does exist, you are not good enough or sensitive enough to detect it.

It can be argued that if belief is a factor, then belief is a cause and the whole energy paradigm is simply a new religion, another faith. Although this is a possibility, it is quickly apparent once you begin to experience your own energy that there is something very real going on and that there is an exciting new world to discover. It also becomes evident that your experience can be verified, duplicated and corroborated by other people's independent experience. However, the first steps require a willingness to allow your own experiences to be your teachers.

Because of this, it will be helpful for you if you approach the ideas that you will encounter in this book with a spirit of experimentation. This requires a mind that is open to trying things that are new, even (and especially) if they seem strange and if they challenge what you presently believe. As an old friend often told me, "If you're going to change, you have to actually CHANGE." Awakening starts with the realization that the world is much more mysterious and wonderful than you have believed in the past. A step in experiencing this is to learn to experience yourself as a field...

Chapter 4
Energy and fields

The limits of my language mean the limits of my world.

Ludwig Wittgenstein, 1922. Tractatus Logico-Philosophicus

New opinions are always suspected, and usually opposed, without any other reason but because they are not already common.

John Locke, 1690. Essay Concerning Human Understanding

There are many sorts of fields. The kind of field most non-physicists generally envision is a place to grow something—say potatoes or wheat, or a place for physical activities, like a football field.

However, in physics, a field can be considered as a space of two or more dimensions in which each and every point contains structured information. For instance, a computer screen operates in two spatial dimensions plus time, and it contains a certain number of points called pixels. Each pixel represents a quantity of structured information indicating a location and a colour value which changes over time. Since the information contained by each pixel is communicated, as well as mediated, by an electric current, the change of value in each pixel also creates a tiny magnetic field, and this field can be detected at a distance from the screen.

A computer screen, therefore, is an informational field. It is composed of components that appear to be solid (the physical screen), components that change easily (the colour state of each pixel), and components that are pure energy (the electric signals that mediate the colour changes). Given a sensitive magnetic sensor, information on the screen can be detected without actually seeing, or touching, the screen.

This analogy can be applied to help visualize the human body as a field. The human body operates in three dimensions plus time, and the information carried by our field is much more complex than the information carried by a computer screen. However, we are, at our most fundamental level, a collection of electromagnetic interactions, all working together within an informational space that can be thought of as a field. Our physical body is the densest part of this field but is not the only part. Our field also extends out from the physical part and interacts with the fields of other living and non-living things around us. Our fields help to extend our senses and perceptions.

For the purposes of visualizing the human body as an energy field, we can start with an image of a kind of field with which most people are familiar—a field of wheat. The wheat field is defined by a physical boundary—the edges of the wheat mark the boundary of the field. It is contiguous (continuously connected) over a certain area and an observer would notice that it has a look of similarity throughout—same crop, same general colours, etc. Although the field is filled with millions of individual plants, from a distance the individual nature of each stalk of wheat is hard to see. Go a bit closer and these individual plants can begin to be discerned. Closer still and details of each plant can be seen—the tough hollow stalk, long slender leaves and terminating seed head of lumpy kernels, each with a long protective spike. Walk through this field and all of one's senses can be engaged—the feel of the wheat brushing past one's legs or the rough hardness of the kernels in your hand, the smell of earth and the light pungent scent of the ripened plants, the resistant hardness of a kernel in your mouth and the crack and crunch as it gives way followed by a flat and floury taste, the sound of wind rustling through the leaves and the image of a golden ocean, waves rolling ahead of breezes playing in the fields.

From the physical perspective, walking through the wheat field with all of our senses engaged is assumed to give us an accurate picture of reality. However, even staying with what can be discerned with the five senses, the experience of a wheat field is very different for different people. A hunter may walk through the field and hardly notice the wheat at all as he is intently focused on looking for a pheasant. A farmer may notice the wheat itself in great detail, checking for disease, looking for weeds, noticing the overall health and stage of growth, but perceiving it all through the lens of understanding that this is a *crop* and seeing it on a macroscopic level. A scientist may study an individual wheat plant, take tissue samples, and examine individual plants under a microscope. She may see the cellular structure but may miss the interactions of individual plants with each other, with the soil, and with the micro-organisms present in the soil and air. What we focus on—and perhaps more importantly what we don't focus on—puts huge limitations on what we perceive.

Focus is only one of the limiting factors on what we are able to perceive. Our senses are also severely limited, each capable of perceiving only a very small range of their respective media. The eyes, for instance, can see approximately 3×10^{-15} percent (that's a percentage that begins with 14 zeroes and ends in 3 or 0.000000000000003%) of the entire electromagnetic spectrum by wavelength. To put this in perspective, the entire surface area of the earth is around 510 trillion (5.1×10^{14}) square meters. If we saw only as much of the earth's surface area as we can see in the electromagnetic spectrum, we could only see a piece of the earth about 12 cm on a side—not big enough to contain an adult human foot.

The range of possible sound frequencies is somewhat smaller than the electromagnetic spectrum but we still miss a significant amount of what it is possible to hear. The human ear can hear sounds between about 20 hertz and 20,000 hertz and sounds can conceivably range up to about 34 million hertz at sea level, so we hear about 0.06% of all of the possible sound waves that are out there. Though it is more difficult to quantify the senses of smell, taste, and touch, we can get approximate ideas by comparing our sense of smell to a dog's, our ability to distinguish separate tastes to the number of chemical compounds that exist or our ability to feel to the total range of pressure and temperature that is possible. Even without considering such things as neutrinos (which are constantly passing through us but are virtually undetectable), dark matter and energy (approximately 95% of the known universe), and the possibility that there could very likely be whole spectra that we haven't yet even imagined and so haven't looked for, I think that the point can be fairly made that we miss quite a lot of what is going on.

Scientific sensing devices have expanded enormously the range of what we can detect. Though there are still numerous possibilities for expansion and huge areas where even our devices are deaf and blind, they can help us to become aware of more than what our senses can tell us. Returning to the wheat field analogy, scientific sensors can help us to examine the wheat plants more closely and to see that the apparently physical stalks of wheat are built from cells, each cell with its own ability to produce more like itself and to work together with billions of its fellows to produce a life form. Each cell communicates with other cells and has its own form of awareness in that it is able to fight off attack from enemies, react to environmental changes, and use energy to maintain a dynamic state of equilibrium that we call *life*.

Science can now also tell us that each component of the cell is made of specific molecules, which are collections of atoms, which are collections of sub-atomic particles, which are vibratory phenomena that can take on the aspect of a physical particle, a vibratory wave and at perhaps the most fundamental level, simply a mathematical probability to exist. However, science does not yet have a way of conceiving, sensing, or measuring all the ways in which these components interact with each other.

All these levels, from sub-atomic particles through to the macroscopic wheat field, somehow manage to harmonize with each other in such a way as to produce a form that is relatively stable over periods of time that are perceivable to humans. As we go up the scale from the extremely unstable and ephemeral sub-atomic particle to the slightly more stable atom, the still vibrating but more predictable molecule, the more stable cell, and finally, the organism, we see an increasing degree of stability over time.

This apparent temporal stability is an illusion—no object is actually constant for even a nanosecond. And yet, our human perceptions lead us to believe that the objects around us, our bodies, our universe, are stable and predictable. A person walking through the wheat field is under the impression that the stalks of wheat around her are still the same stalks if she turns around and looks behind her as they were when she first passed through.

She is also under the impression that the person who turns around to look is the same person who recently made the trail through the field. Neither of these assumptions is true in the sense that every atom of every particle of the person, the wheat, the soil, has vibrated, changed, moved, and transformed. Trillions of chemical reactions have taken place, quantum particles have popped in and out of existence, and the entire fabric of what we think of as reality has shifted like restless water. Each particle is a probability field without physical solidity, and our material nature is ephemeral, changing and—at least in the realm of the very small—unpredictable. Still we walk blithely through the world assuming that what we see is based on something solid, stable and knowable.

Another important aspect of our assumption of a solid basic particle from which everything is formed is the assumption that everything can then be divided into separate pieces. A foundational concept of the objective/material belief system is the idea of *reductionism* in which all things are ultimately divisible into inanimate and separate pieces, and the connected understanding that each thing or person that we see is ultimately separate, individual and unconnected to other people and things.

However, this assumption is in complete opposition to what we now know about the nature of the universe[7]. Going back to the wheat field, it is not simply a field full of individual clumps of inert chemicals that have developed an ability to reproduce themselves. It is in reality a vibratory phenomenon composed of harmonic interactions among trillions of energy/probability fields combined in such a way as to produce a relative temporal stability of form that appears to us to be a field of wheat. From the base up, whatever the substance of the wheat field may be, it is not individual and

7 In fact, all of the old paradigm assumptions of physics have been shown to not hold true. The old paradigm foundation stones of *reality* (the universe exists if we look at it or not), *locality* (objects can only be influenced through direct contact by a mediating force or object), *causality* (the arrow of time goes in only one direction and there is therefore a cause-effect connection in all events that cannot be changed), *continuity* (there are no discontinuous jumps in the fabric of space/time) and *determinism* (things progress in an orderly, clockwork sort of way), have all been shown to be untrue in the Quantum world, and are beginning to be questioned on the macroscopic scale as well. One book that discusses the data supporting this is *Entangled Minds: Extrasensory Experience in a Quantum Reality.* (Radin, 2006)

disconnected particles. Each part of the wheat field is a tiny field in itself, interacting in a larger field in which all parts are connected and inter-related.

Visualize the field of wheat, wheat stocks blowing in the wind, stretching out toward the horizon. Now imagine the solidity of this picture dissolving in your perception so that you can see the field in its nature of constant vibrating change. Each particle is a quantum expression of a field, connected in a matrix with all other particles. The wheat field you see becomes a slightly blurry vision of motion, space, and energy moving. Like sitting in a movie theater and suddenly remembering that the story you are watching is simply a pattern of moving lights on a screen, your perception of the wheat field changes to realize that it is a pattern of energy expressed on the background of a connecting field principle. It loses its solidity, its disconnection, its pre-dictability. In this new way of seeing it, the wheat field is completely different from anything you have ever experienced before, or expected. Every moment it is new, renewed, changed—and you are not separate from it. Your own body/mind complex is interacting with the wheat field, is a part of it, and is connected to it.

Although I've repeated this in several ways already, I will say it again because its importance is easy to miss. Like all fundamental, and basically simple, things, the mind tends to miss the significance and float over this kind of idea with a "so what?" attitude. It is not until we begin to experience the idea for ourselves that we realize how deeply it touches our lives. So, to say it again, the important paradigm shift, or change in basic assumptions, that needs to be made here, is that the basic unit of existence is not, as the Greeks believed, a solid particle of matter that is too small to see. We cannot simply keep breaking a piece of matter in half over and over again and finally end up with a piece of matter that can no longer be broken, and that, therefore, forms the basis of all things (as suggested by Democritus in 460 BC). The basic unit of our existence is not something solid, tangible, or predictable.

In fact, the best current estimate of the basic unit of existence is an energetic informational matrix or field[8]. The information in the matrix is the complex set of parameters which determine what sort of particle is going to appear in which specific part of space at what specific time in order for a stalk of wheat, or a human, to exist. At the physical level, the highly volatile nature of the basic units of existence is dampened by successive levels of harmonic interaction. This successive dampening of the volatility results in "matter" and our illusion that the world around us, including ourselves, is solid.

If we understand that the apparently solid objects around us are based, ultimately, on information and that this information is in the form of an energetic field, interacting beyond the boundaries of what we see as the physical form, it can begin to change our perception as well as our ability to perceive. If the world is made from constantly changing fluid fields of energy, it is a very different place from if it is made of solid, separate objects. In one way of perceiving, a field of wheat is just a field of wheat. In another, a field of wheat is an almost magical vibrating mystery, a field of information and energy manifesting in physical form, a field of which we are an integral and intimately connected part.

The shift of perspective that comes from seeing oneself, other people, animals, plants, and objects all as field phenomena is at first very subtle. It does not change the basic experience of our five senses. However, it does open a perceptual door and change the rules with which we interpret the information that our five senses collect. Opening this door allows the mind to become open to the possibility that there is more to see or experience and that there may be new ways to interpret experiences. It also opens the door to the possibility that we may affect the world around us in ways that we have not previously considered.

When this mental doorway is opened it, is the first step in awareness of a paradigm shift that profoundly affects everything from health to relationship

---

8 Further discussion of the possible forms that this field could take, and of the scientific experiments supporting the existence of a field are discussed in *Some Science Adventures with Real Magic (Tiller, 2005), Entangled Minds: Extrasensory Experiences in a Quantum Reality (Radin, 2006), The God Theory (Haisch, 2006)*, and *The Field: The Quest for the Secret Force of the Universe (McTaggert, 2008)*, among others.

to business to lifestyle. For instance, if *I* am a body and this body is made of solid particles that operate in ways determined by specific chemical and physical rules, my physical health can only be affected by direct physical manipulation. Chemical drugs and medicines and surgical procedures are the only things that will have any effect on conditions that are causing me to be ill. Things like touch for health, Reiki, and various other forms of energy healing can only be seen as silly quackery.

If, however, *I* am an informational field, manifesting in at least four dimensions (three physical dimensions and time) as a physical body, it opens rather a wider range of options for how to deal with illness and injury. If the mental step to fields can be made, energy-based practices become much more evidently valid, as they deal directly with the field or with the information from which it is derived. It becomes obvious that dealing directly with energy or information is a deeper and more subtle way of healing than direct physical or chemical intervention. The physical level of medicines and surgery are still valid, but there are deeper levels of possible influence.

One of these deeper levels is demonstrated by the placebo effect. This is the well-documented ability of people to heal themselves when they think they have been given medicine or surgery that will make them better. Many studies have shown that sugar pills work as well as, or even better than, the real medication and that the human body has tremendous powers for self-healing and regeneration. In fact, in order for new drugs to be accepted for commercial distribution, they must undergo comparison tests with a placebo and be shown to have a significantly greater rate of success. Many drugs fail this test.

Another example of healing from a deeper level than traditional medication or surgery is found in the huge numbers of people who have had cancerous growths that mysteriously disappear, illnesses that go away on their own despite the inability of medical science to explain why, and of healing that takes place via the touch of hands or from a distance without touch at all. The placebo effect, spontaneous remission of growths, and healing by touch or from a distance are not possible within the objective/material worldview's physical framework. Since these phenomena are not possible within the objective/material framework, evidence of their existence tends to be actively resisted, rejected, and discounted.

Opening one's mind to the possibility of being more than a simple collection of tiny bouncing pool balls or particles, operating in mechanistic ways also opens the door to many more possibilities. Our concept of who we are and the power of what our minds can do has not caught up with what both science and psychics are telling us, and this disconnect is becoming more dangerous. We need to wake up to who and what we really are.

If *I* am the physical manifestation of an informational field, then changing the underlying information can have huge effects on how I feel. This is seen easily in counselling situations when deep beliefs are examined. People are able to change beliefs that result in depression, for instance, which then has far reaching effects on their physical health, social interactions and general well-being. Changing deeply held beliefs can also lead directly to physical healing such as remission of cancerous growths or of chronic debilitating disease. Although these kinds of remissions and healings are generally anecdotally recorded and do not meet the criteria for full scientific verification, there is also enough evidence building to make it difficult to ignore the possibility that something is happening[9].

A first step in seeing the world as a field, then, is to practice perceiving oneself as a highly complex and structured collection of information which simply manifests as a physical body. Changing the assumption of self as a collection of particles operating in mechanistic ways to self as a dynamic field of information opens the door to slowly redefine everything that we think

9 It is difficult to document these kinds of anecdotal recoveries in a way that can convince those of us who are skeptical about their reality and even harder to explain why they happen. Theories range all the way from divine intervention to mind over matter to immune system activation. In my own practice as a counselor, I have seen physical healing happen when a client changes deeply held unhelpful belief systems or releases guilt, fear, depression, or other negative emotions. There are also many high profile cases of spontaneous healing. Two of these notable stories—those of Ron Hawkins and Apollo Astronaut Edgar Mitchell—can be found on Adam Dreamhealer's website: http://www.dreamhealer.com/testimonials. In the end, testimonials will not convince anyone, but they can help to open our imagination to possibilities. It is helpful to remember that there is much more happening in this universe than we are currently aware of.

we know, perceive, think and do. Opening to this assumption also allows the mind to encompass and explain a much wider range of human experience.

"Self as Informational field" as a hypothesis explains much more and works on many more levels than the solid mechanistic physical hypothesis but also does not deny or discount the physical. Therefore, the idea of fields can be thought of as a deeper or more fundamental truth.

Once again: *You are a being of light and energy, literally made from the dust of stars, which is itself energy and vibration. You are the field, it is you, and everything is connected.*

What would it feel like, to learn from birth that your mind and body are energy and information, constantly changing, completely connected and part of everything around you? How might it affect your ideas about physical health? Mental health? Relationships? What do you reject now that you would embrace then?

Chapter 5
Determining What is Real

Our definition of the physical universe as a collection of isolated objects, our definition of ourselves as just another of those objects, even our most basic understanding of time and space, will have to be recast. At least forty top scientists in academic centers of research around the world have demonstrated that an information transfer constantly carries on between living things, and that thought forms are simply another aspect of transmitted energy. Hundreds of others have offered plausible theories embracing even the most counterintuitive effects, such as time-displaced influence, as now consistent with the laws of physics.

...Every thought we have, every judgment we hold, however unconscious, is having an effect.

The Intention Experiment
by Lynne McTaggert

As we step away from the comfortable boxes of the objective/material world-view, we are confronted with a frightening degree of uncertainty. This step into unknown territory calls into question everything we think we know about who we are, what it means to have a body, to be alive, and to exist in this universe. Realizing that the ground beneath our feet, both literally and figuratively, is less stable than we thought, seeing that everything we believe may be untrue, is unsettling to say the least. At times it can be so unsettling that we wonder if we are losing our sanity or floating off into a mental illness. Many brave people have run back to hide in the old familiar boxes, rather than face the world without the armour of their beliefs.

It doesn't matter if the beliefs are wrong. Our thoughts are powerful things, and the things we allow ourselves to perceive shape what we *can* perceive. We build our worldview to match what we think is true. Take away the worldview and we are left in an unknown and uncharted place—a place where we have nothing on which to base a judgment of what is real and what is not.

Many people who are still resisting the transition from the objective/ material worldview to the energy paradigm will argue that energy awareness is at best imagination and at worst a kind of psychosis. Perhaps the whole idea of energy awareness is just a form of mental illness, or flight of over-imagination. This argument can be valid—it is true that it is easy to let one's imagination, hopes, or desires create things that are not necessarily true, and it is important to maintain a certain degree of skepticism in order to avoid this. The ground between what is real and what isn't is less well defined, simple, or obvious in the new way of seeing things.

The irony of this is that the old definitions that have provided a comfortable sense of reality have been shown to be wildly inaccurate and not real at all. The Bohr model of the atom, with its neatly orbiting particulate electrons, for instance, was a very tidy and concrete way of understanding how atoms work. Unfortunately, it fails to describe accurately what actually exists. Similarly, just because you can point to a cup you are holding in your hand and say "This is solid and real," doesn't mean that you actually understand what it truly is. Your mental picture of a cup likely doesn't account for the fact that it is an energy based wave form, literally shimmering and vibrating in your hand in a state of constant change.

H.L. Mencken noted that "For every complex problem, there is an answer that is clear, simple, and wrong." The objective/material belief that reality is simply what we experience with our five senses, that we are separate and disconnected beings, that objects are solid, even that we are limited to the experience that we now have—all of these things are being shown to be wrong. The magnitude of the potential of being human and of our understanding of what is possible is growing so fast in our collective awareness that it can be very disorienting.

Thankfully, there are some things that can help to maintain a stable footing and to step into these new understandings of the world without becoming lost. This will be discussed later in the sections on Change and Truth. To begin with, however, it is helpful to know that there is a big difference between psychosis and just feeling unsettled by changing experience of reality. Psychosis is a personal experience that cannot be confirmed or shared by anyone else. For instance, sadness is not a psychosis because many people experience sadness. Each person experiences sadness in his/her own way, and it is impossible to directly share one's own experience of sadness—but the general emotion of sadness is one that is consistent among many people.

Hearing the voice of a demon telling you to put frogs into every mailbox you see is probably a psychosis because it is something that is not shared by very many (or any) other people, and it does not fit with any reasonable criteria. The experience is intensely personal and very difficult to connect with wider circles of understanding. In an infinite universe, such as the one in which we live for instance, it is possible that the demon and its message are real. However, it is also quite likely that it isn't. Either way, putting frogs in mailboxes is not a particularly helpful thing to do. Common sense and mental discrimination is still necessary. Even the Buddha is attributed to having said "Believe nothing. No matter where you read it, or who has said it, not even if I have said it, unless it agrees with your own reason, and your own common sense."

Experience of psychosis also generally involves a rapid change of personality, disorganized thinking, speech, or behaviour, and delusions that are unshakable despite evidence to the contrary. Psychosis generally accompanies substance use, unintentional poisoning by environmental toxins, internal brain damage and/or personality disorders. It also accompanies specific mental disorders such as schizophrenia.

Viewing the world from the perspective of fields can be distinguished from a psychosis because energy perception is an experience that can be shared by many people. There are millions of people who are able to experience energy fields directly and many who are also able to influence them. There is also a growing body of scientific evidence that supports the field perspective. Though it can seem foreign and strange, the concept of fields is a basic assumption that is better supported by science than the assumption of basic solidity. It is possible to learn to experience energy and to gradually expand one's understanding through one's own experience. This experience can also be shared and compared with the experience of others. Unlike a psychosis, energy awareness is something to which common sense and discrimination can readily be applied.

It needs to be noted, however, that anything we can know about reality cannot be more than an assumption. The human mind, or at least what we currently know of it, is not capable of understanding the full extent of reality, and there is always room for error in the way that we understand what we experience. Part of learning to navigate in the new paradigm is learning to question and to constantly re-evaluate what we know. It is also being able and willing to maintain our flexibility of thought and mind, adapting and changing our ideas as we learn more about who we are and how our world works.

Part of this flexibility is the willingness to step into new ways of experiencing or perceiving the world and try the new perceptions out. If you do not experience the world and yourself as energy fields, then you may soon be in a minority. You can learn to change your assumptions and change your experiences. Here are some exercises that can help you to get started:

Exercises for practicing field awareness

1. Seeing your hand as a field

Place one hand on a table in front of you. Be aware of the physical sensations in your hand—the texture and temperature of the table, the pressure and points of contact with the table, perhaps the movement of air across the back of your hand, the touch of sunshine, sore places, tingles, aches—anything that is really there as a sensation. Be careful not to imagine sensations. Simply be aware of what you feel in this one hand.

Now open your mind to the awareness that your perception is only an apparent truth. There is a more fundamental truth to what is happening. In your mind's eye, and in your body's awareness, allow the possibility that the table you are touching is not solid, that your hand is not actually even touching the table. Your hand is simply a vibrating field of energy, in contact with another vibrating field that you have, to this point, thought of as a table.

Study your hand and try to see past your own belief of what it is. Whatever you see, the truth is that your hand is made of millions of cells, each cell composed of billions of atoms, each atom composed of particles and energy clouds, each particle simply a condensed form of energy, all of this mysteriously acting in unison to be able to function as a hand. Your hand is made of energy. The table is made of energy. The sensations rushing to be perceived by your brain are made of energy, transmitted by energy, perceived, recognized and evaluated by more energy. For a few moments, put away your idea that you, the table, or any of the things around you, are solid. Let the idea that you are made of constantly changing energy and vibrations sink as deeply into you as possible. How deeply into your belief system can it go? Where do you feel yourself resisting this idea?

2. Walking as a field

In this exercise, take a walk outside. Leave your phone, iPod and other electronic distractions at home. You can do this anywhere and anytime. However, to begin it is easier to find a place to walk that is relatively quiet, preferably where there are trees and in a setting that is as natural as possible.

Keep this simple. Just walk. Let your body relax and your thoughts float by like clouds. Don't get involved with them. As much as possible allow your muscles to relax and your walk to become a smooth and focused flow.

Now allow your mind to open to the possibility that the *you* experiencing this walking is fundamentally based on vibrating energy. Rather than a discreetly separate mass of animated matter, allow the idea to seep through your awareness that you are a self-aware field of energy-based information. Extend this idea to include everything around you. Like a magnet passing through other magnetic fields, your field is constantly interacting with the fields of people, animals, plants, and objects around you. Eventually you will be able to feel this directly. To begin with, however, simply focus on the possibility that this perception could be true.

Walk this way as long as you wish. Take note of the thoughts that try to tell you that only the physical perception is true and also of any new thoughts or perceptions that come along.

Practice this often and note how your ideas about the world around you begin to change.

More ways of exposing yourself to the concept of energy:

- Read *Energy Medicine* by Donna Eden
- Take a Reiki class
- Get a healing touch or Reiki treatment
- Learn about Theta healing
- Take a meditation class
- Practice Chi Gong or T'ai Chi

* * *

Experiencing vs. Contemplating

So far, we have looked at the possibility that the worldview represented by the objective/material perspective may not be able to contain the entire reality that is available to us in this universe. This is not really such a difficult stretch of the imagination. Considering that we live in an infinite universe, it is really not so far-fetched to entertain the possibility that our present understanding of the world may not be the whole truth and that there may be room for the existence of a field state. However it takes time for an idea like this to sink in and become more meaningful than just an intellectual piece of data. This is why practicing is important.

In his story *Stranger in a Strange Land*, written in 1961, Robert Heinlein coined the word "grok". The sound of this word is a bit irritating, but its meaning is quite useful. The meaning that he gave to this word is the experience of transferring something from intellectual knowledge to a processed, understood, full bodied, *felt* understanding. It's a bit like the difference between a computer storing information about something and a human experiencing it.

The human mind is capable of playing with ideas, memorizing bits of data and creating a kind of virtual world that manages to avoid actually taking part in the experience. In the West, and in most of the world at this time, we are taught to think but not to *grok*.

The difference between *grokking* something and thinking it is like the difference between knowing that there are billions of stars in the universe without actually looking at them or standing on a prairie on a cold clear night with a full hemisphere of brilliant stars above your head. Standing in this place, the cold touches your body; the immensity of the sky speaks of insignificance, and yet also can lift you into a connection that realizes, "I am a part of all of this." It is possible to be in this place and remain in an intellectual experience—to experience everything through the filter of the mind. However, if the mind's constant chatter and analysis is let go for a few moments, the experience of grokking the stars can take place. If this happens, the experience of stars transfers from an intellectual understanding to a full-bodied experience and stars will never be the same for you again.

Allowing the awareness of energy and fields into your life is no different than allowing the awareness of stars into your life. It could be easily argued by someone who lives in a big city that stars don't exist, or if they do exist, they don't matter. He never sees them. They are hidden by the city lights, so what evidence does he have? Even if he sees them on TV or hears people talk about them, they are just a mental concept. He hasn't experienced them personally.

Take this same person to a quiet country field on a clear and starry night, and the reality of stars will be much different. Now they are an experience. There is nothing to believe in or not to believe in. They are simply there. When he goes back to the city, he will know that the stars are still there, covered by the lights, and he can still look for them if he chooses to do so.

This is a simple example, but so is the idea of energy and fields. Fields and energy do not need to be believed in—they can simply be experienced. Once they are experienced, they are no different from stars or magnetic fields or electricity or any number of other things that we know to exist, and don't really understand. They are just part of what *is*. Once they become a part of awareness, they simply blend into the world, and the idea of not believing in them becomes kind of silly. You don't believe or not believe in a stone or a tree or the fact that you can push some numbers on a small device and talk to someone on the other side of the world. These are all miracles and also nothing special.

> *You are a being of light and energy, literally made from the dust of stars, which is itself energy and vibration. You are the field, it is you, and everything is connected.*

Chapter 6
Change

One should count each day a separate life.

Seneca (3 BC—65 AD)

People who have examined the question of pain and suffering in the world in a very deep way have come to the conclusion that there is a fundamental difference between *pain* and *suffering*. *Pain* is a physical phenomena and is inherent to being a biological life form. *Suffering*, however, is something that can exist with or without real physical pain. Suffering is a layer of fear and struggle that is spread on top of pain or even that is inserted into situations that are not painful but which we dislike. Pain happens, and though we can do many things to avoid it, we cannot eliminate it completely from existence. Suffering, however, is another matter. Suffering arises because of a deep misunderstanding about the nature of the universe and because of the struggles that this misunderstanding creates.

This misunderstanding is deeply embedded in the objective/material worldview. As has been discussed, this worldview is founded on the principle that the universe is somewhat like a vast machine—it runs on immutable laws, its behaviour is ultimately predictable, and if we just learn enough about it, we will be able to control it. If we learn enough, we will be able to make life safe, to control pain and suffering, to stop losing what we love. The attempt to control our world and each other, and thereby avoid loss and suffering, is a deep driving force behind the objective/material worldview, and also a driving force behind much of the aggression and cruelty that our race has invented.

None of this is innately *bad*. However, nearly all of it is in fundamental opposition to the most basic and obvious property of the universe. As wise people in the past knew, and as science has now discovered, everything—including every aspect of a human being—is based on vibrational energy, and even this vibrational energy is ultimately a function of probabilities. Vibrational energy is constantly changing, and therefore nothing ever remains the same. Since change is an unconditional fact of existence, resisting change is not very helpful. No matter how much we want to believe we are in control, the fact is that we are not.

The idea that things change is not new, complex, or even very exciting. It is a very simple fact, and one that is known to everyone. In the way of simple things though, it is extremely difficult to fully apply this idea to oneself. Flowing in a waterfall of being, this thing called *"me"* is never motionless, so any image of it, or belief about it, can only represent an aspect of what it *was*—never what it *is*. There is nothing in this universe that does, or will, continue to exist and nothing that will last forever. Fighting this simple fact is what most of our energy is spent upon, and it is also the source of what we think of as suffering.

Like it or not, change is our most fundamental and basic reality, and there are really only two ways of meeting its challenge. The first is to resist it, which is the basis of fear, sorrow, hatred, depression, and violence, and the second is to embrace it, which is the basis of love, joy, and peace. Although we are remarkably capable of the self-delusion necessary to hide this simple truth, and incredibly creative in the lengths we will go and the stretches of imagination that we will use in order to avoid it, this truth is still the *Truth*. Things change, we change, and nothing remains the same.

Although, as I said, this is a very simple and well-known idea, experiencing it is difficult. Most of us experience ourselves mainly through our thoughts. The words and pictures that run nearly constantly through our minds are taken to be the expression of *self*, and we constantly identify ourselves with these words, thoughts, and feelings. Unfortunately, a conscious thought can never be a fully *present* experience and can never be an experience that fully understands change. This is because in order to think about something, the mind must take a little piece of the reality around it, freeze its motion, and examine it. Time does not stop while this is happening, so the mind is constantly behind. Every time it reaches to try to understand what is happening around it, everything changes. By the time the mind is able to come up with words, the information is already old, the instant has passed, the world has moved on.

Rather than being expressions of what we are, thoughts are actually one of the chief ways that we fight against the experience of change. Thoughts are both the images that we use in an attempt to maintain who we think we are and reactions based on our history and expectations that tend to lock us into repeating patterns of often unhealthy behaviour. The thoughts and images that we cling to with such desperation actually represent much more of what we are **not** than what or who we are.

As we experience and learn about our world and then react to what we experience, the experiences and reactions form a template of beliefs and programs that we then identify with and call "*me*". In a self-sustaining and self-confirming circle, these beliefs and programs also determine what we are *able* to experience and what we *expect* to happen. The idea of *self*, therefore, fights change by filtering out experiences, concepts and images that do not agree with what it already believes. It also perceives as suffering any experience that threatens the stability of these beliefs and images and any experience that results in loss of beliefs, images, objects, or people to which, or to whom, the sense of *self* has been attached.

All of this happens below the level of conscious thoughts. What we think of as conscious thoughts are actually secondary aspects much like echoes, bouncing back from belief systems stored deep within the subconscious. The thought echoes maintain and reinforce the template of *self*, but neither the thoughts nor the template are truly who we are. Rather than representing who we are, thoughts—as well as the experience template from which they arise—represent programs that we have learned in order to interact with other people and the world around us. They are repetitive, reactionary, and conditioned.

As people grow older they generally become more rigid and set in their ways, and they find that the world around them confirms their expectations of it. This is because our expectations not only filter and colour what we *can* experience but also actually create the circumstances that will confirm our expectations. If I believe that people are basically self-centered and thoughtless, for example, I will find numerous examples to prove this point to myself, and I will grow increasingly convinced of the truth of my convictions. I will also react to situations around me in such a way that I will create my expectations—my attitude toward others will generally cause them to behave toward me in the way that I expect.

Ultimately, all beliefs are wrong simply because a belief cannot be in the present moment but must be something that represents a past understanding—something that is already gone. Who I was yesterday is similar to who I am today but not the same. Who I will be tomorrow could possibly be completely different. What I believe is coloured and contained by the limits I have placed on who I am—I can't understand beyond the bounds that I have placed on my world. As my mind and understanding expands, what I know to be true must also expand, and I will find that what I believed in the past was not the whole story.

In the objective/material worldview, it made sense that we would gather experience, learn from this experience and use our learning to better understand what was happening in and around us. It also made sense to expect that the future would be similar to the present and that cause-effect relationships from moment to moment would provide a degree of predictability. In a world of solid particles and predictable interactions it makes sense that the future moves in a somewhat ponderous way and that it depends completely on the past.

As we make the shift to the energy or quantum, worldview, we begin to realize that the future is not as determined as we had thought. We have the ability to let go of limiting beliefs, and by doing so it is possible to experience a complete shift in both how we see the world and how the world seems to respond to us. We also have the ability to let go of the confining predictions of the past and realize that each moment is an opportunity for everything to be completely new and completely different.

Each time you expect your wife or husband to be as they were yesterday or last year, each time you attempt to retain your belief that who you are fits the image that you have built for yourself and placed in the mind of others, each time you name an object and think you understand what this means—each of these actions is an act of resistance to change. Each time you find yourself living through an "ordinary moment" or thinking that life is dull or feeling caught on a treadmill of repeating actions, realize that this is resistance to change.

When you can see yourself and everything around you as a waterfall of flowing, vibrating energy, and realize that no image, or thought, can possibly represent the living reality of a person or object right NOW, you will begin to understand the significance of the simple truth of change. As a small bonus, you will also understand why many religions have placed a taboo on images, idols, etc. When change is understood, it is obvious that no image can ever represent reality, and therefore an image is not worth worshiping. This doesn't mean that images are bad—just that they cannot represent the real nature of the present moment.

This is the secret of the simplicity of change. When change is fought—as it is to one degree or another by all humans—change is the source of all of our fear, loss, suffering and insignificance. When embraced, it is the source of our connection with the universe, with who we truly are, and with safety.

Letting go and diving into change is an essential part of opening to the energy worldview and conversely it is a reason that many people will choose to fight this paradigm with all of their strength. For many people, the idea that they may not be right and that there is nothing solid to hold to is so terrifying that they would literally prefer to kill and/or die than to accept it. This is unfortunate, as there is so much beauty and nobility of spirit that comes from simply letting go. Embracing change is like embracing wonder and stepping into a rapturous world of mystery, beauty, and love.

It is fear of change and of letting go—not the devil—that causes us to suffer in this world.

Affirmation:

There are no ordinary moments, there is no such thing as repetition.

* * *

Exercises for awareness of change

1. I don't really know what this is or what it is about.

Think of something that happens often in your day—like seeing a window, walking through a door, answering a telephone, etc. Make a mental note to yourself to use this as a cue. Each time you see the cue (answer a phone for instance) take a quick internal glance at what you are seeing, feeling and thinking. Look around you and for everything you notice, remind yourself: I don't really know what this is or what it is about.

This is true because all that you are seeing is your image of what you think is there. A desk, a window, a person—none of these are static, or even truly solid. What you see is limited by your own beliefs, preconceptions, training, and ideas that things remain stable over time. Stretch your mind and imagination by beginning to undo this delusion.

2. This person is not the image that I have made. I do not truly know who this person is.

Apply this similar concept to someone with whom you have a close relationship—your spouse, partner, friend, child, parent etc. Feel the stretch that happens in your mind when you consciously, and with a sense of awe, curiosity and love, look at a person and realize that they are a mystery beyond your comprehension.

If you are struggling in relationship, if you have found that your sex life has become stagnant, if you are locked in conflict—practice saying to yourself, "This person is not the image that I have made". If you do this with sincerity and willingness to be open to curiosity, love, and openness, this single practice can revitalize a relationship and your sex life. More on that later.

3. Follow your breath.

When you wake up in the morning, and when you go to bed at night, spend a few minutes lying on your back. Place your hands on your stomach and put your attention in your hands so that you can be aware of the sensations as they touch your stomach. Pay careful attention to the movement of your hands as your stomach rises and falls with your breath. This is also a good time to let the question "Who or what is aware of breathing?" sink softly under your thoughts. If you practice this, you will begin to notice several things:

- There is constant change in your body.

- There is even more rapid and constant change in your mind.

- It is difficult to keep your mind on the sensations of your breath and hands.

- There is no stable or constant "you" to identify in all of the shifting thoughts and sensations of your mind and body.

Use this practice to help you see how your mind resists being aware of change as it happens in the present. If you practice this consistently, you may also find that it helps you to sleep more easily, and to feel more rested when you wake up.

Note: Don't fight the change as your mind flits about. When you become aware that your attention has drifted away from your breath, calmly and patiently bring it back again. Don't judge any of your thoughts or feelings, and don't get upset if it feels difficult. If you have to be upset, or judge, don't be upset about being upset or judging. The point here is to practice not being caught in the habitual practice of struggling with the reality of change and the reality of the present moment. What is, IS. Stop struggling with it and just breathe!

4. Practice the Present

Just as a photograph can never represent the full and living reality of a person, so a mental image of anything at all cannot represent its full and living reality. An image, perception, or idea in the mind is always a photograph, recorded and examined after the event has actually happened. The time lag between the actual event and the image may be a few milliseconds or many years, but the result is the same. If you can put words or pictures to a thought, you are not operating in the present.

Even if the image in your mind seems to be a moving image in real time as you have a conversation with a friend, for instance, everything that is perceived is still filtered through the mind. It is essential to understand that the mind is simply a recording and processing device. YOU ARE NOT YOUR THOUGHTS. YOU ARE NOT YOUR MIND. In the energy paradigm, you are a being of energy that operates through a body. You are a field, based on information, actuated by a flowing potential to be what we refer to as energy. The reality experienced by the five senses of the body, and the sixth sense of the mind and its thoughts is only a tiny fraction of what is really happening. The awareness that the mind provides with its words, evaluations, and feelings is always behind and never actually present in the moment.

To understand this, imagine a time that you have watched a waterfall. It seems nearly impossible for the eyes to follow the flow. They jerk up and down, fixing on one spot and attempting to follow it, losing it, fixing on another, up and down, back and forth, always moving. Contrast this with standing under a waterfall. The full body experience of water pouring down is beyond thought. It is immediate, present, stable, and changing at the same time. This example is only an approximation, but it gives some idea of the difference between thinking about something and simply experiencing the moment.

Now remove yourself from the waterfall a step further. Remember a waterfall that you have seen in the past and find the picture in your mind. This waterfall picture is a recording of something that no longer exists. The water in the picture has long ago fallen and gone its way, the waterfall has changed, the plants around it have grown and died and grown again, the rock has worn and changed, nothing in the picture is what is truly there.

If you have a sense of the difference between your mental picture and the reality of the waterfall, try to use the same process with your picture of your spouse or of someone with whom you have a close relationship. Examine everything that you think you know about this person and realize that it is all a picture of a waterfall. Everything you know is in the past.

Now apply this same awareness to yourself. Imagine that every part of you is constantly changing and that every second your physical form is completely remade and renewed. Try to stand in the waterfall of this awareness, letting change be a full bodied experience rather than a thought. Allow your thoughts to exist like a TV in the background, or a movie that you're not watching. Ignore them, and realize that they, too, are in the past.

Allow your mind to open to the possibility that its labels, names, and explanations are all simply defenses against reality. Open to the possibility that you are capable of being intensely aware, intensely present, and that to do this you will have to relinquish the attempt to understand, explain, control, grasp, fix, change, judge, evaluate, repress, ignore or analyze your experience. In the words of a wise monk and teacher from Thailand, "Let go, let it be, do nothing".

Practice "Let go, let it be, do nothing" often in your day. Look up from whatever you are doing for five seconds and open to the flow of the waterfall.

Chapter 7
Living from the inside–out

I am immersed in the One and that One manifests Itself in all.

Kabir, circa 1450

From the perspective of today's science and psychology, it is beginning to make sense that belief systems have a strong effect on what we actually see and experience—expectations are filters of what we can perceive and conditioners of our reactions. It is also beginning to make sense that our internal choices, feelings, and actions affect our state of mental and physical health. All of this is now strongly supported by research in neuroscience, biochemistry, and psychology.

The jump from here to understanding energy and field concepts is not great. Mainstream science has not yet made this jump, but when it does, whole new worlds of understanding will open as well. Until that time, however, I can only offer the field and energy perspective as one that is lived and shared by a rapidly growing number of people worldwide.

Imagine a waterfall again. A visitor looks at the waterfall, looks away for a few seconds and then looks again at the waterfall. The visitor is under the impression that he is looking at the same waterfall both times. In reality, the water that he saw the first time has already fallen, and he is seeing all new water moving past his eyes. The water is supplied by a water source that is connected to all of the water in the world through the water cycle. Water evaporates into the air, disperses over the land as clouds, falls to the ground, and runs back to the sea. The few seconds of waterfall that the visitor saw are simply a moment's snapshot of a cycle that is both the changing falls in its individual beauty and a part of the cycle of water of the whole planet. If the falls had a concept of *self*, it could say that it is, indeed, different from other falls. But the water that is its being is the same in every falls, river, lake and ocean.

In a much more fundamental way, we—and all life forms—are waterfalls. We are systems of organized vibrational change and we must keep flowing. Energy must continue to enter us, move through us, and be released because this is the definition of what it means to be alive and to exist within this universe. To exist is to be connected to, and constructed from, the energy of the universe, and to remain alive requires that this energy be constantly flowing.

On a biological level, this is evident in the way that we must constantly take in oxygen, water, and food for energy and nutrients and excrete our waste. We can survive for a few weeks or even months without food—but only because the body is able to use food that it has stored in the form of fat, or in extreme cases to metabolize muscle and other less essential parts of the body in order to keep the vital organs and brain going. Without a constant and flowing energy supply, the life process supported by these organs will shut down.

Without water, we can only survive a few days, and without oxygen only a few minutes. The physical flow of energy represented by food, water and oxygen must be constantly present and moving continuously for a human (or any other carbon based oxygen using life-form) to remain a *life* form, and the input and output must remain roughly balanced. If the life form continuously uses more energy than it receives, it will eventually die. On the other hand, if it continuously takes in more energy than it can use, it will eventually poison itself.

Water is essential, but too much water can kill us. Food is essential, but too much food eventually destroys the body. Oxygen is essential, but too much oxygen can poison us. In all things balance is essential because all things are a flowing waterfall. If too much water goes into the falls, it overflows its banks and loses its shape. If not enough water goes into the falls, there is only a channel left with nothing in it.

On a psychological level the waterfall-like flow principle is less evident but still observable. Our minds are constantly ingesting ideas and information and excreting thoughts. In our western society, we have mistakenly identified ourselves with our thoughts, acting from Descartes' "cogito ergo sum" or "I think, therefore I am" statement[10]. Unfortunately, Descartes got it wrong. He didn't understand that conscious thought is only a small boat floating on the sea of a deeper energetic process that is a human.

As one example of this, what most people think of as emotions originate far below the level of conscious thought and propagate through the body via a variety of chemical messenger molecules as well as electrical nerve impulses. The result of these messengers and impulses is a complex of physical sensations in the body. The physical sensations are recognized by a part of the mind that is closer to the conscious part—but generally still not directly in awareness. A determination is made—"bad" or "good"—and a message is passed to the conscious mind. Finally, the conscious mind becomes aware that it is sad, or angry, or jealous, etc. The conscious mind, which tends to think that it is in charge, is in reality simply reacting to deeper processes that have already occurred.

Mystics and people who have studied in meditative traditions have taught for thousands of years that it is possible to experience the deeper realities beyond thought and that when this happens it becomes clear that what we think of as conscious thought (and the idea of *me*) is very close to the idea of a boat floating on the water, reacting to the movements of the powerful depths below it. We think, but we think *because we are* and not the other way around. Who we are is deeper than what we think and—completely contrary to Descartes—who we are comes *before* what we think.

We are constructed from the organized flow of change that comes from the movement of energy. We are phenomena of information and energy

---

10 This is one of the most well known quotes in the history of philosophy. It was first published by René Descartes in French (Je pense, donc je suis) in his *Discourse on the Method of Rightly Conducting One's Reason and of Seeking Truth in the Sciences* published in 1637 and later in its Latin form in *Principia Philosophiae* (Principles of Philosophy), published in 1644. Isaac Newton was strongly influenced by Descartes' writing and Descartes' principles have become foundation stones for modern thought.

organized within an informational field, connected with every other point of the fundamental field. At the quantum level, we are a universe of sparking change and vibration. Huge voids of empty space are populated with pulsing sparks of energy that pop in and out of existence in response to probabilities that are woven into the informational fabric of the entire field. There is nothing solid, nothing constant—our physical, mental, and energetic selves are based on flow, vibration, and change.

Beyond even this is the realm that is beyond change, beyond thought, beyond opposite polarities, reported to us by a few highly attained mystics. In this realm—be it conceptualized as Nirvana, or God, or simply the Field—is the stillness and formlessness from which all movement and form arises. Perhaps there is something that is also beyond this—but it is here that the record of human attainment has thus far ended.

It is not possible to prove the truth of these statements at this time. However, as Ken Wilber has attempted to show in his book *Integral Psychology*[11], modern science, and particularly modern psychology, understands only a tiny fraction of the range of experience that has been reported to us by mystics over the course of the millennia of human existence.

Although many of these deeper levels remain beyond the ken of most people, huge numbers of people are taking a new step into the understanding that I think of as Awakening. These people are going beyond understanding, or even belief, and entering into the experience of the energy of the Field. Some people see aspects of it in what they call the aura or energy field around the body. Others see the entire body in its field state, recognizing the essential state of energy and the holographic informational matrix that underlies and creates the physical. Some don't see energy but feel it as vibration, tingling, or temperature change. Some simply intuit the energy—connecting with the

---

11 Ken Wilber, *Integral Psychology*. (2000) As part of this book, Wilber outlines the various levels of consciousness that have been reported by mystics and accomplished practitioners from a large number of different traditions. He has correlated these to show where they overlap and to show the range of possible experience that has so far been reported. It is interesting to note that modern cognitive psychology addresses only a small fraction of this range of possible human experience.

informational matrix of the Field and knowing things that have not been communicated in normal or physical ways.

However it is perceived, awareness of energy is becoming more normal, and very soon it will be understood by a majority of humans that our nature, existence, essence, and purpose is far greater and far more beautiful than we have ever imagined. As we awaken to the awareness of the Field, and our part within it, this awakening expands the horizons of our intellect and imagination into whole new realms of beauty, interconnection, and possibility.

This new experience of the beauty and interconnection of life does not negate or deny previous beliefs or experience—it simply informs and expands them. For those who believe in God, the Field is simply a greater understanding of the expression of God's thought, and the beauty of God's creation. We are literally made of God, connected to God and a part of God.

For those who do not hold religious beliefs and do not wish to use the name "God", the Field still exists and can be understood from a more scientific viewpoint. The truth of the existence of an entity called God is still unknown, but the experience of the Field can inform and expand our self-understanding either way. If we are Christians, it can make us better Christians. If we are Muslims or Jews or Atheists understanding of the Field and its related energy informs our interpretation of reality, expanding and broadening it so that we can reach more deeply into the potential of being human and more deeply into the truth of our belief. Eventually, and at their core, all belief systems are one and all paths lead to the same place. This does not negate the worth of individual paths.

However, to this point in human history, most people have believed (and most faiths have taught) that God is outside us. God is someone, or something, to be attained by searching on the outside. The awakened perspective brings God much closer. The Field consists of all things, and all things exist within the Field. All things exist because of the Field, are animated by the energy of the Field, informed and made manifest by the Field. In this way of understanding, an individual human is not only connected to the Field but actually IS a microcosm of the Field. A single human cell plays its role as a part of the overall system that is a human, but each cell also carries the information and potential to become an entire human. One could ask, is the human in the cell, or the cell in the human? Really, both are true.

This perspective is also critical for understanding the idea of the Field. The question of "Is the Field in me or am I in the Field?" is actually a confusion of what the Field really is—and of what I really am. The same confusion is evident in the question "Is God in me or am I in God?" From the perspective of energy and the Field, the confusion is unnecessary. A clay jug and a clay cup are shaped differently, but they are still clay. Although they are separate in form, in substance they are one. As Kabir, a 15th century poet and mystic wrote:

> Inside this clay jug
> there are canyons and
> pine mountains,
> and the maker of canyons
> and pine mountains!
>
> All seven oceans are inside,
> and hundreds of millions of stars.
>
> The acid that tests gold is here,
> and the one who judges jewels.
>
> And the music
> that comes from the strings
> that no one touches,
> and the source of all water.
>
> If you want the truth, I will tell you the truth:
> Friend, listen: the God whom I love is inside.

* * *

The universe as our mirror

From the perspective of the Field, I am a node of self-awareness, constructed from the material of the Field and ultimately one and the same in substance with all things. Looking outside myself I see the "thousand things"—all that is manifest in the world of form, and looking inside I see that all of these things are a part of me as I am part of them. As Kabir says, "Inside this clay jug there are canyons and pine mountains—and the maker of canyons and pine mountains." I am a mirror of the universe, and the universe is my mirror, or, to paraphrase Kabir's more poetic way of saying it, looking either in or out, I will find both pine mountains and their maker.

Though the mystical understanding of the inward journey and the way in which the Field informs and supports this view may still be difficult for many people to accept, it is growing very difficult to deny the psychological understanding of the human mind. From a psychological perspective, we perceive the world through the filters of who we are; we see what we expect to see and call this *reality*.

Because what I *can* see is filtered by what I *expect* to see, what I see outside myself has more to do with who *I am* than with what or who I am looking at. If I am annoyed by a certain person's personality, it is almost certain that I have similar traits lurking somewhere in my shadow;[12] when I admire or love someone this love springs from the well of love that I am able to have for myself, when I withhold love from another I withhold it from myself as well, and when I hate, this hate begins with the self-hate that lurks in the dark places within me.

There are two possible perspectives then. We can call one the "external viewpoint" because it assumes that my feelings are caused by what happens outside myself. The other perspective is that of the mirror. In this perspective,

---

12 Carl Jung used the term "shadow" to denote the part of the human psyche that is disowned and hidden in the subconscious. We have an image that we portray to the world, and we have a shadow that contains all of the things that we reject, hate, and fear. Learning to love and accept the shadow and to usefully integrate these unwanted parts of ourselves, is an aim of Jungian therapy.

my feelings are a result of my own perceptions. The way I act or react to a situation is greatly affected by my perspective.

An example of this difference in perspectives that comes from my counseling practice can be seen in a man who came to me with problems of anger and anxiety. He could speak very knowledgably of spiritual practice, love for others and living a life where spirit is a central consideration. In fact, he would spend a great deal of time in the sessions lecturing me about these things. When faced with even small irritants, however, his reaction was to immediately blame whatever or whoever had offended him. His blame was accompanied by what was, to me, a very palpable energy blast of anger and guilt that came from the area of the solar plexus chakra and of the navel chakra—centers of power and of emotion.

This man was certainly not alone in his difficulty hearing that he was not practicing what he preached. Many people are highly unreceptive to self-reflection, or mirroring, that shows the disparity between what they say and what they do. For most of us, when a mirror is held in our face, we simply close our eyes.

When applied, however, the mirror concept completely reverses the normal point of view about cause and effect and places the responsibility for one's own feelings and actions more squarely on the shoulders of each individual. It also refutes the objective/material worldview that we are just meaningless cogs in the wheel of a great machine. If we use everything we see as a reflection that helps us know and understand ourselves better, then outside experience becomes useful and purposeful. This will be discussed in more detail in the section on using negative emotions as allies. What in the objective/material way of seeing the world are random events beyond our control can become instead useful learning opportunities when we apply the idea that what we see outside ourselves is a mirror for what is going on inside.

To continue with the example, my reaction to the man's anger and energetic attempt to take away my energy and confidence could be to become angry back, which would of course result in more anger for both of us. As a second option, I could allow myself to be overpowered and give him my energy and power. This would result in me feeling used and abused and would encourage him to be angry with me more often.

A third option is to use the mirror to see the reflection of my own anger in his actions. As my anger flares and my mind begins its circles of blame and accusation, I can direct my thinking back to my own hypocrisy. This anger is also in me. Here is the mirror of my shadow. Here is an opportunity to accept what I have disowned. By not reacting with more anger, I learn to manage my own feelings. By not allowing myself to be overpowered, I learn self-confidence. By accepting the person behind the emotion, I learn to love myself in spite of my shortcomings.

The perspective of the mirror creates a spiral of integrity, self-worth, and internal strength.

The external perspective initiates a spiral of escalation of violence. This violence acts both internally and externally.

Every instant is a new opportunity to decide which perspective we wish to use.

Worldviews and Perspectives

Here is an imagination experiment to try. Imagine three small children. One child is taught from birth that she is bad, that she is alone and disconnected from the universe and that the world is a dangerous and cruel place. It is expected that she will be willful and that her traits of sinfulness will have to be suppressed through hard discipline and careful watchfulness by her parents and elders. She is taught that though this world is cruel and hard, there is another world that is much better—and also a third world that is full of torture and torment. These last two worlds are possibilities for her when she dies. Her basic nature will automatically take her to the third world—the world of eternal torture and pain. Her only hope, therefore, is to accept that her own internal feelings, voice, and desires are bad and that she must obtain her information from something outside herself that is good and that knows better. Without this help, she is eternally damned.

From conception forward, the cells in this little girl's body grow marinated in the implicit awareness that every part of her is bad. In order to

59

be saved, she must attend a physical place of worship, accept the authority of a God that is outside her and who acts as her master in all things, and strive to do good as defined by the authorities around her. Sometimes this good may involve helping starving people to have food. Sometimes it may involve dropping bombs on people who believe differently. For her, good is defined by a set of parameters for what is included in her beliefs and what is not. These parameters cannot come from her own voice. They must be interpreted by her elders, ministers, or priests. Authority must come *to* her from someone or something that is outside.

This child's sense of self must, therefore, be dependent on the opinions of those who are outside her. If she *does* good and is praised, she *is* good and vice versa. Deep inside, her sense of existence will be dependent on what happens outside her, denying anything that comes authentically from within. What she owns, what she wears, how she acts—all will be seen from the outside-in as if she is looking in at herself through the eyes of others.

When self-concept comes from the outside-in, ideas must be more rigid because one's own judgment is not trusted and one's own sense of self is like a fragile piece of glass, easily broken by any outside influence. When self is broken, defenses suddenly kick in and the person or event who did the breaking becomes *bad*. Anything is justifiable in order to see that this person is hurt as badly as "I" was, that this person's self is also destroyed, that this person pays for how they have hurt me. By believing that I am dependent on what happens outside me, I make myself fragile and then I believe that I must protect myself from a world that will try to hurt me. The more I protect, the more fragile I become; the more fragile I become, the more power and protection I need and the more deeply I become disconnected from my authentic internal voice and from my true power.

A second child is conceived in a family that has no religious beliefs. This child's prenatal experience is in connection with a mother who believes that the material world is all that there is, that when we die there is nothing more and that what we can normally perceive with the five senses is all that exists. From birth forward, this child is taught to use his own judgment, not to believe in anything unless it has been experienced and to treat others with respect because it is part of social responsibility. There is no implicit spiritual or energetic connection in the material world, since these things are not part of the objective perception of material science (yet) and so the child understands that he acts on his own power and initiative only. He is separate and ultimately alone, he is responsible for his own actions, and he is his own ultimate authority.

For this child, his own perception of what is happening around him is more important than any external authority. However, he sees his actions as isolated and individual, with only a veneer of social responsibility—or perhaps fear of retribution—as a reason to stay within the laws of his society. He reacts to the world that he sees from the understanding that he does things *to* it and it does things *to* him. If someone does something he doesn't like, this person *makes* him angry. His anger is the fault of other people and their actions with respect to him.

This child mistrusts authority of any kind, especially religious authority, and makes his choices based on his own desires and beliefs. Because of this, he may believe that he is acting from the inside but his choices are all based on an understanding of the world in which the outside reality is the most important. He does not understand the deeper processes of his body, the interconnections of his actions, or the way in which his thoughts create his experience. For him, there is only the solid and physical world and because of this he is constantly stuck in patterns of reaction to what he sees outside himself. He has taken command of his world, in a way, but he has also limited his awareness to a small and quite rigidly defined slice of what is available to him and of what his mind/body system is capable of experiencing. His authority comes from his concept of *self*, and this self acts in isolation. Whereas authority comes *to* the first child from the outside, for this boy, authority comes *from* him. However, his authority is his conscious mind and his awareness of material reality. He is not able to perceive, acknowledge, or make use of his connection with the Field.

A third child is conceived in a family for whom the awareness of energy fields is an everyday experience. This family understands the energetic lesson of the waterfall and the changing, flowing nature of all forms. They understand that what they think of as "self" is a process, not something that is constant and that this self both affects, and is affected by, interconnections with other people and things.

This child grows up with the understanding that she is a node in the vast field of information and vibration that is the universe and that she is a holographic reflection of the universe—as it is of her. Her actions and experiences are connected to the whole, and she is neither good nor bad but rather an active awareness in an infinite field, with infinite potential.

This child is encouraged to look beyond the apparent reality that is reported by her five senses and to trust in her own abilities to understand and see the interconnections around her. She understands that her actions are all ripples in a pool of cause and effect and that each choice made in the present moment has a strong effect on the content of the next present moment. Because of this, she is empowered with the understanding that she is always intimately connected with all that is—both part of the ONE that is the Field and part of the adventure that is individual awareness. Her actions are a flowing dance with the universe and she is a co-creator in her own reality. Although she is not in control of the dance, she is also not powerless within it.

As this child grows, she learns to experience herself as a vibrant and creative expression of flowing interaction with all that it is. She understands from the level of deep body awareness that she is energy and that this energy is always moving within her. She learns to quiet her mind and to allow the natural process of flow to remove blockages caused by fears. As she does this, her body grows more supple, healthy, and vibrant. She also learns that there are many voices within her, all with different feelings and needs. She sees that she contains a voice for every aspect of what she sees outside herself—she could be the murderer or the saint, the thief or beggar or politician. She begins to understand that everything that she sees outside has a correlation inside, and that—though she is not able to control directly what appears to be outside her—she is able to affect and quiet the voices and feelings that are on the inside.

Gradually, as she works with this inside/outside paradox, the line of cause and effect reverses itself. When other people see an external cause and *react*, she sees an internal cause and *acts*. She begins to understand that everything that she experiences begins somewhere deep inside and that her choice of focus is a determining factor in what actually happens around her. By paying careful attention to her own body and mind, and by applying her understanding of interconnection and flow, she begins not only to understand, but grok (as explained in chapter four) her part in the field and in the flow of life. For this girl, authority is something that flows *through* her, coming both from who she is as an individual and from her connection and existence within the universe of all things. She understands that though she has an individual self that contains the whole, she is ultimately a tiny drop of water in the vast sea of all that is.

These descriptions are not intended to be value judgments. Each has its own strengths and each is necessary. It is up to you which is more desirable for you, at this time.

Which child best fits the perspective in which you were raised? Do you think authority comes *to* you, *from* you, or *through* you?

Exercise: What is your worldview?

We each must choose what and how we want to see. Each of the examples above represents aspects of a particular way of seeing and experiencing the universe in which we live; each is an outline of a worldview.

Which of the three examples fits most closely with the belief systems in which you were raised? Which of these systems best fits how you see the world now?

If you could choose to support fully just one of these worldviews, to put all of your power of thought, belief, and creativity into manifesting one of these systems of thought in your world, where would you choose to put your energy and belief?

Think about this last question a bit more. Do you put your energy and choices into building the world the way you want it to be, or do you make choices that build the world the way you were taught it was?

Internal Orientation

External orientation, especially when blame is used, puts all focus on avoiding the real issues—which are located inside. Instead of addressing the discomfort where it truly is, the external perspective requires that we expend vast amounts of energy fighting with external factors in order to get rid of a perceived problem. Of course, this seldom works for very long. The problem can't be killed, and the scapegoat only takes the brunt of the negative energy for a little while—then a new scapegoat is needed. Throughout history, humankind has repeated the cycle of blame and sacrifice over and over and over in a wearying repetitiveness that defies rationality. Finally, people are beginning to wake up to the reality that blame only increases our pain, misery, and smallness, and they are waking to the awareness that there is another way.

This other way is part of waking up—but it is not new and does not depend on what is written here. It was stated by Jesus when he said "love one another". It has been stated by great spiritual leaders throughout all human history. It is just now that, finally, a greater number of people are beginning to understand.

To "love one another" requires an internal orientation that can be focused on seeing things as they really are. This means removing the filters of judgment, fear and expectation and understanding the paradox of being both powerful and powerless, both responsible and guiltless, both connected to everything and alone in a choice of action. Seeing things as they truly are requires clear self-knowledge and awareness in order to separate what I want, or what I expect, from what is presenting itself to me.

Ultimately, the lessons of change, of the Field, and of the mirror, help me to understand more clearly and to use this clear understanding to choose actions that are truly in my own best interest. If understanding is clear, it becomes obvious that my best interests cannot be separated from the best interests of the people and environment around me.

Acting from an internal viewpoint, therefore, is a move away from the historically prevalent human tendency to find scapegoats and external reasons to blame for all problems. It replaces blame with responsibility, denial with integrity, self-deception with rigorous truth, automatic reaction with considered action, dependency with personal power, and victim/martyr mentality with the courage to take charge of one's own fate.

There are many people, however, who still are not willing or able to accept this kind of clarity or personal responsibility. Like the two first children in the examples above, they may have been taught from birth to live with an external orientation, or they may not have had the good fortune to be loved and cared for enough to be able to look within themselves. Their experience generally involves a greater degree of suffering, but it is not wrong. The whole point of an awakened worldview is lost if it becomes another religion bent on changing the viewpoint of others by force.

When the Field, and the flow of energy and information within it, begins to be understood, power over others becomes irrelevant, since there is no need to have power over something that is a part of oneself. One part of a waterfall has no need to control the other parts. It simply takes part in the exhilaration of existence.

Falling awake, like falling asleep, can't be forced. It can, however, be prepared for. The point to consider as you read these words is what reality you want for yourself. If you prefer to remain asleep, then practicing the external viewpoint will help you with the necessary denial, blame, and violence. Practicing living from an internal perspective and seeing the world as a mirror of who you are will help to prepare you for the experience of flowing with the Field as a co-creator of your own life.

Exercises for changing the locus of control

For all guilt is a state of being lost in the past; all anxiety is a state of being lost in the future.

Ken Wilber, No Boundary

People so often say the world will never change; it's not the world that needs it—it's people. If you spend time looking only at what you want to see, for whatever reason, you really don't want a change.[13]

1. Noticing blame—journaling exercise

The first step in changing something is simply being aware of it. To help yourself become aware of places where you may be placing blame or relinquishing your own power, give yourself some time to sit down with your journal.

Take a few deep breaths to calm your mind and give yourself the intention to focus on seeing the conflicts that you have in your life. Once your intention is set, allow your mind to picture the people or situations with whom or with which you are in conflict. Conflict includes arguments, anger, strong disagreement, traffic anger, feelings of powerlessness, political, ideological, or religious beliefs which portray other groups as being wrong or bad. It also includes derision, belittling others or self, things that you don't like about someone else or yourself, things that irritate you about someone else, and any other case in which "I" am good or right and someone else is not or in which "I" am bad or less than someone else.

As each case comes up, write down your name and the name of the person or situation, and then move on. Stop when you can't think of any further conflicts.

---

13 Written by an American convict named Russell in a letter to Bo Lozoff, and printed in Bo's book: *We're All Doing Time* (Lozoff, 1985).

Now go back through the list putting an arrow in each case pointing in the direction that blame is going. If you blame yourself or see yourself as bad or wrong, the arrow points toward you. If you blame the other side or think that they are bad, wrong, irritating, inferior, or otherwise unworthy, the arrow goes toward them.

It is possible, and very common, to apply blame internally. Blame's focus is on making someone guilty, not on finding solutions and not on healing. Blame is about retribution, and we exact this retribution from ourselves as much as from others. It is equally destructive in either direction, and in fact all the arrows have two heads, pointing in both directions. You cannot blame yourself without also blaming others and vice versa. However, for the purposes of this exercise it is useful to know in which direction you generally direct your blame.

Not all conflict involves blame. It may be that this is a healthy conflict in which you see yourself and the other person or situation as equals and you can feel a sense of love and respect for yourself and the other person while still disagreeing with them. In this case, put a circle around both your name and the name of the other person or situation.

Note which way most of the arrows point. Do you apply blame outwardly more often, or do you apply it to yourself?

Would you like to resolve any of these conflicts? How could the concept of the world as your mirror help to change the way that you see your conflicts?

Important note: This exercise is also a good measure of your degree of self-awareness and self-honesty. Everyone has some conflict somewhere, so if you don't have much to write down, you may want to think about this a bit more. Also, direct conflicts with a person are easier to see or admit to than conflictual states of mind, such as religious or political views that single out particular groups as being good or saved and other groups that are not, or internal blame or generalized guilt that is carried around as a sense of being bad or not good enough.

2. Exercise for seeing another person

In the practice of tantric sexuality, partners attempt to reach awareness of God through a process of truly seeing each other and understanding that they are mirrors of the divine for each other. How might it change your life if you used every interaction with another human as a way of seeing the mystery and divinity of all things more clearly?

This exercise can be practiced anywhere, anytime. Try it while standing in a grocery line-up, driving in rush hour traffic, meeting with your boss, putting a child to bed or making love with your partner. Release the world you think you have made and understand that you cannot see what is not already within you. Choose to see your own divinity in others and you will find it in yourself. Choose to condemn others and you will also condemn yourself.

3. Forgiving God

This is a somewhat advanced exercise and may require a heavy dose of sedation for the internal skeptic. However, the idea of a creator or some divine life source has been with the human race for as long as we have history, and it is deeply embedded in our collective psyche. No matter what your current beliefs are, the concept of God is in your background in one way or another.

Except, perhaps, in the case of some highly accomplished mystics, the human relationship with God always involves an element of anger and need for forgiveness. Either it is God who must forgive people or, particularly in this time period, people who are angry with how badly God has messed up.

Either way, the lesson of the mirror is that *God* and *I* cannot be separated. A finger cannot be pointed at one or the other without the mirror reflecting it right back again in the other direction as well. The lesson here is that forgiveness is not about saying everything is OK and letting someone get away with rotten behaviour. Instead, forgiveness is about freeing myself from the anger, blame, guilt and hatred that I have been holding.

To practice this exercise, take a few moments several times a day to notice the people, animals or objects around you. For anything that comes into your awareness simply say *"I release you from my expectations and judgments. I forgive you, and I ask for your forgiveness."* Hold in your mind the intention of seeing everything around you as an aspect of Divine Mystery, part of the universal field, part of God and part of yourself.

It can also be very helpful to try this exercise with God—whether you believe in God or not. Try addressing your conception of God and see what it feels like to release him/her/it from your expectations and judgments and to accept that you and God are one. Is this difficult? Does it feel blasphemous or frightening? What emotions come up when you do this?

4. Committing to Love

As we learn to look from the inside out and to come from an internal locus of control it becomes increasingly clear that it is impossible to cause harm to another in any way without harming and undermining ourselves. Though it is possible, through ignorance, to hide from this truth, hiding does not make it less true. Ignorance can provide some anaesthesia when we hurt ourselves and others, but it does not protect us from the wounds.

Looking deeply inside also puts us more deeply in touch with the foundation energy of the Field, and it becomes clear that this energy is love. The Hawaiian Huna practice of Ho'oponopono is a very concise synthesis of the perspective that all that is outside is also inside. Huna was repressed in Hawaii for many years. However, like many other ancient paths, it is now beginning to be more widely known and the once outlawed wisdom is again beginning to be taught and respected.

In the practice of Ho'oponopono, it is understood that we are not separate and isolated beings. We are each connected to each other, and we are in touch with this connection through the unconscious mind. In Ho'oponopono, it is understood that I am 100% responsible for everything that I see as a problem, no matter how far away from me it is or how disconnected from me it is. This is different from blame—I am not to blame for the problem, but I am responsible because I am holding it in my mind and supporting it with my belief and energy. By removing my support for the problem, I help to heal the collective unconsciousness of the human race which holds so many thoughts of war, death, and suffering. I also move myself, and the world as well, in a direction of returning toward the zero state, or God.[14]

Ho'oponopono is just one part of the very deep practice that is Huna. However, it is also a simple and powerful way of cleaning up our relationships with the people in our lives and of bringing a greater sense of harmony to ourselves and to our relationships. In its simplest form, Ho'oponopono can be stated as a single prayer, repeated like a mantra to yourself whenever you are having difficulties with a person, situation, or feeling:

I'm Sorry. Please Forgive me. I Love you. Thank you.

As you are saying this, put your conscious intention into each statement, allowing yourself to feel the words rather than just reciting them. Let this intention expand into the Field, letting go of a need for particular results. This is a freeing exercise and can be used for healing yourself and others—physically, emotionally and energetically.

---

14 Further information about Ho'oponopono practice is easily available with an internet search for the word. A good book on the topic is *Zero Limits: The Secret Hawaiian System for Wealth, Health, Peace, and More* by Joe Vitale. (2007)

The idea of having 100% responsibility for what we perceive, and of saying "I am sorry" or "please forgive me" can be difficult in situations where there has been abuse and cruelty. How can I, or why should I, say I am sorry or ask forgiveness of someone who has been abusive or cruel to me? There are so many examples of heinous cruelty and abuse, and the villains often seem to get off with far less than what they deserve.

This is discussed further in the chapter on forgiveness—but there are no easy answers here. The most important thing to remember is that we are discussing changing the locus of control, and as long as we believe that we are victims, our locus of control is located outside of ourselves. Taking responsibility for my own perception does not mean condoning what someone else has done to me. It does, however, mean realizing that I am the only one who can set myself free of the pain and trauma that holding onto blame and victimhood entails. If I am abused, it is like having a hot coal thrust into my hands. I don't often have a choice about receiving the coal but I do have a choice about what I do with it once I have received it. Ho'oponopono helps us to remember that we have the option of dropping the coal so that we are not continually burned, even when the abuse is over.

Chapter 8
Boundaries

And this is one of the major questions of our lives: how we keep boundaries, what permission we have to cross boundaries, and how we do so.

A. B. Yehoshua

It is impossible to have a healthy relationship with someone who has no boundaries... It is impossible to learn to be loving to ourselves without owning our self—and owning our rights and responsibilities as co-creators of our lives.

Robert Burney

Boundaries are actually the main factor in space, just as the present, another boundary, is the main factor in time.

Eduardo Chillida

Thus far, we have been looking at the ways in which the energetic basis of who we are is connected to, and in many ways one and the same with, all objects and people. We have also discussed the importance of bringing our perspective to an internal point of reference so that we can understand the world as a mirror, reflecting who we are. However, it is also true that we are separate beings with separate thoughts and experience, and our physical bodies do not generally experience the connection that is inherent in the Field.

Though it may seem somewhat paradoxical, in order to have a good understanding of the concept of the interconnection of all things, it is also necessary to have a good understanding of the boundaries that seemingly separate things. Although we, along with all other beings, are connected and *One* through the Field, we are also unique within the boundaries of our own fields.

Boundaries can be experienced on many levels. We have energetic boundaries marking the outer edges of the body's energy field. We also have psychological boundaries, emotional boundaries, verbal boundaries, and physical boundaries. Bringing awareness to all of these levels of boundary can be helpful, as boundaries are intimately associated with conflict. Understanding boundaries helps to better understand conflict and how to work with it with skill and effectiveness.

Boundaries are, in many ways, psychological constructs and are very useful psychological tools. As my experience is centered on the psychological implications and uses of energy and fields, this chapter will be focused mainly on the psychological aspects and implications of boundaries. However, boundaries also have a basis in energy and in the way that our individual fields interact with each other. Psychology, like biology, cannot be separated from the basic matrix of energy that supports all things.

No matter if we are considering an energetic, psychological, or physical boundary, at its simplest, this boundary is just a line that denotes where one region stops and another begins. The region in question can be anything from a country to a belief system, from a property line to a code of conduct, from a cellular membrane to a human being. The word "no" sets a boundary, all laws are boundaries, and each choice about what we will and will not accept into our lives is a boundary.

Our bodies also have boundaries. On the physical level, the skin is the obvious boundary that divides what is physically *me* from what isn't. The skin is a flexible barrier that allows passage of some materials, blocks others, and provides a sensitive antenna for sensing the outside world through touch.

In addition to the skin, however, our bodies have another layer of boundary that is experienced by many people. My own experience, and the experience of many people I know, is that the human body has an energy field that extends outward from the body a variable distance. Actually, this field has several layers, and each layer has its own boundary. However, for the sake of simplicity, we will think of this energy field as forming a single boundary layer, completely enclosing the physical body.

The boundary layer formed by the human energy field is very flexible, elastic, and durable. It can be so small as to touch the skin and so large as to encompass a whole room, or house, or even at times to extend beyond the earth. This boundary is a very subtle line, somewhat like a thin membrane that denotes the place where *I* stop and where everything else begins. It must be noted, of course, that in a very real sense, the distinction between what is *I* and what is outside of *I* is an artificial one. On the level of the basic field, we are all connected.

However, on the level of individual organisms and objects—humans included—there is a need for some distinction, and there is a reality that we live in a separated state. My body energy field is the container that helps to define who I am, and that holds all of me together.

A very helpful way of understanding the idea of energetic boundary is to consider a cell membrane. The membrane is an extremely thin layer of lipids—literally much like a film of oil on water. However, this thin membrane fulfills a large number of functions. It protects the interior of the cell from unfriendly or unhealthy substances with which it comes into contact. It permits the passage of nutrients and useful substances into the cell and the passage of waste substances out of the cell, maintaining an equilibrium so that the cell always has the right amount of what it needs. The cell membrane is also a sensing device that is able to sense chemical messages sent from other cells or from elsewhere in the body, react to electrical signals, communicate and send messages to other cells, and sense the chemical composition of the cell's immediate surroundings.

Most importantly, the cell membrane is an elastic and flexible container that defines the outer limits of the cell and holds all of the parts of the cell together. If the membrane is removed, a cell becomes just a bunch of tiny components floating apart. The cell can't be a cell without the membrane to define its edges.

Similarly, the human energy field defines the outer limits of a person's personal space; it is the container that holds all of my parts—emotional, physical, mental and spiritual together. Within this field is the dynamic, energetic, changing process that is called "I". This "I" is not, in an ultimate sense, a real thing, nor is it actually separate. Like the parts of a cell, it is merely an aspect of a larger reality. However, also like a cell, it does have a separate physical existence, and it can be useful to know about the boundaries that define this existence.

Before we go on, it would be helpful for you to get a sense of what it feels like to be gently contained. To do this, first try putting your hands in front of you, arms straight, palms out, held about chest level. Tighten your muscles and push out with the intention of holding away from you whatever may be attacking. Imagine that you are trying to push away all of the problems, people and issues that are out there, push away the world, and protect yourself. Get a sense of how this feels in your body—what do you notice about your state of mind, tension, and breathing?

Now relax your arms for a few moments and take four or five deep breaths. On the last deep inhalation, raise your arms up to chest level again. This time however, turn your palms in to face your chest and bend your arms and lift your elbows slightly as if you were holding onto a large round pillow in front of you. Exhale and relax, holding your arms in this position. Feel your arms defining the edge of a field that surrounds you on all sides and that gently contains you. It is elastic and strong, so you can relax and let who you are simply fill it and push out against its edges. Relax so that you can be gently contained by this elastic boundary. Again, notice what your body is feeling. What do you notice in your state of mind, body tension, and breathing? Notice which of these two feelings (pushing away or containing) you feel most often. Do this before you read on.

Generally, people experience the pushing out exercise as one that is quite tense. It requires more effort, and it often coincides with a sense of insecurity, worry, or fear as I push the world away, knowing that it is ultimately bigger and stronger than I am. Some people, especially men, experience this exercise as a sense of strength and defiance—a kind of "just try it, I'm ready for you" attitude. However, even when it feels strong, the pushing out position requires more effort and tension. The pushing out exercise is also an example of old paradigm thinking where problems are solved by pushing against, or fighting with, what is outside of *me*.

The containing position generally feels more relaxed, and many people find it to be an unfamiliar and unexpected relief to just relax and expand out against the edge of their own space. However, it is also a very unfamiliar feeling for many people and so can be uncomfortable to start with. If we have spent most of our lives pushing out against the world, it can be very difficult to relax into our own container. This is especially true for people who have difficulties trusting. Remember that what we see on the outside actually originates from what we feel and deeply believe on the inside. If you have difficulties trusting others for instance, it is likely that you will also have difficulties trusting the integrity of your own space and your ability to relax within it.

Here are some exercises that you can use to begin to experience your own boundary:

Boundary exercises

1. Individual boundary

1. Cut a piece of yarn or small diameter rope at least 5 meters long.

2. Sit in a chair or on the floor and take a few deep breaths with your eyes closed.

3. Think of someone about whom you have a neutral feeling—not a strong attraction or a strong dislike. Imagine this person moving slowly toward you. How far away from your body would you want them to stop?

4. Use the yarn or rope to mark the line showing where you would want this neutral person to stop coming closer to you.

5. Notice if you have made a complete enclosed space or if it is open in one or more places.

6. Try to notice what you feel in your body that tells you that the string is in the right place. Where in your body do you feel this?

7. Once your string seems to be in the right place, try moving it a bit. If it is open, try closing it to make a complete enclosure. If it is large, try making it smaller. If it is small, try making it larger. Each time you change something, take a minute or so to sit still, breathe, and notice your body. What do you notice when you change the size of your boundary? Do you feel comfortable inside your boundary, or do you want to get outside of it?

This exercise can be very helpful for children. I will often ask a child to mark out his or her personal space with a line of yarn. Sometimes the child will mark out a space but not put him or herself inside of the space. Interestingly, children who don't have a good sense of their own space are more likely to either be bullied or be a bully. Learning about personal space and boundaries is a very helpful first step toward building confidence and can also be a helpful tool in bully-proofing.

Once you become familiar with the idea of marking your boundary with string, you can practice visualizing it at any time. Visualizing your boundary is a very helpful tool to use in situations of conflict with another person, when you have feelings of insecurity, or when you need to sort out what part of an issue is yours and what part belongs to someone else.

Your boundary is the dividing line between *you* and *not you*. Everything inside the line, including all of the feelings, needs, desires, and thoughts belong to you. They are your direct responsibility. Everything outside the line belongs to someone else and is therefore not your direct responsibility. It is much more effective to focus your energy on changing what is inside your boundary than to focus energy on trying to change what is outside of it.

2. Boundary with a partner

1. Ask a friend to sit down about 10 feet away from you. Make a boundary as you did in exercise one.

2. Ask your friend to move slowly toward you—perhaps one foot at a time, waiting for a few seconds before moving closer. Note how your body reacts as your friend moves closer.

3. Usually, there is a particular point that is close enough. When your friend moves beyond this point, you will become less comfortable. Note where this point is. Is it outside your boundary? Are you comfortable having someone come inside your boundary? Do you feel better as they move toward you, or do you feel more uncomfortable the nearer they approach? What is your body's reaction in each of these situations?

4. Have your friend move away again. Do you feel sad or abandoned as they move away, or more calm, relaxed and relieved when you have some space again? What is your body reaction as your friend moves farther away from you?

5. Switch around so that you are the one approaching and moving away from your friend, then repeat this exercise. Notice what you feel as you approach and as you move away again.

If you try this exercise with different people, you will find that the distances change. We have different comfort levels with different people, and this is OK.

You may find that you don't have a strong boundary, or any feeling of boundary at all, and will welcome most people all the way inside your space. Consider how this plays out in other aspects of your life. Do you feel that people abandon you often? Do you often seem to be on the needy side of a relationship? Do you crave closeness and never seem to quite get enough? Do you feel like a victim often, take on feelings from others, or feel overly sensitive? Are you the one who generally tries to hold on to relationships, fix them, find a way to connect?

On the other end of the spectrum, you may find that the boundary exercise is empowering. Finally, a way of saying "keep out" and "stay away". You like to have your own space and hate to be invaded by others. Sharing your feelings and being "close" is uncomfortable. You can instantly relate with the idea of space and boundary, and it feels like a relief to give yourself permission to have your own space.

This is a spectrum and most people fall somewhere between the two extreme ends. However, spouses or partners are often near different poles. It can be helpful to do this exercise with a partner and understand the different requirements and expectations around space that you have. This can help both partners to find ways of moving closer to the middle.

* * *

It is helpful to think of boundaries as circles, or spheres, to put it in three dimensions. Like the example of a cell, we each have a boundary that denotes the edges of our own container. Inside the container is *me*. Outside the container is *everything else*. Of course, these distinctions are of diminishing importance as we move more deeply into the awakening. As we realize our oneness with all things, keeping separate a little bit of that oneness becomes unnecessary. However, we also live in a three dimensional reality where distinctions of separation do make a difference. Using boundaries skillfully requires understanding that they are arbitrary, flexible, and ultimately imaginary while at the same time having a sense of impeccable integrity about what belongs inside and what belongs outside. This is a paradox that the mind doesn't like very much, but that's OK. Don't be worried about what the mind says, and keep returning to the body awareness that you practiced in the exercises above.

Knowing what is inside your circle and what is outside is essential for relationships, and is also a step in developing the integrity necessary to move out of the victim-perpetrator cycle. In a relationship, this means understanding that the feelings, desires, drives, and needs that come from within my sphere are MINE. I own them, I take responsibility for them, I create them, they are MINE, regardless of what may appear to be happening in the spheres around me. Any attempt to make my feelings the fault of someone else is a misunderstanding of the way the world works, a misunderstanding that always results in increased suffering.

As you may remember from the section on the universe as our mirror, a fundamental difference between the objective/material worldview and the energy worldview is a shift in the direction of the arrow of causation. In the objective/material worldview, I am basically a helpless victim thrust into the world to survive as best I can. I can dominate or succumb, but one way or the other what I experience is a result of what happens to me. My feelings, thoughts, and actions are therefore the result of what is imposed on me from the outside and my only hope for peace or security is to change or fix what is *out there* so that it will meet my needs more effectively.

As we awaken into the energy perspective, and beyond, it becomes clear that the arrow of causation is actually the reverse of what we learned from our objective/material teachers. From the awakened perspective what I see, say, do and experience is a result of who I am and the filters through which I view the world around me. Therefore, what I say and do is an expression of how I see and understand myself and my world.

For example, imagine that you give me a gift. You made it and it comes from you. I accept the gift but decide I don't like it. I get angry and throw it back at you. I add a few more gifts of my own and throw them at you too. You accept my gifts dramatically, and enthusiastically throw more gifts back at me. We keep doing this until we run out of energy or get tired of it. Sometimes this can take a lifetime. Sometimes it goes on for generations.

Put like this, the whole process seems a bit silly. However, this is what happens when we experience the world without boundaries and without understanding what we are doing. You give me a gift that is all about YOU, but I think it is about ME. I use it as evidence to support my lack of self-worth and my belief that you are an idiot and a jerk. I give you more gifts, in the form of my thoughts, words and actions, and you make the same mistake that I have made. You use a reaction you are used to using—aggressive or passive aggressive or victim/martyr or whatever other story you are fond of—and the conflict builds. The ego loves this because it can build a huge bonfire of drama very quickly. If I like drama and suffering, then this is definitely a good way to get what I am looking for.

If I am getting tired of suffering, however, there is another possibility. You offer me a gift. From within my own boundary I understand that this gift is an expression of who you are and what you are feeling in this moment. I understand that the gift is not about me at all. I don't like it very much, and so I let it go. Perhaps I return it to you. Perhaps I throw it in the garbage. Maybe I just drop it and forget it. In any case, I know I'm OK. I choose to see myself as OK and I choose to see you as OK. That's it. It's so simple that most of us will do our best to completely misunderstand it for as long as possible. But that's OK too. Just know that every moment is another opportunity to realize how OK you are, regardless of what is happening around you.

One real life and somewhat extreme example of this is given by Victor Frankl from his experience in a Nazi concentration camp. In one instance he was strapped to a table so that he couldn't move. Rather than succumb completely to fear and hate, he began experimenting. He realized that he could still move his eyes. He could still wiggle his toes. He could move some fingers. He was still in charge of his own mind. He still had freedom. By doing this, he was able to stay out of terror, or hate, or insanity. He lived through the concentration camp experience and managed to use it as a basis for helping many people.

What was different from Victor Frankl and others in the camp? Why, under the same conditions, was he able to emerge whole and capable of loving and helping while others were not? I think it is because he knew that he could choose his own perceptions and he chose to see what was whole and life-giving, even in conditions of extreme fear, suffering, and imminent death. He later taught his students to see people for what they can be, not what you think they are. Find the spark of possibility in each person and you will help them to find it in themselves.

The lesson of boundaries is that the responsibility for this choice lies inside my own sacred circle. If I choose to see another as unworthy, or to accept an attack, then I am also choosing to see myself as unworthy, as a victim, without the integrity to be responsible for myself. As I understand the true direction of the arrow of causation, I also understand that when I see the spark of possibility in another, I affirm and promote it in myself. Boundaries are a useful tool to sort out what is mine, what is not mine, what I can control and what I cannot. Using this tool well can mean the difference between enmeshed, co-dependent, resentful relationships and loving, freeing and uplifting relationships.

As always, it is a choice, and it is much simpler than it seems. Own what is yours. Don't take personally what belongs to others. Know and express your feelings and desires respectfully. Don't expect others to fulfill your desires. Believe in yourself and look for the spark of light within all things. Tell the truth, especially to yourself.

These are boundary lessons. As always, we have the choice to love or to suffer. Boundaries help to give more skillful means of making the choice to love.

Chapter 9
Healing the Past

I'm here little one. I believe in you. I love you. If you need to cry or scream or hate or resist I will stay with you. If you are lonely I will give you courage. If you are sad, I will listen. If you are angry I will keep you safe. If you are frightened I will protect you. I will be with you until you die, and after your death I will still be with you. I am stronger than your fears and you cannot lose my love.[15]

The wound is the place where the Light enters you.

Rumi

Although the Awakening that is taking place in the world is a process of opening to a wider perspective of what is real and what is possible, it is also a process of healing the psychological and energetic wounds that follow us

---

15 At about 18 months old I had an operation to remove my cancerous right eye. The aftermath of the operation involved not only the painful recovery, but also multiple episodes of being held down, unable to move, while things were repeatedly inserted into the eye socket in order to form and fit a prosthetic eye. Although I had no memory of this for many years, it profoundly affected my mind, body, and way of being in the world and has been a focus of many hours of therapy. I wrote this affirmation as a message from my current self to the little boy screaming bloody murder and unable to move or escape, and to all subsequent ages of myself when I didn't believe that I was OK. The children that we were, and who still exist within us, need this depth of love and commitment. If we have children, then they need it as well.

through generation after generation, handed down by parents who were also struggling with wounds. Strong negative feelings result when we come into contact with situations that remind us (consciously or unconsciously) of past pain. In order to free oneself enough to step into new ways of experiencing the world, it is often helpful to first step back and heal or release the perceptions of wounds and challenges that come from childhood experience.

There are many misconceptions about this sort of healing. Since Freud first began refining his idea of psychoanalysis, the idea that there are things hidden in our past that will come out and bite us later has taken hold in our cultural belief system. Today, many people fear going to see a counsellor precisely because they think they will have to talk about their childhood or spend lots of time and money discussing memories of things that have long since passed. The worth of this seems highly questionable to many people, and the desire to do it, regardless of worth, is even more questionable.

Fortunately, healing the past does not require spending hours on a couch talking to a psychoanalyst. In fact, in my opinion at least, the effectiveness of rehashing one's history in this way is somewhat over-rated and is actually missing a very important understanding of the way the mind works.

Adyashanti, a spiritual teacher from California, defines the ego as *a repeating pattern of circular thought, based on separation.* This is a simple definition and is also a very useful, far-reaching, and deep definition—one that can help a great deal in clarifying what is or is not useful when working to dissolve past patterns and heal past wounds.

From the perspective of the Awakening, it is important to reiterate that a human being is much more than the mind/body system defined by the science of the objective/material worldview. A human is an entity ultimately based in a Field of infinite probability and consisting of vibrational patterns of energy that manifest as physical, emotional, and mental constructs. The objective/material perspective recognizes the physical, emotional and mental components of being and is therefore not wrong. However, it misses the deeper aspects on which these surface constructions are based, and therefore limits the possibilities for understanding and for healing.

A human personality, or ego, is a relatively shallow aspect of a human entity. It is, as Adyashanti says, basically a repeating and circular pattern of thoughts—like a set of computer programs that determine the behaviour and responses of a computer. The programs that define an individual ego are the result of genetic influences (which are of course derived from millions of years of history), from cultural influences, family and community influences, life events and experiences, environmental influences and economic influences, to name only a few of the factors. All these programs, however, are based on a single very important idea—the idea that there is a difference between what is *me* and *not me*.

On a physical level this me/not me difference is quite obviously true. It can also be true on some energetic levels, and it can be hard for the mind to accept that two (or more) conflicting realities can be present in the same space at the same time. That's OK. The mind is not at all good with paradox, and this is one reason that paradox is so useful. A human personality is only the surface aspect of the being that is a human—the part that can be accessed and experienced through thought and emotion. As explained earlier in the waterfall analogy, a waterfall can be identified as having different characteristics from the river and as being separate from other waterfalls, but it still is a function of the flow of water. Many falls can exist even in the same river; each waterfall both is and is not separate from the river and from the other falls.

The deeper aspect of who we are, both below and enveloping the layer of ego and personality, is unaffected by whatever changes we may or may not make to our personalities or the coping mechanisms that we use in order to get by in the world. Like the depths of the ocean that are unaffected by the storms and waves above, the deeper aspect of being is not affected by experience or actions. There are also no separate and individual waves—no *me* or *not me*. There is just water. This is the level at which, as my teacher in Thailand would repeatedly say, "Everything is already OK".

In most Western psychological approaches to therapy, the idea is to define a problem and then fix it using one method or another. Generally, the patient implicitly agrees that he or she is damaged, and the therapist agrees to help fix him or her—or as is becoming currently more popular, the therapist facilitates the patient's self-healing. Either way, both the therapist and patient assume that the patient has a problem and that something must be done to resolve this problem.

From the perspective of the Awakening, however, the foundation of therapy is different. Beginning at the center of *being*, there is no problem and there is no separation. There is nothing that can be a problem, nothing that can be lost and nothing that can be gained. There is nothing to fix, and anything that is perceived as a problem is simply an error of perception. It is a program, a repeating system of thoughts, an ephemeral and changing bit of nothingness to which we have given some attention.

Healing the past, from this perspective, is quite a lot simpler and less traumatic than it is from the perspectives usually presented in the objective/material worldview. There is no need for methods or techniques, although they can still be used if desired. The patient/therapist relationship can still be important but not as a relationship in which one person needs to be fixed and the other helps or facilitates the fixing. The relationship is useful because it provides a safe place where two beings who believe themselves to be separate can come together and in an act of dynamic co-creation of experience, remember and reflect their wholeness to each other. There is no more powerful catalyst of healing on the personality level than a single moment of Presence from the being level. In this state of Presence, *you* and *I* are just like waves on an ocean—simultaneously different in form and *one* in essence.

Of course, the rational mind will read all of this and miss the point that there is nothing that really needs to be done. The rational mind still wants to do something and wants to know how to do it. This is OK too—we have rational minds for a reason after all. It is just important for this mind to begin to realize that it is not the whole of what we are—nor even close. It has to realize that it does not need to be in control all the time.

While the rational mind is learning to let go of control and to just relax into the wholeness, stillness and peace of what it already is, here are a few things that it can do:

Noticing Thought Loops

A thought loop is a circular and repeating pattern of thought. Thought loops are also often connected with emotions and behaviours that increase in strength as the loop continues. Thoughts are transient, biased, and unreliable things. Like stereotypical used car salesmen, it is not a good idea to trust them.[16] Paying attention to thoughts can be helpful, but mainly in order to identify the loops.

As discussed earlier, the ego is actually constructed from these thought loops, which repeat and strengthen themselves. Bringing non-judgmental awareness to a thought loop is like bringing water to a bowl of sugar. Sometimes the sugar will dissolve away immediately. Other times the sugar is hard and crystalized and will resist the water for quite a while. However, no matter how long it takes, patiently, quietly, without judgment or hurry, the water and sugar always become one with each other.

Also patiently and without judgment, bring your attention to the thought loop just long enough to identify it. "Ah, here you are again," you may say. Once you have noticed the loop, stop looking at it. You have already given it more attention than it needs, and there is no reason to give it more. Each time it pops into your mind, patiently, but briefly, notice and then let it go. Like a cloud, like water flowing in a river, like soap bubbles in the wind, these thoughts are just passing by. Relax. Leave them alone. There is nothing that you need to do. Just notice and let go. Eventually you won't even need to notice. Everything is already OK.

Paying attention to body sensations

When thought loops become very strong, they can be quite difficult to notice and then ignore. Conversely, there are times when thought loops exist but are very hard to identify. In both these cases, the body can be an important helper and source of information.

The mind and the body are in fact not two separate things. There is no thought that arises without some sensation in the body—with or without

---

16 This is not to say that thoughts are worthless. They are very good for doing things like designing bridges or cell phones, or planning a vacation or figuring out a budget. They are just not good when they become identified with *self*. They are tools, not identity.

awareness of the connection—and no sensation that is not in some way connected to a thought. Much of the difficulty we get ourselves into arises simply because we choose to believe our own thoughts, and then we become negatively or positively attached to the sensations that go along with them. No thought is worth believing, as there is no thought that can be present. All thoughts are actually the past considering itself or the past considering the future. It is not possible for them to exist in the present.

Most thoughts are difficult to detect in the body because they are small and fleeting. We get into further difficulty, however, when a thought loop begins to cause strong emotions and sensations in the body or when a strong emotion or sensation begins to cause strong thoughts. Either way, each step of the loop strengthens the next, and on each turn of the circle, the whole system becomes both stronger and more persistent.

It can be very helpful to train yourself to notice when a thought loop and a sensation or set of sensations and emotions arise together. When you notice a thought loop or strong emotion happening, ask yourself where you feel it in your body. Use physical feeling words such as hot, cold, hard, soft, smooth, acidic, warm, burning, tight, sharp, achy, scratchy, itchy, full, heavy etc. to describe the feeling.

As with thoughts, don't give the sensation too much attention. Allow awareness to sink in around it and then leave it alone. Be patient when it comes up, and don't become frustrated when it doesn't go away immediately. If you can't manage that, don't be frustrated with being frustrated. At some point, there will be a place where you can realize you are OK. Let the OK settle into the cracks and openings of your mind and body until it is all that is left. This, after all, is the only truth that matters.

Viral Thought Loops

Minds like to make things complicated, and they often resist simple things like letting go, relaxing, or being OK. If you have noticed your thoughts and identified the associated physical sensations and you are still having difficulties, it is likely that you are experiencing a thought loop that began long ago and has now become very strong and tricky.

Thought loops have a reason to exist. They are shortcut programs that our brain uses in order to protect us and to help us to react quickly in dangerous situations. They are also intelligent programs that thrive on attention. They recognize any situation that has a similar feeling to the experience in which they were created, and they expand their reactions to include these situations. The loops that control the most reactions get the most attention and literally gain energy, substance, and endurance, thereby out-competing other possibly more positive thought loops.

A further difficulty with thought loops is that they often get confused about who or what they are protecting. Thought loops, when joined together into a mass of beliefs, images, and experiences, begin to believe that they are an identity. When they get to this stage thought loops and beliefs do not, however, care what their results are or what the quality of feeling is that they elicit. They exist in order to exist and they propagate themselves with no consideration of anything else. For this reason, a thought loop like "I'm stupid, ugly and worthless" is actually quite successful. It is difficult to ignore, it joins up with very deep physical feelings and emotions, causes a large variety of behaviours which make it stronger, and generally thrives once it gets introduced into a system. It also bounces from internal to external and accuses others with "**You** are stupid, ugly and worthless." This further increases the scope of the program and helps to infect other people with the same thought loop.

In fact, thought loops, as well as beliefs of any sort, can behave a great deal like viruses. They attack a host, use the host's own systems to replicate themselves, and infect others around them. The positive or negative nature of the belief or thought loop is irrelevant to the survival of the loop itself. The only thing that is relevant is the amount of attention that it gets and the number of feeling situations into which it can hook itself. These are the things that make it stronger and more successful.

One very common example of this is the thought loop "I'm bad." This thought loop usually develops very early in life, often in response to a relatively minor incident. It can even develop before birth, in response to a situation like an unwanted pregnancy or as a hand-me-down from a mother and father's belief systems. If we take the unwanted pregnancy as a specific example, a child who is subjected in the womb to a mother's distress at being pregnant begins its life soaked in a feeling of being unwanted and disapproved of. It has no way of understanding why this is happening, but it also has no escape from the negative feelings. There are only two places the feelings can be directed—internally as "I'm bad" or externally as "you're bad". Both these conflicting directives are internalized and become part of the program.

Once begun, the program starts to react to any situation that has even a slight feeling-resemblance to the feeling environment in which it was created. Disapproval from others, making mistakes, not being pretty or handsome enough, not having a good enough job, not feeling popular... the list of triggers just keeps growing as "I'm bad" finds more things to hook itself into. The opposite polarity of the loop also grows into an expanding list of "you're bad". The person finds more and more people and situations that seem to be threatening or unsafe and, if left without larger awareness, the underlying "I'm bad/you're bad" program becomes increasingly dominant as a part of the person's personality. It also becomes the filter through which he or she sees the world and therefore biases all incoming information in such a way as to strengthen itself. As the person gets older "I'm bad" can become the dominant personality characteristic, and a kind of prison with no windows from which the person cannot even conceive of escaping. From a defensive program it has become identified as self, and the human entity in which the program is running has lost the ability to see beyond it.

Often, programs of this sort start to get out of hand, crossing lines of behaviour that are socially unacceptable. When this happens, counter programs are developed that run on top of the old program and limit what it can do. The deeper program still can use these new programs, however. To continue with "I'm bad", a child may hit someone and be punished for it. He learns that he can't hit people every time he wants to and changes his behaviour—a new "I'll be nice" program develops. However, he also learns that he's bad for hitting, bad for wanting to hit, and bad for having to use the "I'll be nice" program. The two programs run in opposition to each other, which works rather well for the programs because fighting with each other helps them to gobble resources and to keep running in the circles that help them to be stronger.

So, a thought loop is a kind of program that is originated in an experience, often negative or traumatic, and often very early in life. Successful thought loops are ones that become stronger over time, that hook into a wide variety of feeling situations and triggers and that therefore receive large amounts of attention and resources from the host in which they operate. Thought loops can be positive or negative. Unfortunately, the human brain and body chemistry is set up to react strongly to situations that it perceives as being dangerous and so negative thought systems often receive preferential focus.[17]

As discussed earlier, thought loops are only a surface phenomenon in a human entity, comparable to waves on a deep ocean. They will lose their strength if the wind of attention is directed elsewhere or stilled. They can also lose their strength if the sensations that accompany the thought are recognized and non-judgmental awareness is brought to the pattern, remembering that it is only a surface aspect of being and does not need to be acted upon. Everything is already OK.

The history and development of a thought loop is essentially irrelevant. This is because the present moment is the only moment where an action can actually take place, and the present moment does not depend on anything from the past. It is a completely free moment. Thought loops create the conditions that then appear to be a problem or an injury. Step aside from the loop and release the past and it becomes evident that there is nothing that needs healing or fixing.

---

17 This is true on a social as well as a personal level. A nation is much more likely to allocate resources to a war effort than to an initiative for peaceful action because there is so much strength of focus and attention on anything that is perceived as a threat. Thought loops and the programs that they represent operate in relationships, families, countries, and cultures as well as in individuals.

Homeland Security, in the United States, is an excellent example of a protective thought loop that continues to expand its control, influence, and filter of perception. Since the tragedy of 911, Homeland Security has helped to create an almost permanent state of perceived emergency—one that supports, condones, and promotes the continued growth and necessity of Homeland Security.

However, getting outside the circle of a thought is something that minds tend to resist. In order to help with this stepping outside the thought loop circle, it can sometimes be helpful to find the source of the loop and to bring this source into the present. Looking for the source of the loop can look suspiciously like delving into one's childhood and can resurrect all of the associated images of pipe smoking therapists and patients on couches. The difference here is that the past is not the focus, and neither is the *story* around what happened. The focus is on bringing awareness to a thought/feeling that originated in the past so that it can be experienced in the present. Bringing this thought/feeling into the present allows it to change. The story around the event is important only in that it is something to forgive and release— not something on which to focus time and attention.

Finding the source—the regressive slideshow

The regressive slide show is a tool that can help to identify the beginning of a thought loop. In order to use it, you must have already identified both the thought loop itself and the body sensations that go with it. Once you have a clear sense of the feeling that goes with the loop, ask yourself the question "When and where have I felt similar feelings in the past?"

Allow this question to take you back through time, bringing up thought/feeling images like slides in a slideshow. Each time you identify a time where you felt a similar feeling, briefly acknowledge it and then ask yourself the question again. Let the current slide go and allow the next to float into your awareness. Keep doing this until you have arrived at what you think is the earliest memory.

You may be surprised at how early this memory is. Since it is a feeling memory as well as a visual one, and it does not rely on words, it can come from before you were born. Some people may even find images arising that can't be explained in terms of the life they have lived. Sometimes thought loops actually originate in a time or place that is beyond this life—but don't get caught up in where the images take you or in the story of what happened. Getting caught up in the story just strengthens the original loop, and so it is not helpful. Instead, just acknowledge the image and its story without judgment.

Once you have found the earliest image, hold it gently in your mind. It can help to surround the image with light—choose a colour that feels good to you. White is often used, or gold for love and compassion, or violet for transformation. However far in the past this image appears to be, acknowledge that it is with you here and now. In this here and now, give love and forgiveness to yourself and anyone else who is in the image with you. What message can you give to yourself in order to be able to forgive and release the image? What does the former you need in order to know that he or she is loved, that he or she *is* OK and *will be* OK? Allow these questions to answer themselves, and watch without interfering as the image changes itself. The message that I wrote to myself, quoted at the beginning of this chapter, is an example of the sort of message that can be very powerful to send back to your younger self.

If nothing happens, if you can't forgive, if a gift of words or feelings or images does not appear, don't worry. Remember that this is just a mind tool—a kind of hide and seek with yourself that helps you remember what is already true. Everything is already OK. You can do this exercise again another time, or try something else, or do nothing. Ultimately, all that matters is to know that it doesn't matter.

It can be quite helpful to write down what happened in this exercise in your journal and to come back to it from time to time. It may take some time for the thought loop to lose its power, and so it is helpful to remember the message you gave yourself. Whenever the thought loop starts to take over, just acknowledge it without judgment and replace it with your message. Remind yourself that you do not need to believe this thought any longer.

Who is experiencing this?

There is a question that comes from the teachings of Zen Buddhism which is to ask oneself "Who or what is experiencing this?" At first this seems a bit trite—the answer is "me" of course. However, if you go beyond this first obvious answer, you will find that it is very difficult to pin down exactly what *me* is. You will also find that whatever name or shape you can give to *me*, it is contained in and experienced by something else. Who or what is this something? If you follow the question "Who, or what, am I?" your mind will very quickly arrive at a kind of precipice or jumping off place. On the edge of this precipice is the dividing line between what can be imagined in shape and form and time, and what has no shape and does not exist in time. Your mind cannot go there, but *You* are already and eternally there.

Keep asking yourself this question. As Mukti says, "Hold the question like a smooth stone, and drop it from the top of your head all the way into your being, down into your gut."[18] Let the question move beyond words and beyond the story, blame, or emotion that is trying to repeat itself and get your attention. Let it take you to the edge of the silent stillness without trying, like relaxing into a soft cushion and letting gravity do the work of putting your body at ease in the softness. Then let the question go.

The mind is always intent on answers and we are trained from birth to expect to find answers to questions. Working with questions like "Who or what am I?" requires a different understanding however. This is a question that is meant to lead the mind to the edge of where it can go so that it can see the jumping off point and become comfortable on this edge. The mind cannot go beyond this point, and any answer that can be contained in thought is the wrong answer. However, you can sense what is beyond this point, and bringing yourself into contact with the edge can help you to glimpse the great stillness that lies beyond the changing perceptions of thought and identity. This can be very helpful, especially when you are feeling caught up in turbulent thoughts, feelings, and perceptions.

When working with this question or other questions such as "Is this thought true?" the answer "I don't know" is perhaps the best and only answer that the mind can come up with. It is good to become comfortable with "I don't know" because this is a very liberating truth. In reality, all we know is what we perceive and as I have discussed already, the best that can be said about perception is that it is severely limited and almost completely inaccurate. It is much more truthful to understand that I don't know who I am, I don't know who my partner or friend or enemy is, and I don't know what life is about. Not knowing, if properly perceived, can open up new space and expansiveness inside as we learn to release the need to know and control and instead begin to relax into the mystery of being. When Jesus said that we

18 Mukti, *Stillness*. Interview with Renate McNay.
  https://www.youtube.com/watch?v=vT2P6kByKhI

must become like children, I think that is what he meant. Like children who can see the wonder and mystery without needing to understand or control it, we can open ourselves to the freedom and expansiveness of the great mystery of being. This is, in itself, a great liberation.

Letting go

The tendency of the mind/body system to hold on to what it knows, or what it wants, is very strong. In a recent incident, I was spending some time with a student who wanted to download a movie on the computer. There were a number of reasons I wouldn't help him with this, but there were also some reasons that even if I wanted to help, I couldn't in that situation. The network speed, the lack of a program that would do the task, lack of time—there were many reasons that made it completely undoable in that situation. However, no matter what I said or how I explained the facts of the situation to him, he was completely unwilling or unable to let go of his conviction that if he just wanted it badly enough, it would happen. Eventually, he went away angry and I was left to consider what had gone wrong in what I was doing. As I was considering this, I saw what a powerful mirror this student was for me, showing me what it looks like when I hold on to things despite what is real or true.

From the outside, letting go seems to be such a simple thing. From my point of view, understanding that there is no way that a movie can be downloaded should be enough to make it reasonable to let go of the expectation. From this student's point of view, no words or explanations were enough, and there was no alternative but to be upset, disappointed, and further convinced that the people around him didn't care for him. As he left with middle finger extended, he also showed the "I'm bad/you're bad" dichotomy to be alive, well, and fully functional. When you are caught in your own desires and expectations, it does not seem to be an easy or simple thing to just let them go.

Letting go is, however, the single most liberating and healing response that we can make to a situation. In the deepest sense of what we are—beings of flowing change in an eternally changing universe—any action that is not letting go is a resistance to life itself. When we cling to an image of who we are, cling to the story of our trauma or triumph, cling to our pain or our pleasure, cling to what we want or to what we don't want, cling to what we believe or what we don't believe—all these types of clinging and holding are what cause us to suffer.

I was on a long drive at one point, enjoying the passing scenery and the freedom of letting my thoughts run free. In a quiet and empty moment, it occurred to me that I had been looking through a filter all my life that filtered everything I perceive with the idea "this is not it". In some way, everything that I saw came into my perception with the pre-labeling of "not right, not good enough, not Nirvana..." This included all perceptions of myself of course, which helped to explain the life-long "improve Todd" project I'd been on. The feeling in this moment was a bit like peering around the edge of a vast movie screen and realizing that everything I had thought to be real before was a projection on the screen. The screen had been the whole world, but suddenly I realized that it had edges and there was more than what it showed. I went immediately back to seeing the screen, but the glimpses come back from time to time, reminding me of the limitations of believing what I believe.

Religious teachings, Eastern and Western alike, share a commonality in presenting the world as a place of suffering and something to escape from. Human history abounds with teachings of how wrong we are, bad we are, dirty or unworthy or sinful we are. It also abounds with stories of how we can get to better places if we are good and worse places if we are bad. Generally, it seems that the bad is emphasized and we are guilty until proven innocent.

I don't know the truth, or lack thereof, in any of this, and for once I am beginning to be less concerned about that. What I do think to be true, in this moment at least, is that we cannot be but what we are, and it is only in our insistence on making this a bad thing or a good thing that we lose track of who and what we *really* are. In the story of Adam and Eve, when they ate of the fruit of the tree of knowledge of good and evil, they unwittingly learned how to judge themselves and others. I don't think that God threw them from the Garden of Eden, though. Actually, they never left the garden at all. However, they thought that they had been expelled because suddenly everything was different. Now they were able to decide for themselves what was good and what was bad, and they began to want good things and not want bad things. With all this judgment, wanting, and not wanting the garden was no longer an Eden. Now it was a scary jungle, full of danger and pain.

Letting go is the way to return to the garden, but letting go is very confusing to the mind. The mind thinks that letting go is an action, something that it has to do. It is necessary for the mind to be open, ready, and willing for letting go to happen, but letting go is not an action or a thought or something that the mind can do. Letting go is something that happens on its own while we are not looking—like falling asleep (or falling awake), like a cloud that has passed, like water in a river, like time. Letting go is happening in us and around us in every instant, and it is only our insistence on preventing it that makes our problems appear to stay.

Imagine everything you know about life to be wrong. Imagine everything that you believe to be unimportant. Imagine everything that has happened to you to be irrelevant. Imagine everything that you think and feel to be without substance or ability to endure. What is left is the mystery of not knowing, and in this mystery is the possibility of freedom from all that has been. Let go of the past and it can no longer determine the future. Let go of who you were, and it will no longer control who you are. Let go of what you want and don't want, and these two imposters cannot cause you pain. Let your mind move to the edge of paradox, the edge of the abyss where it cannot go, and understand that letting go has already happened. This is the place of trust, or faith, or grace, emptiness or acceptance or whatever word works for you. In this place, the garden is still here, all is well, and there is nothing that can happen that can be wrong.

Resist this if you wish, with all of the mind's complaints about the terrible wrongs in the world, both within us and around us. The mind is correct, as far as it can tell, and on its screen of projection the wrongs and iniquities will continue to build into mountains as pain and trauma pile up and the corresponding need for healing and for righting of wrongs grows. Play this game for as long as you wish, but know—somewhere deep inside—that we will all return to the garden eventually, and in our returning we will find that we were never really away at all.

Chapter 10
From Fear-based
to love-based thinking

Part 1: Awakened truth

Small truths divide, great truths unify.

Todd Blattner

I don't know what I may seem to the world, but as to myself, I seem to have been only like a boy playing on the sea-shore and diverting myself in now and then finding a smoother pebble or a prettier shell than ordinary, whilst the great ocean of truth lay all undiscovered before me.

Sir Isaac Newton (1642- 1727)

Truth is something that tends to be badly misunderstood, much to the detriment of the world in general. In the traditional way of seeing it, Truth (with a capital "T") is an absolute. It is fixed, unchanging, and solid. Truth is a period. There is nowhere else to go.

Traditionally, truth is something that is disagreed upon by a variety of groups—especially religious groups. Since it is an absolute, it follows that one of the groups must be right and the others must be wrong, and this is where the unfortunate and detrimental part comes in. People are often ready to kill each other in an effort to establish whose truth is *The Truth*. This human tendency is even more unfortunate when seen from an understanding of the fundamental nature of the universe as it is now known by science.

If Truth, with a capital "T", does exist, we now know that the universe in which we live is far too complex and mind bogglingly huge for a human mind ever to comprehend it. The conscious part of the human mind is not even capable of understanding itself. How can we possibly claim to understand the whole and entire Truth of existence? Seen from the vantage point of an infinite universe, in full view of our own tininess, the idea of killing each other over who has the correct truth is a bit like two colonies of ants deciding to fight over which one owns the earth. No matter who wins, the purpose is kind of silly.

Truth, it turns out, is not an absolute at all, but a *process*. Fortunately it is quite easy to determine the relative usefulness of a truth by using a simple principle. Small truths (I like dogs, you like cats) tend to cause division and separation. Greater truths (we both like some kinds of animals) tend toward unification.

As a human mind develops, it moves through a series of approximations of truth, from relatively small and divisive truths to larger and more unified truths. Growth is the process of using an approximate truth as a stepping stone to find a more powerful truth. For instance, a child may first learn that water is wet—this is true in some situations. Later, he will find that water is hard and cold, or soft and fluffy—this is true in other situations. Another time he will find that water is like air—this is also true. Eventually, he will learn that water can change its form—this is a more complete understanding. At some point, this child may understand that water is a form of energy and vibration and that he is not separate from water or its transformations. This is still a deeper understanding. In this way, we progress from truth to truth, moving from relatively confined truths toward truths that are more universal.

The greater the truth, the more of reality it can reliably explain, and the more it can unify apparently disparate ideas. This is a very important point, because people tend to cling to their own perception of truth out of fear that if they let go they will be lost with no way of knowing in what to believe or how to order their lives. Many religions strongly encourage their followers to believe that there is only one truth, that all other systems and religions are wrong, and that it is dangerous to have new or different ideas. Letting go of or changing this kind of belief can be very frightening—both because of fear of Hell and damnation and because of the fear caused by loss of certainty and structure. It can feel like one is lost without any points of reference when questioning a strong and controlling belief system.

However, we do not have to give up all previous beliefs or limited truths in order to incorporate new ones. All smaller truths have aspects of larger truths in them. By looking for points of inclusion and similarity between ideas, ideologies, or faiths, we can gradually expand our understanding and increase the flexibility of our thinking. This process can be greatly aided by using these *rules of inclusion*:

- It is only possible for a human being to know approximations of ultimate truth.

- Development of the mind involves progression from lesser to greater truths.

- Greater truths can be known by their quality of universality. The more a truth explains, encompasses, and accepts, the greater the truth.

An example of the principle of inclusion in action can be seen in the subject of this book. Most people still believe that the world they live in operates on the principles of Newtonian physics and that they are made, at the most basic level, of solid physical particles. This belief is truth. It explains and even predicts a huge amount of what can be seen and known in the physical world, and it has brought the human race from the dark ages into the space age. It is a powerful truth.

However, as we have progressed and used the truth as symbolized by Newton's ideas and the worldview of objective materialism, we have begun to discover many things that this truth cannot explain. It cannot explain quantum phenomena. It cannot explain the experience of human energy fields, spontaneous healing and many other aspects of human experience that are entering into mainstream acceptance. It can explain much about the world from the outside in—looking at it as an outside observer. However, it is not very good at explaining the world from the inside out, as experienced and lived in a human body. The old truth is powerful, useful, and still has its place. However, a new truth is needed.

The concept of fields is a part of this new truth. It is a more powerful way of seeing the world because it does not have to deny the old way, but it enables conceptualizing and utilizing a much wider range of experience and a much wider degree of flexibility. A *field* can conceptually encompass everything from the basic information underlying the energy of a subatomic particle to the way that this particle behaves when combined with trillions of others in the macroscopic world. Since it is more inclusive than the previous truth, it is more powerful and more developmentally advanced.

In a similar way, all religions claim to have their own Truth. If one looks carefully at these truths, however, one will find that there are points of similarity between different religions. These points of similarity, by the rule of inclusion, are more powerful truths than ones that are only claimed by a single religion. Truths that can be found universally in all religions are far more powerful and developmentally advanced than truths found in only one. Moving to a more unified religious truth does not mean having to dismiss or let go of a truth that was previously cherished. It means only that the old truth must take a new place as a part of something larger.

Using the rule of inclusion, we need not become lost and confused by the plethora of possible partial truths that are thrust in our direction. We can choose the truth that is the most inclusive, and when it no longer explains things sufficiently, we are ready to step up the ladder and learn a new, more inclusive and more powerful truth. This process never ends. To be human is to always have the possibility of further growth and learning.

Understanding the rule of inclusion is a very important part of stepping into the Awakening and the paradigm of energy and fields that is part of it. This is because there is a great deal of fear associated with letting go. Realizing that truth is a process allows us to slowly soften hardened belief systems and safely move from one level of understanding to another without becoming completely adrift in confusion. The rule of inclusion is like an anchor for a ship in dark and stormy waters. It provides a point of reference and something to hold on to—but it also allows movement, flex, and the ability to ride with the waves.

Without an anchor of this kind, it is easy to become stuck in the trap of Truth with a capital "T". This can be seen in instances where people have become mired in fundamentalist religious dogma, unassailable political beliefs, or beliefs of any kind that are hardened, inflexible, and unchanging. Anything that makes a rigid image of how the world should be and how it should not be creates a division and a polarity of good vs. bad and this in turn creates repression and conflict.

Beliefs of this kind are clung to because they cover a very large shadow. The person who is clinging so desperately to the belief has an unconscious (or sometimes even conscious) fear that they will lose who they are and, at times quite literally, be lost to the demons and fire if they allow change. The harder they try to keep the belief pure or to resist the forces of evil, the greater the division and polarity and therefore the greater the conflict. It is interesting to me that the people who fight the devil the most ardently are usually the ones who promote conflict and division most strongly. If there is a devil, these people are unwitting vehement supporters.

Learning to Let it Be

There is an important measuring stick that can help to let us know if we are learning the art of truth as a process or if we are stuck in rigid truth. This measuring stick is, very simply, our ability to *let it be*.

When we need to control others, assert power over others, or manipulate others, it indicates deep insecurity and fear. Why would I need to control or manipulate others if I were not afraid of them in some way or afraid of not getting what I want? When we need to take from others or use others for our own purposes, we demonstrate that we are not capable of relying on ourselves, trusting ourselves, or being content with our lives as they are. When we need to fix others or change others, we demonstrate the shadow of our discontent with ourselves.

A great mark of a person who is in secure contact with his or her inner nature is the ability and desire to let others be as they are. An advanced person has no need to change the world, only to love it as it is. He or she has no desire to control others—far greater power is available when it is accessed from the inside out. Self-mastery is far more fulfilling, powerful, and joyful than mastery of others.

The ability to let it be is also founded in the understanding of the Field and all it entails. To let it be does not mean to condone and uphold violence, pain, and suffering. It does mean, however, an understanding that where we put our attention and our will, we also put our creative energy. To fight something is ultimately to increase its energy and power. By letting it be, we can build the power of the thought form of peace and withdraw from the thought form of domination and control. This kind of action sends ripples through the fabric of the world that have far greater effects than we can see or even imagine. One person, simply through their being, can radiate a healing energy of change to many.

On the other hand, people who need to control, manipulate, convert, dominate or in any other ways inflict their own needs on others are still operating from the insecurity of rigid truth. If you find a place in your life where you cannot let something or someone be as they are, it is a good sign that you need to examine your own beliefs to see what is hiding in the shadows behind them. Don't judge yourself harshly when you find these areas. We all have them to one extent or another. Simply use the healing power of awareness and continue to practice. Let the violet flame of transformation burn within you and transmute the desire for control of external things to the knowing of mastery from within.

Truth with a capital "T" can be a dangerous and uncomfortable master, and the polarization of opposites that it produces causes great suffering and pain. On the other hand, truth, as a living flame of expansion and growth, can become a joyful and playful guide on the journey of life. As always, we are free to choose which experience we prefer.

Some exercises for distinguishing truth

1. Character opinions Venn diagram

Think of someone with whom you have a long-standing conflict. Make a list of as many aspects of this person's character and personality as you can. Try to find some positive things to say, even if this is a challenge.

Find someone who also knows your conflict person but who likes this person. Ask them to do the same exercise.

Draw two large circles about one inch apart, side by side on a blank piece of paper. Draw a third circle that partially overlaps these two circles. Put opinions that only belong to you in the circle on the right. Put opinions that only belong to the other person in the circle on the left. Put opinions that are similar from both of you in the circle in the center.

Note that the opinions in both the left AND right circles are true, the opinions in the center circle are probably more true, the entire diagram with all aspects present is still more true, and the person that you are describing with this diagram is much, much more than what you have described. There is still more truth to be discovered.

2. Belief Venn diagrams

Try the same exercise with any belief that you feel strongly about. Find some conflicting points of view and compare notes. For example, if you are a Democrat, consider the Republican perspective (and vice versa). If you believe that you are good, find some of the lingering thoughts and possibilities for bad or evil that lurk within you. If you believe that abortion should be abolished, try to understand why others feel it is necessary. If you believe that your religion is correct, try to understand how someone else could have similar feelings about another religion. Put the opposing beliefs in circles side by side. Join the two circles with a third circle and try to find at least one thing that is common between the two. While you are doing this, notice your resistance to allowing the possibility that your truth is not the only one.

3. Listening without judgment

Find someone with whom you do not agree or perhaps a person with whom you disagree on a particular point. Make a pact with yourself really to listen to this person.

Listen *through* the resistance that you feel. Just listen. Mentally note your resistance and arguments, but don't give them your attention or energy. Take notes. Do whatever it takes really to hear and understand what this person is saying. Find at least three ways in which what this person has said could expand your ideas about the world.

The resistance you (and all people) feel when you come into contact with new or contrary ideas is a part of your protection against awareness of change and part of your struggle against the reality of the universe. The extent of your anger, irritation, desire to think of this exercise as stupid, or other ways of avoiding or disliking this exercise are a measure of how frightened you have become of change.

Remember to smile and be gentle with yourself. Struggling with the struggle doesn't help. If you can't, or don't want to do this exercise, just relax, and let the awareness that you are changing settle gently through your cells. You wouldn't be reading this book if you weren't ready for new awareness. Let it come to you in its own time and in its own way.

4. Releasing "Bad" and "Good"

Think of at least one thing you strongly believe to be wrong or bad. If you can, try to locate where in your body you feel this badness or your resistance to it. Name the physical sensations—hot, cold, tight, tingly, dull, numb, aching, poking, whatever is really there. Imagine this badness as a container of hydrogen.

Now think of the opposite to the wrong or bad you found. Notice where you feel this in your body and name the physical sensations. Imagine this goodness as a container of oxygen.

Now allow the hydrogen and oxygen to run together in your imagination. Feel the energy of the two combining in your body and your mind. Light them on fire and give them a violet flame. Forgive the badness and the goodness both and let them join back together into the love from which they came.

Notice how the sensations in your body change. Forgiveness is an act of release, freeing yourself from rigid bonds that have held you in pain. Forgiveness is an act of love for yourself. Practice forgiving yourself by forgiving your judgments of others as often as you can.

Part 2: Awakened thoughts

We are shaped by our thoughts; we become what we think. When the mind is pure, joy follows like a shadow that never leaves.

Buddha

Drag your thoughts away from your troubles... by the ears, by the heels, or any other way you can manage it.

Mark Twain

In the Awakening, thoughts are both more important and less important than in the objective/material paradigm. Thoughts are more important in that they are understood to come before action, and therefore they are more powerful than action. Thoughts determine what we perceive and how we act (or react). Thoughts also are important in focusing and directing our intention and our energy; the direction, intention, and focus that we choose plays a powerful part in manifesting our experience of each moment.

However, in the objective/material worldview *my thoughts* and *me* are generally considered to be one and the same thing. The brain is understood to be the center of thought and the center of self. I *am* my thoughts, and as Descartes said "I think, therefore I am". This worldview tends to inflate thought to a place of power and importance that is overly grandiose and to emphasize the material separateness of individual brains. When seen from this viewpoint, thoughts are both a source of power (I am in control) and a source of fearful aloneness (I am ultimately alone, inconsequential, fragile). According to the objective/material worldview, the ultimate source and home of my consciousness rests in my brain—a fragile bundle of nerves with the consistency of custard, protected by less than a centimeter of bone. This is not a secure place in which to exist, and so it is natural to be afraid. It is also natural to try to hide from the fear by finding ways to have power over others and over the physical world.

In the awakened understanding, however, thoughts are themselves affected by deeper processes and are only the tip of the iceberg of what is possible in awareness. I have said several times before that thoughts are like a boat floating on a vast ocean. This analogy is useful, but as is true for all attempts to imagine or describe the Field, it is only an approximation. In order to understand thoughts, it is helpful to remember that the Field is both around us and in us. Rather than a boat on the water, we are a submarine within it. Even this, however, implies a separateness that is not really there. There is no separation within the Field and so both the submarine and the passenger are made of the water in which they are traveling.

The step to new understanding often requires some initial trust or at least willingness to be open to the possibility that what we know right now may be limited or even wrong. I have been fortunate in that through my practice of Vipassana meditation, I have occasionally had an opportunity to glimpse the vastness that is beyond thought, and in my time spent with monks in Thailand and with other teachers, I have had the opportunity to learn from people who seem to have access to a much wider range of experience than is normally attained. These experiences have helped me to release some of my assumptions about who I am and the role that my thoughts play. They have also, however, made me aware of how tightly I cling to what I know and how frightening it can be to let go.

In one experience during a meditation retreat, my body seemed to dissolve until it felt like vibrating air, transparent and formless. In another, the world as I knew it simply disappeared, and for a very brief moment I understood fully and throughout my entire body that there is no solidity, no me, no other, no solid and material world, and no thought. I can't say what is beyond all of these things, only that there was an experience of existing but not in any way that is a part of normal experience. In my conscious mind, this experience was exciting and pleasurable. Somewhere in the depths, however, it must have stirred a deep fear, because shortly afterward I nosed into a depression that came and went for several years.

At another time, while living with my Thai teacher, I went walking down a jungle path late at night. The moon was bright, shining through a slight haze so that it seemed that the air was almost glowing, and the distant hills were visible as dark silhouettes against a starry sky. The night was touched with a comforting coolness after the heat of the day. Frogs and jungle insects croaked, buzzed, and sang. Fireflies flitted in and among the trees, little magic sparks and fairy lights in the forest. The intensity of life around me was almost palpable, saturating my awareness with the fervour of a monsoon storm.

As I stood in my own silence, I suddenly became aware of a feeling of rushing movement. The trees and life around me seemed to shimmer and dissolve so that the solid forms were flowing and less distinct. I was aware of a great wanting—not in desperation but in the sense of energy being pulled into the plants as a result of life's desire for itself. For a moment, I understood all the form around me, and including me, to be a part of this flowing energy. Far beyond thought, the structure of the world was no structure at all—a flow of energy sucked from the source by life's desire to continue itself. My experience of this exhilaration was brief, and then a terror from somewhere deep within me kicked me back to normal experience. It is not easy to face the unknown, and our fears lie far below the level of the conscious mind—far below the level of our thoughts. I was not ready to let go, release my imagined control, and enter so deeply into the flow.

Experiences come and go and are subject to the interpretation of the mind of the person doing the experiencing. Their content is true only in the sense that it stretches and grows the individual, expanding the range of awareness. Reality is always stranger and more ineffable than we can imagine and peak experiences of this kind are very individual in nature. I have related these stories not to say my experiences represent a universal truth but to illustrate that conscious thought is by far not all that a human is capable of experiencing and that conscious thought is only a tiny part of all there is to being human. In the Awakening, huge numbers of people are beginning to experience these greater depths in their own ways. Whatever the individual experience, the common denominator is the realization that human potential is far greater than the objective/material worldview has allowed us to imagine.

In a strange juxtaposition, in the worldview of energy and fields, humans are both more and less powerful than in the objective/material worldview. We are less grandiose and less in control of each other and the world around us. However, we are far deeper, far nobler, more connected, more worthy, more responsible, more filled with potential to achieve a kind of greatness that is beyond the imagination of those who maintain the rigid limitations imposed by materialism. As we realize that our power does not come *from*, but *through* us, and as we take steps to move beyond the limitations of identifying ourselves with our thoughts, the universe of our own experience expands for us and we expand with it.

This expansion is a process of the Awakening. Energy awareness is something that can, and in many ways should, sneak up on a person. As we expand, and the conscious mind sets the intention to allow and encourage this expansion in whatever way it can, we open a door to expanding our understanding of both thought and all that lies beyond it. The conscious mind can open the door, but the expanded awareness must come of its own accord. It generally arrives quietly, in small ways, when it is not expected.

* * *

Thought, in the material paradigm, tends to take over and obsess in its own neuroses. Awakened thought, however, is a very powerful tool for transformation, change, growth, and even the artistry of creating one's own life moment by moment.

The idea that energy exists is not difficult to comprehend if a mind is open to the possibility, and this is the first task of a mind that is ready to awaken. The second task is to learn how to remain open. When the door is opened it becomes clear that reality is not what was believed in the past and that the ramifications of a world that is based on energy and change rather than matter and predictability touch every part of one's life. Opening the door of the mind is a bit like taking the red pill in the movie *The Matrix*. Everything is changed—and this is why it is still resisted with such vehemence by many people.

Once the energy paradigm becomes real for a person, however, a number of realizations begin to happen. One of these is that, although we are not our thoughts, still our thoughts have more effect on the world around us than was previously believed. In the objective/material worldview, thoughts are hidden things that don't have any particular effect on the world around us. We can have whatever thoughts we want, let our brains run wild on whatever crazy fantasies and dreams that they come up with, and these thoughts have no consequence outside ourselves. The only things that really matter in this worldview are physical actions because it seems that the world is a physical place.

However, if we accept the premise that the physical body is simply the densest portion of an energy field system, thoughts take on a much more important role. Though there are levels of awareness that are beyond thought, thought is still the starting place of action for most of us. Thought is energy in a more pure and less dense form than matter. Creation or manifestation is a process of holding the focus of a thought. The degree of focus, certainty, and energy placed in the thought determines how quickly it becomes physical and what people and events are attracted by it.

The depth of mind from which the thought comes also has a great deal to do with the power of that thought. Some people are able naturally to access very deep levels of consciousness, where at least some of their thoughts have very little static, or conflict within them. Other people access thoughts at a level where they are more conflicted; these people have more difficulty manifesting what they want in the world.

Although there are many schools and teachers who provide instruction for how to manifest, how to focus, and how to use thoughts to create what we want, my experience is that using thoughts in this way is not necessarily beneficial.

Thought and the idea of Self

Some of the changes of perspective in the Awakening are truly radical when seen from the old worldview. One of these perspective changes is the perspective of what it means to have a self.

For most of us—certainly for me for the greater part of my life—there was no question in my mind about my own existence. Beyond even believing, I simply knew that there was a *me*. The obvious nature of this observation rendered it beyond question.

When I looked into the nature of my being through meditation, however, and when I studied with accomplished teachers, this certainty in the idea of *self* was badly shaken. When my wife died of cancer, when I watched helplessly as her body lost its vitality, when I watched her ashes disperse in the place she had requested, the foundations for my denial of death were destroyed and with them the foundations of my idea of a permanent self.

Of course, there *is* a *me* in the sense of a mind/body/consciousness with a personality living a life. That is true. However, there is a deeper truth that this *me* is always changing. This *me* has a beginning, and it has an end, and there is nothing that I can do about it. Perhaps the *me* continues into other lives or other worlds, but even so, it will not be the *me* that is writing these words right now, just as I am completely different than a child with my name who lived over forty years ago.

The idea of *me* is a thought—a changing, powerful, intelligent thought, but still a thought. The deeper one looks into the nature of this thought the more inescapable the conclusion that it does not have a center. When one looks very deeply for a self, one finds there is nothing there.

This seems, at first, to be very bad news. In this place of naked honesty, the ego must see that it will die. Not only will it die, but all its dreams of control, safety, and security are without foundation or substance. There is nothing in this world that it can own, can keep, can control for very long, and there is nothing that it can take with it when the body dies—not even itself.

This can be a very solemn, depressing, terrifying place. It can also be a dangerous place, this place where death tramples through the walls that hold him out, and his spectre breaths directly on one's soul; it is the place that we each avoid with all our strength and ingenuity.

But truth is never a chain that binds. Truth is a light that shines on the chains with which we have imprisoned ourselves and shows them to be unreal. In what seems to be the darkest moment, where self is finally seen to be a fiction, the light of freedom begins to shine. Nothing is changed, there is still this me, but there is a shift. Instead of a *me* living a life, there is LIFE living a me. Sometimes suddenly, usually gradually, the fear and defensiveness of the little me softens and dissolves, and it begins to see that all life is an expression of the same source, all is truly one, and in this realization that is beyond thought, beyond sensation and beyond emotion, it realizes the freedom of going beyond the story of me.

Thoughts continue, emotions continue, body sensations continue, a life story continues. Nothing is lost, but now there is less attachment to any of these things. Thoughts can come and go, but they are not constant, and there is less desire to become stuck in them. Emotions and body sensations come and go, but their demands are not chains and compulsions. The story continues, but it is not so serious or frightening. For those with the fortitude to look truthfully and deeply, this is the opening and emancipation of loosening the death grip we have on life. When we finally relax this grip of the fear of death, when we look death fully in the face and accept him and her and it peacefully and gently and without resistance, we begin to touch that which has no ending and no beginning and that in which there is no fear.

Practices that teach focus, manifestation, development, and use of powers of mind can be very helpful for achieving material goals, and this can be a useful skill for living. However, it is also important to realize that intention is a focus of desire and this focussing of desire will strengthen the ego self from which it came. Like Aladdin in the cave of wonders, people who begin to see the possibilities of the powers of mind are initially enthralled by the treasures that can be had. However, eventually they also realize that all these treasures are temporary and that they only prolong the illusion that satisfaction can come from something that is temporary and external. The only real treasure is what is found in the lamp—the Genie which is the symbol of the light.

Part 3: Attention

In the past, "saving the world" has been understood to require heroic actions, travel to foreign places, battle against the forces of evil, and strenuous work to right the wrongs and injustices that surround us. These things are not wrong, and often they are also necessary. However, many people who have been involved with aid programs, or who have fought for peace and justice have become jaded, disappointed, and discouraged by the lack of results or the way the battle never ends.

Part of what is missing in the "save the world" approach is an understanding of the basic nature of the Field, the forces that animate it, and the ways we can influence our experience within it. A place to start with this understanding is the power, and role, of *attention*.

In the objective/material worldview, where everything operates on physical principles, the way to stop something is to oppose it. Indeed, the only way that an object will stop its motion is if it is forced to do so. As pointed out earlier, Newton states:

> "Every body continues in its state of rest, or of uniform motion in a right line, unless it is compelled to change that state by forces impressed upon it."

If an object is moving in one direction, application of a force in the opposite direction will slow it down and eventually stop it. This simple principle is used in most human situations as well—when we see something we don't like, our first reaction is to oppose it in whatever way we can. If we want to stop someone from doing something, we oppose them. If they don't want to be stopped, we increase the amount of force. They also increase their force, and eventually a fight develops.

Over and over again, we have put our energy into fighting things, believing that by doing this we will be able to stop the evil that we see and create something better. Obstinately, and against the evidence of the results that are attained, we apply this principle of force against force and think that we can stop something by opposing, or fighting with it. We fight global warming, fight terror (with terror), fight disease, fight cancer, fight abortion, fight any number of things, and then are often puzzled when things just seem to get worse despite all our energy and effort.

The reason for this is much clearer when looking at it through the perspective of fields. It doesn't matter if you put energy into a field positively (actively try to increase it) or negatively (actively fight it or try to destroy it). Either way, you are putting your energy into the thought form, or idea, that is contained in the field and in that way you are adding your support to it. Supporting or opposing, you are actually increasing the power of any field you put your attention into by giving it your thoughts and energy.

It is easiest to understand this concept from the basic level of fear. From the energy field paradigm, fear represents a certain tone or vibrational energy level in the field structure. This tone is like a radio channel—it is something that has to be tuned into. However, unlike a radio station, tuning into the channel is a two way communication. If a person tunes into the fear station, he or she receives the fear vibrations and enters the fear tone. This causes the person's personal field also to vibrate at the fear level and since the field underlies the physical biology, this in turn effects the emotions, thoughts, and biological functioning of the body.

Once a person is tuned in to the fear channel, he or she begins to broadcast fear on the energy level and manifest fear on the physical level. Since the physical body is in a fear reaction, thought will be fear based and strongly influenced by the instinctual reactions of the brainstem rather than the logical and more discerning prefrontal cortex. On the energy level, energy goes to maintaining the fear vibration frequency, and this energy feeds back to the fear channel. Unlike radio, when a person tunes his or her field to a specific emotional frequency, he or she adds his or her energy to the frequency and help it to grow stronger.

On the psychological level, the meme[19] of fear transmits itself as the ideas, justifications, and thoughts that support fear. On the physical level, fear

19 A meme is a self-replicating thought or idea that is transmitted from person to person, somewhat like a virus. Memes can have a wide range of complexity from ideas associated with the latest fashion fad, to a particular prejudice, a political or religious doctrine, or an entire worldview.

manifests as everything from individual anxiety to acts of violence. When enough individuals focus on fear, it then emerges on a national level, ultimately manifesting as increased levels of control over citizens by the government and increased levels of protectionism/aggression against other countries.

It doesn't matter if a person believes in the fear-based propaganda, motives, ideas, memes, actions, etc. or if he wants to fight and stop them. From the field paradigm, in order to have access to a particular tone, you must be tuned in to it, and if you are tuned in to it, you are giving it your energy. Trying to get rid of fear by fighting it is like trying to get rid of darkness by blocking out the dark. From an energy basis, all that matters is that you are giving something your attention. The polarization (good or bad, for or against and so on) of your attention doesn't make a great deal of difference.

An example of this from my practice is an eight-year-old girl who came to see me because of anxiety attacks. She lived with her mother part time and with her father part time and would often have panic attacks at night because when she was with one parent, she missed the other and vice versa. The attack would start with her feeling of separation anxiety and then grow as she worried both about the parent she was not seeing and about the frightening feeling of her attack.

Of course, there were many issues and much history beneath her reactions. However, her immediate need was to learn how to manage the attacks. I taught her how to breathe deeply into her lower abdomen and how to track the body sensations that arose as the panic attack came on. By using her body sensations (things like a strong butterfly sensation in her stomach, tension in her shoulders, etc.) she was able to recognize the panic early. She then learned that she didn't have to be afraid of these sensations. She could recognize them, give them calming messages with her thoughts—messages like "you are OK" and "I love you", and focus on breathing deeply. I gave her the homework to go home and have a panic attack but to do it with awareness—taking her conscious mind as far into the attack as she could and noting what she was feeling. For each sensation, she was to say "you are OK" and "I love you", and to continue breathing.

This girl was a fast learner. The next week she reported that she hadn't been able to have a panic attack, and as far as I know she hasn't had one since. By doing these exercises this young girl was able to learn that she was not a powerless victim of her panic. She was also able to learn the importance of where she put her attention.

Placing attention on the panic, the reasons for the panic, and the objects of the panic simply made the panic bigger. Placing attention on stopping or fighting the panic also made it bigger. Either way, the power of her mind was used like gasoline on a fire, adding to the fuel and building the fire higher.

Placing her attention on her body sensations allowed her to be in touch with the truth of what was happening inside without blocking the flow of energy. Accepting and giving loving messages to herself focused the power of her mind on calming the storm of chemical arousal that was brewing inside her. Breathing deeply gave her an anchor to help to hold her thoughts steady in the storm and also affected her physically, activating the parasympathetic nervous system which is involved with relaxation.

Although this is a simple case, the principle is the same if it is a small child's panic attacks or a national emergency. Attention is powerful, and what we place our attention on grows larger. It doesn't matter if our attention is directed toward fighting an issue (fighting terrorism for instance) or promoting it. Either way, the power of attention operates within the Field, increasing the strength of the thought-form, broadcasting the frequency of the issue (fear for instance), and multiplying the effects of the issue in the minds of more and more people. In this way, intention literally creates reality. It is the precursor of the conditions that govern our thoughts, which then govern our actions, which then create our next moment's experience. Attention literally directs our life force, and it is through our attention that we spend this force. That on which we place our attention, either negatively or positively, gets bigger.

The importance of this principle cannot be overstated, and is a critical part of the new awakening that is happening worldwide. As people become aware of the energy paradigm, they also become aware of the extreme importance, and power, of the choice of where they put their attention. *Your attention is your most powerful, and precious, possession.*

Every moment of every day, there are thousands of people, activities, and things that compete for our attention. The choice of where our attention goes is a direct choice of where our life energy is spent, and of the feelings, practices, and ideas that we have chosen to support. Since attention governs the direction and focus of thought, and thought is what initiates action, attention is literally what creates the reality that we experience. _We give our life energy to, and thereby strengthen, the things to which we give our attention._ This can be a sobering thought for many of us.

Despite the urgency of this call to direct one's attention, there is a deeper level which is a middle way. It does not involve being stuck in a particular pattern of reaction, as the young girl in the example initially was. It also does not involve a need to place focus on sensations or feelings or to direct or control attention at all. As was discussed in the short section on thought and the idea of self, at the deepest levels of awareness it can be seen that self is only an idea and this idea is constantly changing. Since everything about this idea of self is in constant motion, there is no need to pay attention to any of it. Everything that is thought or felt will eventually change and become something else. There is no need to try to force attention one way or another. It can suffice to simply turn the volume down a bit so that the tumult of panic or fear or anger or worry is a bit less obnoxious, and then to allow the mind to settle on its own into its natural place. This natural place is peace.

This deeper way is very simple but also harder to understand and explain. The mind wants to have things to do and is initially frightened and confused by ideas of this sort. Therefore, there are times when techniques and practices can be helpful. However, it is always best to remember that practices and methods all have limitations. The ground state of being is beyond the need for any kind of practice or method.

Sitting Like a Goat

There are many practices that teach ways of increasing focus and ability to direct attention. Each of these practices has its own merits and can be useful. However, I have found that the practice of directing and controlling

121

attention can be paradoxically counterproductive. From an awakened perspective, the ground state of all beings is one of stillness, balance, and flow. Anything other than this is the result of interference by the desire of mind and body to control and shape what is happening. Further practice in controlling and shaping can create many experiences—some of them very pleasurable but is also a further step away from the natural state.

It seems somewhat paradoxical to be saying "be aware of where you put your attention" on the one hand, and "don't try to control your attention" on the other. Explanations are only words; your understanding will come of its own accord. However, one way of unifying this apparent contradiction is to see it as a difference in depths. On the conscious surface, there are many thoughts that, if given energy and action, will cause problems. It is better to remove attention from these thoughts before they become actions. However, the imbalance at these surface levels comes from a kind of meddling with what is already OK deep down in the depths. The most powerful way of controlling our attention is therefore to realize that there is ultimately nothing that needs to be controlled. Don't try to figure this out, because it won't work. Allow your experience to give you understanding in ways that are sensed rather than cognized.

The technique of "sitting like a goat" is not really a technique. It is just a way of taking time to be without purpose and to practice the idea of *stopping*. Almost every waking moment of the day is spent with an idea of needing to do something, obtain something, avoid something, be entertained in some way. To *stop* is to let everything be as it is without trying to change it. It is to see the story of who we think we are and what we think is happening to and around us without grasping at the story, identifying with the story as *me* or *mine*, or trying to push it away.

I like the name "Sitting like a Goat" because it gives me the image of a mountain goat, sitting on a mountainside in the sunshine, looking out into the space and wilderness. It doesn't need a purpose, a direction, a goal, a reason, a desire. It doesn't need to fix anything, change anything, create anything, worry about anything, stop anything, or start anything. It is just there.

With this in mind, try making some time in your day to "sit like a goat". Watch your attention as it moves, bounces, flits about, becomes dull or sharp, sticks to particular thoughts or feelings or worries. Watch it like a goat watching the flies and sunshine, feeling the wind whispering in the grasses and the clouds floating by. The flies are there, buzzing about. The clouds come and go. The goat doesn't pay any attention—it just lets them be as they are. You can do this in stillness. You can also do this in motion, in walking, or in a grocery line.

If the mind persists in following particular thoughts, you can try gently asking "Who or what is thinking this thought?" Let the question take your mind to the edge of where minds can go, and then be still on that edge for a moment. Whatever racket or mayhem may be going on around you, or even within you, the stillness of what is beyond this edge is always there.

For these moments, touch nothing, identify with nothing, own nothing. For however long you wish or are able, let everything be OK, just as it is.

Part 4: Awareness

As discussed earlier, the *me* is only a relative truth—a constantly changing construct of mind, body, and memory. When the *me* observes itself, it begins to understand that it is constantly changing and that there is a deeper reality than it can comprehend. It may then begin letting go of beliefs, programs, and images of itself. Stripping away these things opens more space, flexibility, and adaptability. Self-observation and stripping away old programming can also can be an aid to realizing a different kind of awareness. Like a name of God which is "I am That", this other awareness is an entering into *Awareness-that-is-itself*, as opposed to awareness *of* self. Awakened awareness is what we enter into when we release the notion of a *me* that is separate and self-serving.

However, I will talk here mainly about the kind of awareness which is self-awareness because this is where most of us are still functioning. In addition, self-awareness can be practiced and is very useful in making life a more pleasant and productive experience. It can also be a step toward realization of Awareness-that-is-itself, though the two are not necessarily linked.

The importance of self-awareness, or mindfulness, on a psychological level, is that it is the doorway out of repeating patterns. Without awareness, the human mind/body system is basically a highly advanced robot running on programming that comes from its genetic code and from its training. This robot is able to learn and to develop new software on its own, but once it has developed a program for coping with a particular situation it will tend to use the same program over and over again, whether it works well or not.

For instance, if a child learns from its mother or father that spiders are nasty and frightening, this will embed a whole complex of associations in her mind/body system. Each time she sees a spider, her unconscious mind recognizes it and associates it with "bad" and "scary" and therefore "dangerous". Her body dutifully reacts with feelings of fear and disgust, including all the hormonal, chemical and electrical changes in her body that this entails. All this builds up enough to finally (a few milliseconds later) come into her conscious mind, and she screams and runs away, thinking that she chose to do this.

If self-awareness is inserted into this pattern, and the girl becomes old enough to be able to hold her focus and direct her attention clearly, she will see that she actually did not choose anything at all. Her body simply ran an old program and reacted to what it perceived as a threat before she had time to consider what was going on. Awareness is the part of us that can watch the programs in operation and question—why am I doing this? It is also the agent of change and of freedom from the suffering that we bring on ourselves with the old programs that we repeat.

When I work with adult clients, I often start with what, from my training background, is called a *Primary Scenario*. The primary scenario is a kind of genographic map that lays out all the client's family relationships from grandparents forward, charting salient characteristics of each person, relationship patterns, physical issues, substance abuse, context in terms of place, time and social situation, and many other aspects of the person's life connections and development. Charting and mapping all this information provides a detailed map of the history of the programs that a person learned and inherited as a child and helps to see how many of these programs are still in operation, causing repeated reactions of anger or anxiety, relationship problems, or other issues.

The primary scenario is one tool for bringing awareness to these programs clarifying and illustrating the way in which reactions in the present are generally based on programs from the past. Often people will experience an emotional reaction to a situation that seems out of proportion to what has actually happened. They will react with rage to a relatively small slight or with abject fear in response to a boss giving them a mild reprimand. Situations like these, where the emotion involved is out of proportion to the actual event, are always ones in which the present situation has simply reminded the unconscious mind of a similar situation in the past. The emotion that is developed, and reaction which ensues, has everything to do with running an old program and very little to do with what is actually happening in the present. Without self-awareness, this will continue for a lifetime, and nothing will change. Without self-awareness, our childhood and genetics would be like the bars on a prison cell, holding us in bondage for life. With self-awareness, however, we have a key that can set us free.

Many, and in the past perhaps most, people have not understood the power that they hold within themselves in the form of awareness or the precious gift of freedom that it offers. In this time of awakening, however, more people are realizing that they are able literally to change their past, by becoming aware of how it affects their present.

Awareness is like a solvent. When water is mixed with sugar, the sugar dissolves on its own—there is nothing else to be done. If the sugar is in large crystals rather than fine granules, it will take longer to dissolve. Stirring the mixture can make the sugar dissolve faster, shaking it may break up some of the bigger crystals, heating the water can help—but stirring, shaking, heating, and any other action, is ultimately unnecessary. It is the nature of sugar to dissolve in water. In the same way, it is the nature of awareness to dissolve old programs and patterns so that they can soften and change.

Awareness is the key that opens the door to the discovery of freedom and the potential of being human. All the practices, techniques, methodologies, therapies, etc. that one can find are just shaking, stirring and heating. They can speed up the process a bit, break up the bigger lumps and crystals perhaps—but ultimately they are unnecessary. Awareness is the first, most important, and last key, and, in its awakened state of Awareness-that-is-itself, it is ultimately all that is needed.

Working with Awareness

It is very difficult to be aware of the origins of thoughts or to maintain an equanimous (meaning balanced, not craving or wanting, and not disliking or trying to get rid of or change) mind frame while in the throes of anger, grief, passion, jealousy, despair, or other strong emotions. Even with the very strong intention just to be present and watch what happens, it is extremely difficult not to get caught in the thoughts that come with strong emotions and allow them simply to carry us through the emotional wave—a wave that often breaks and crashes leaving us feeling afraid, guilty, depressed, or worse. For this reason, it is best to start practicing awareness by watching something that is related to the mind and one's thoughts, but is not as insidious as thought. This "something" is the body.

Since the mind and body are not separate but completely connected, everything that happens in the mind is also reflected in the body and vice versa. There is a constant flow of communication between the body and the conscious mind through the medium of body sensations. Other communication is happening more rapidly between the body and brain at many levels— electrical, chemical (via hormones and other chemical messengers), and of course on the quantum level through the properties of field interconnection.

Seen from the perspective of the Field, a thought contains a certain vibrational frequency, and this frequency travels throughout the body and surrounding area similarly to the way that ripples from a stone travel out in the water. The thought produces a certain frequency and this frequency is communicated on a variety of levels and via numerous pathways throughout the body/mind system. Some of these levels and pathways include:

- chemical and electrical signals

- changes in muscle tension

- vascular tension and heart rate

- changes in breathing including:

  - depth of breath

  - rate of breath

  - muscles used to activate the lungs (diaphragm, ribs, shoulders, back)

- physical movement and changes in posture

- facial expression

- body position

- body alertness and readiness

- the physical sensations that accompany all of this activity that are often finally recognized by the conscious mind as an emotion.

All this is constantly flowing and changing in a circular system that feeds back on itself. A thought produces physical sensations which then feed back to change or increase the intensity of the thought, which produces different or more intense sensations, and the circle continues.

Although this may sound somewhat complex, it is actually part of everyday common experience. It is not difficult to see that when one focuses on loving thoughts that the body tends toward pleasant and loving sensations; focus on angry thoughts and you have angry sensations, jealous thoughts and you feel jealousy in your body, fearful thoughts and there are fearful sensations. The opposite is also true—fearful sensations create fearful thoughts, angry sensations enhance or create angry thoughts. The system is always working, always changing, always balanced in a loop where sensations and thoughts are intimately linked and connected.

✓ Because of this intimate and subtle linking of thought and physical sensation, a thought or program can be watched either in the mind or in the sensations that happen in the body—it doesn't matter which. Becoming aware of the body is a powerful way of connecting the conscious mind with subconscious processes because the body registers these processes as physical sensations. Generally, the conscious mind ignores all these sensations and therefore misses what is going on. By training yourself to notice what your body is feeling, you will begin to connect your conscious mind with deeper and deeper levels of the subconscious and therefore be able to bring awareness to the programs that are running at these levels.

For example, a client with whom I worked found that he was constantly uneasy, especially around other people. He wanted to please others, help people, and just be comfortable with and be accepted by others, but something always seemed to get in the way of this. He was intelligent, good looking, capable, and well educated, yet he always felt like he was somehow outside the circle, even with friends, and he generally felt alone and not understood.

This man began to practice awareness of his body. Through directed breath and movements he became more and more sensitive and in touch with the location and description of physical sensations in his body.

When we began, he at first felt a bit silly when I asked him what he was feeling in his body. Men aren't taught to feel particularly, and our bodies tend to be tools to use and otherwise ignore as much as possible. Gradually, however, he began to discover that he could be aware of the location of physical sensations. He found anger in the chest, fear in the stomach and shoulders, anxiety in the stomach, chest, shoulders, throat and forehead. Taking steps into understanding subtler levels of experience, he became able to identify the feeling of sensations in these areas: anger was heavy and compressed, like a hot weight on his chest and explosive feeling in his head. Anxiety was a quavery vibration throughout his body, a tight and painful knot in his stomach, rapid and shallow breathing in his chest and a feeling of emptiness in his heart, tension and constriction in his throat, and a foggy achy feeling in his forehead.

All these sensations had always been there, but they were subtle enough (and he had learned to ignore his body well enough) that he had generally not been consciously aware of them before. Even when they did become strong enough for his conscious awareness to notice them, he did his best to ignore them. He'd take a Tylenol for a headache, try to ignore what he was feeling by working too much, or find numerous other ways to distract himself enough to be able to ignore what his body was feeling.

Although it was unfamiliar and uncomfortable, he began to learn that he didn't have to run away from the sensations in his body. Even when his sensations became very strong and frightening, and his mind was bent on getting away from or stopping what was happening, he learned that he could use his awareness to soothe the frightened thoughts. Where he would previously have begun to feel the anxiety and have immediately started to move, fidget, change the subject, or distract himself, he learned that he could simply stay still, breathe deeply, and allow the feelings to wash through him.

When the mind stops reacting to the sensations, as this man learned when he stopped trying to run from what his body was feeling, the sensations bring up thoughts in the mind. Like a wind-up toy when the spring is released, the tension and energy that has been built up begins to unwind, and this appears as thoughts that can sometimes seem frightening or crazy. By learning simply to watch—building his awareness—and staying focused on his breath and the changing sensations in his body this man began to be able to stay with his feelings and not react to the anxiety as he had done in the past.

Instead of reacting to his anxious feelings and thereby practicing them into an increasingly pervasive habit, he learned just to breathe, stay still, and be aware. This man who had initially had difficulty accepting that his body felt much of anything at all was eventually able to stay with his physical sensations so well that he could begin to trace the feelings back into his past. He learned to experience a strong feeling—for him the anxiety was the main issue—and then to look for other times when he had experienced similar physical sensations. He learned to play a slide show of his own past, allow the images and memories to come forward, briefly experience them, and then move to the next slide, always moving toward earlier memories.

Eventually, this process of remembering, watching and accepting, and moving further back, brought him to pre-verbal memories from before he was born. His body memory (later confirmed in a somewhat uncomfortable discussion with his mother) still held the experience of being inside a mother who was frightened, in a bad relationship, and badly wanting to not be pregnant. From his earliest experience, this man had been in a situation of not being wanted, and this experience had left an imprint on all his cells—both brain and body. Realizing this, he was able to understand that the little child was not at fault, that the fear was not his and was no longer necessary, and that he did not have to be afraid anymore.

Before practicing awareness, this man's anxiety was a blockage in his system on all levels that left him unhappy and often close to incapacitation. After practicing awareness, this same anxiety became his pathway to understanding his past and changing his present, his path to energetic, mental, physical and social healing, and his key to release from old patterns and programs that were causing a great deal of unhappiness and suffering in his life.

Awareness is the key to changing the suffering and difficulties in our life in a positive way. Without awareness, each time we repeat an old pattern, become angry, become anxious, or fall into our programmed reactions, we simply increase the suffering in our lives by increasing the physical addiction to the habit. With awareness, these same incidents can become pathways to healing and release.

Although this man's therapy process involved using his body sensations as a bridge to remembering his past, it is not absolutely necessary to dig out everything that has happened to us and to understand how it connects to present patterns. It is the awareness of the body sensations, along with developing an ability to accept them without judgment, craving, dislike, or an attempt to change them that is the key. It is not necessary to understand or analyze body sensation—only to be aware and accept it, knowing that it will change.

In fact, even awareness is not necessary if one is able to simply remain in a state of acceptance that everything is already OK. In this case, there is a deep acceptance of *what is* that simply allows it to be without any need for judgement at all. The paradox of this kind of deep acceptance is that when we truly accept *what is*, then we also give it the freedom to become something else. Most healing practices that actually work are just different ways of convincing the mind to let go, stop judging and allow change to happen.

As water dissolves sugar naturally and on its own, so healing happens as soon as we get out of the way, stop resisting and trying and let it happen on its own. As is true in many situations, it is easier to understand this from an energetic perspective than from the objective/material perspective. In the energetic perspective, *health* and *flow* are synonymous. This is related to a very fundamental property of the universe in which we live called the law of entropy. The law of entropy is one of the most firmly established and apparently immutable universal laws that is known. It states that the universe—and everything in it—is constantly moving toward a greater state of disorder, randomness and chaos. Life appears to be defying the law of entropy and creating order and complexity wherever it goes.

In reality, however, life has only signed an uneasy truce with entropy. In order to work within the physical laws of the universe, life must actually increase the speed of flow of energy from a state of order to disorder. This means that life creates a structure within which energy is dissipated much more quickly than it would if the structure was not there. Energy flows in, creates temporary order, and flows out again, in a more disordered state. Life can therefore be understood as the temporary structure and organization that results from the flow of energy being used more quickly than it would be if life were not present.

There are many examples of this, or ways of visualizing the principle. For instance, when you turn on a light switch, electricity flows through a tiny filament in the light bulb and makes it hot. The heated filament glows brightly and we see a light. The light results from concentrated and useful energy moving through the bulb, creating heat, and in the process, dissipating. The electricity is not able to be used again. The energy is still there, but it can't be recaptured and recycled. In this example, the light is dependent on the flow of energy. Stop the energy and you stop the light. While the light is on, it is increasing the flow of entropy—helping the universe to become ultimately more dispersed and chaotic. However, it is also creating light in the darkness.

Life is essentially like the light bulb. Although the levels of complexity cannot even be compared, the idea is essentially the same. We have to have flow in order to exist. On an energetic level, this flow is represented by the concept of Chi energy, or Prana as discussed earlier. On a physical level, flow is represented by intake of food and oxygen, excretion of wastes, and free circulation of oxygen and nutrients in the body. It is also represented by physical flexibility, resilience, and a lack of hard, knotted, or restricted places in the muscular structure.

On a psychological level, flow is represented by a flexible mind that does not attempt to grasp onto things. This is the ideal that is written of so often in texts about Buddhist, Taoist, Christian, Sufi and other mystics who search for the ability to "do without doing", "act with no action", be "present in this moment", and be "mindful". All this, including such peak experiences as Satori, meditative bliss and experiences of oneness with the universe are ultimately based on releasing the tendency of the mind/body system to attempt to grasp, hold, or find security in something that is constant. Entering into the flow is entering into the energetic force that allows life to exist. It is worth taking a moment to let this sink in. It is a statement that can easily be passed over without really understanding how fundamental it is. Really get this, and you won't need anything else.

In order for life to create order in this universe, it must constantly maintain a flow of energy in order to sustain itself. We create order in many ways. The physical body is an obvious form of order. Beliefs of who and what we are, what our story is, where we come from, what we love and what we hate—all these are forms of order as well. Our physical and social creations, from buildings and machines to governments and religions are also forms of order and all of these require energy to flow in and flow out in order to be sustained and maintained. A building will decay without maintenance. A religion will die without followers. A government will fail without resources, belief and people who give it their energy. Stories of hatred, victimization, or pain (which are already blockages of flow) will no longer exist if given no energy or attention.

However, the flow of energy that sustains a system also changes it. Change is generally seen as threatening and so individuals, and systems, tend to resist change. Resistance to change is also, by definition, resistance to flow and so as we fear and resist and attempt to maintain things as they are we gradually cut off the source of our life energy. Any stoppage, blockage, or slowing of the flow of energy through a living system, or any system for that matter, represents a place where that system is in effect saying "no" to the energy that sustains it.

Without realizing it, we are constantly repeating this "no" in our day to day lives. Resistance to change, resistance to new ideas, being set in a particular way of thinking and unwilling to consider other viewpoints, rejecting and limiting thoughts, clinging to a particular idea, person or thing, identifying one's self, partner, or others with particular images or ideas of what you believe them to be—all of these are ways in which we limit ourselves and say "no" to flow. Muscle tension, resistance in any form whatsoever, clinging, holding, fear in any form—there are many ways that we say "no" to our own lives.

A son or daughter dies and grief is normal and important. Sometimes, however, this grief is held for many years and becomes a filter through which life is viewed. This clinging to what is beyond one's control is a blockage of the flow. It will decrease vitality, and if it is severe enough, it will eventually manifest as some physical ailment or another.

This same daughter or son, or perhaps parent or friend, is murdered or badly hurt by someone else and we cling to not only the grief but the anger and desire for retribution. This is an even more serious and deep blockage. It will create great tension, stress, and internal mental and physical damage.

My wife (or husband) fails to fit the image that I have created for her; she fails to be what I want or what I expected. In my mind I hold a picture of what I want and think I need, and she does not fit my picture any longer. I cling to my picture and what I want, and again I block the flow. In my body I suffer the tension, stress, and mental/physical/energetic blockage of clinging to something that is not real. In my relationship I create tension and blockages in intimacy because I am trying to shape my partner to fit a picture that is not her. I create disappointment, anger, distance, and discord, and I am unable to see what and who my partner truly is. Much of my energy is diverted to the attempt to create something that is not real or true, and in this way the energy is wasted, and my ability to flow is blocked. Not only am I blocking my own flow, but I am also limiting, disrespecting, and blocking my partner by attempting to make her fit into the box of my own beliefs, impressions, and desires.

Without awareness we would be stuck in these patterns with no way of freeing ourselves; we would be doomed to lives filled, and shortened, by automatic attempts to be secure, to avoid pain and linger in pleasure, and by fear of change that blocks and strangles the flow of our own life energy.

Awareness can be a key that allows us to experience our actions as well as the effects of our actions and to put these two things together. Although this seems a simple thing, it is much harder than it sounds. Increasing the depth of our understanding of the effects or consequences of our own actions is a lifetime job that entails practicing to increase our awareness of subtler levels of thought, body sensation, and subtle energetic experience.

While practicing meditation in Thailand, I had an opportunity to watch my own mind and its expectations of continuity. I would sit for an hour, and both my mind and body would become involved in an experience of one form or another. Sometimes this experience would seem very deep, pleasurable, or spiritual. Other times the experience was full of anger, frustration, sadness, or physical pain. In each case, it felt like the experience was something strong and lasting. However, I would get up for a short break, come back five minutes later, sit down to start again, and find that something completely new had arisen. The images, thoughts, feelings and body sensations that had seemed so deep and solid when I got up had evaporated like a dream; in sitting again, I was watching a new dream unfold.

Each time one sits for meditation, a new experience arises, independent of what was happening before. In the flow of energy that is the basis of our minds, bodies, and universe, nothing is constant and nothing remains the same for even a nanosecond. This lesson can be applied in our lives with the people with whom we live and work. Just because my spouse has seemed to be the same for twenty years does not mean that it is true. It is my expectation and my image that has remained the same.

Truly letting go of an expectation or image is an act of love—both for myself and for others around me because it releases the blockage to flow that the image creates. Being in the flow IS being in love, and releasing another from my expectations allows both myself and the other to be more free and more IN love—literally. In meditation, each time one sits, one starts again with an experience that is new. It is the same with relationship. Each morning, practice seeing the person beside you as someone new. Release your images and expectations and see what happens[20].

Whether the issue is relationship, work, anxiety, anger, the existential questions of life, or any of the possibilities of human experience, awareness is the catalyst that makes the difference between an experience that is healing and beneficial and one that is a repetition of old programs and old patterns. Awareness shines a light on what *I* am doing so that I can see it; if I can see, I also have a choice to release or change what I see.

Beyond awareness is, of course, simply resting in the peace of being-as-it-is. Awareness is an important and useful tool, but it also has an end point. Paradoxically, the end point is always present and does not need to be obtained. It is already yours, should you choose to know this. There are many tools because there are many minds. Ultimately, you need to choose

---

20 There are references in Christianity, as well as other religions, forbidding graven images, or images of any kind. With the understanding of energy, the reason for this is clearer. It is not pictures on the wall or sculptures on the floor that are the problem. It is the images that we engrave in our own minds and then stubbornly cling to. A graven mental image is an attempt to stop the change that literally gives us life. Release the images graven in your mind and it will give your life new freedom and vitality.

the tool that is best for you—and also know when you are ready to discard it for something more fundamental and simple.

* * *

Awareness exercises

Awareness starts with attention, and so the practices listed in the attention section are all helpful in developing awareness as well. Here are a few other ways of practicing awareness:

1. Awareness of thoughts: Self-talk

Self-talk is the chatter that goes on inside our heads on a nearly constant basis. Often this self-talk is very negative, judgmental, and nasty. The messages that we give ourselves are generally repeating tapes and reactions that we learned as children and that we continue to repeat to ourselves for a lifetime. By learning to watch our thoughts, we can begin to recognize these repeating tapes and learn to stop reacting to them.

The primary purpose of this exercise is to change your mind from a habit of reacting with fear-based thoughts to a habit of reacting with love-based thoughts, and it is therefore a cognitive exercise. However, changing your thoughts will begin to change your entire mind/body system as well. On an emotional level, it will help you to feel confident, secure and loved more often. On a physical level, it will help you to feel less stressed and healthier. On an energetic level it will help you to attract people and events into your life that bring more love, abundance, peace, and beauty into your world.

All these levels—mental, emotional, physical and energetic are an interlocked system. Change one, and the others change as well.

Self-talk can be particularly helpful to pay attention to when you notice yourself feeling angry and is, in fact, one of the primary tools that is used in anger management programs. It is not only useful for anger though—any time you are feeling a strong emotion or you notice the negative messages that you are giving yourself, self-talk is a great place to start.

To work with self-talk, it is helpful to make a "T" chart. Draw a line down the center of a piece of paper. On the left hand side make a heading saying "unhelpful thoughts" and on the right hand side make a heading saying "helpful thoughts".

Under "unhelpful thoughts" write down all of the negative, angry, depressed, cutting, and unhelpful thoughts that are running around in your mind concerning a particular incident or problem. Pay careful attention to the ones that repeat like a broken record over and over again.

Once you think you have most of these thoughts written down, look through them and try to find one that you can see in another way or with another perspective. For instance "I'm a failure" could be replaced with "I have succeeded at some things I have done". This second statement is more true than the first because everyone has succeeded at something—even if it is only the fact that they succeeded in getting up in the morning. Note that the second statement is made possible by a change in perspective. In the first case, I am focused on all that I have done wrong. In the second case, I am acknowledging that life is difficult and even little things make a difference. It can take a huge amount of courage sometimes just to get out of bed and face another day. I did it! What courage and perseverance I have! I even had breakfast, got to work on time, spoke with someone I was scared to talk to, and so on. When you look in the right way, you will find that you can see the world differently.

In each case, look for a statement that looks at the issue from a different perspective and that can be both more true and more helpful. Here is an example of a "T" chart:

Unhelpful Thoughts	Helpful Thoughts
I'm a failure	I have succeeded at some things
I'm not good at anything	I can: (make a list)—cook a meal, change the oil in my car, run 1 km. Everyone has something they can do...
I can't control my anger	I can be aware of my anger. I can ask for help. I can change if I choose to.
I'm stupid	I can do my best with whatever talents I have. I don't need to compare myself with others.
I always mess everything up	Sometimes I succeed. I can focus more on what I do right than what I do wrong.

A "T" Chart like this helps to make it clear that there is a choice. Either side of the chart can be true but without awareness, it is easy to remain stuck in the habit of tearing ourselves down with our thoughts. When you become aware of your self-talk, you then have the opportunity to choose which thoughts you want to invest your energy in; you will see the results of this choice in the way you feel about yourself and also in the way others see you.

2. Awareness of Emotions

Awareness of emotions can be kind of tricky. If one becomes angry, for instance, the anger carries a momentum of its own, and the more one thinks about it, the stronger it gets. The same is true for any strong emotion—sadness, jealousy, fear, and others. Rather than trying to be aware of the emotion, therefore, it is more helpful to be aware of the physical sensations that go along with the emotion. When you are angry, what do you notice in your body? Are your ears hot? Does your jaw clench? Do your fists clench? Does your chest feel tight? How about your stomach? Pay attention to what is happening and see how early you can catch it. Can you find only the strong sensations or can you start to notice the more subtle markers that happen long before you realize that you are actually angry?

Many people are unaware that they are angry until they have nearly reached the point of explosion. They think that they are unable to control themselves because they miss all the signals their body gives them until the anger effect is so strong and the fight or flight reaction is so far along that their conscious mind no longer has any control. Then they say "I just snap. I can't help it".

It's true that you can't help but snap if you get to the point where your conscious mind has been over-ridden by the fight or flight mechanism. That is why it is so important to be aware of the body signals that arise before you get to this point. They are like messengers saying "Look out! You're getting angry. Change what you are doing!"

Depression, sadness, fear, jealousy—any strong emotion is bound to come along with physical sensations in the body. If you put your focus on the physical sensations, you will begin to make an interesting observation: They change. While you practice awareness of the sensations, focus on your breath and tell your mind to be still—or practice something like Ho'oponopono to give your mind a more positive focus. Sooner or later—generally sooner—the strong emotion you are feeling will change.

It is also helpful to understand that all emotions come as waves. They have a building phase, a peak, and a falling phase. If you catch them early enough, they can be gentle waves, rippling quietly. If the triggering event is strong or if you let things build up too much, they can be like tsunamis ripping through. Awareness of your body sensations will help you to learn to ride the waves with more comfort and ease and to keep the waves from gathering the strength needed to do damage.

It can be very helpful to work with a mind/body therapist who can help you to become aware of your body sensations and to track how they connect with your emotions[21]. Massage is also a very helpful form of therapy for people who have difficulty with awareness of their body.

3. Meditation and Awareness

There are many forms of meditation. Generally speaking, meditation requires an object of focus—a physical object, a word or sound, an idea, an activity, physical body sensation, or breath. Through dedicated focus on a chosen object, it is possible to quiet the mind and gain more skill in working with the mind/body system. However, not all forms of meditation are created equal. If you choose a form of meditation, it is helpful to understand what your purpose is—why are you doing it and what you hope to achieve.

The objects of meditation can be broken into categories of visual objects, sound objects, or activity-based objects. Each of these categories can be further broken down into physical or mental—i.e. real objects or mental constructions or images of objects.

Visual objects can be anything from a candle flame to a picture of a god, goddess, or any object of worship. Sound objects can be anything from a single tone to a repeated word or phrase (mantra) to complicated chants. Activity based objects can be any action done mindfully, from fishing to yoga to washing dishes to driving a car.

There are different benefits to different kinds of meditation. Focusing attention on an image (physical or mental) of a god, goddess, symbol of a religion, or object of worship (such as the Christian cross) is a way of focusing the mind while also working

---

21 There are many forms of mind/body therapy. One that I am trained in is called Integrated Body Psychotherapy (IBP). You can find a worldwide list of IBP practitioners at this website: www.ibponline.org

to take on the qualities of the object of focus. Meditation on the face of the Buddha, for instance, would be with the intention of developing more of the qualities of the Buddha: compassion, love and mental clarity.

Sounds carry their own vibrations and some of these vibrations can be very healing. Repetition of a mantra, chant, or tone creates these healing vibrations and helps the practitioner to take on the qualities of the sound being created. Some sounds, like the famous OM mantra, for example, carry very powerful transformational vibrations that can help to sensitize the mind/body system to more subtle realities and levels of awareness. Other mantras are thought to help activate or open specific chakras in the body.

It is important to remember, however, that focus on a single object can also be limiting. We live in a universe of change, something with which most of us have a degree of discomfort. Focus on a fixed object can actually increase our tendency to become rigid or to try to control or stop the change. It can also set up thought forms and vibrations in our energy fields that, while initially helpful, later become thick and block the natural flow of energy and change in our system.

A practitioner of energy healing once told me of an experience with a man who had practiced meditation with a mantra for many years. Normally, a person's energy field is reasonably open and, with permission, an energy practitioner can help to open blocked channels and create more movement within the field. This man, however, had such a strong shell around him that she couldn't do anything at all.

The shell that this man created through practice of his mantra had both helpful and harmful effects for him. Like a castle wall, it gave him strength and protection. However, it also made him somewhat emotionally isolated, and it was beginning to have connections with physical stiffness and pains—which was the reason he had come to the practitioner in the first place. He didn't want to hear about his shell though, and so the practitioner was unable to help him.

In my own experience, I practiced Vipassana meditation for over twenty years. During this time, I generally spent two hours per day with the practice. I believed (and still believe) very strongly in the freeing power of this practice because, unlike other forms of meditation, Vipassana focuses on something that is always in motion—the physical sensations of the body. By focusing on an object that is always moving and changing, Vipassana gradually builds an internal and strongly felt understanding of change. More than just an intellectual idea, the reality of change as it applies to *me* and *my body* becomes a deeply sensed and "grokked" (physically experienced and understood) personal experience.

However, when I spent time with my teacher in Thailand, he told me to stop meditating—that it wasn't good for me anymore. I was initially quite angry about this and spent a week or so fuming about it. How could I let go of something I had spent so many thousands of hours on? "I have attended fifteen ten-day retreats, practiced daily for years, based much of my way of life, on my practice and used it as my way of managing my emotions and dealing with difficult situations... how can you ask me to stop?" I thought.

As I began to get over the anger though, I realized that my practice was supposed to be teaching me to let go into change. Increasingly, however, I had been using it to control my feelings and to give myself a sense of something solid to hold onto. What was supposed to be a practice in accepting reality as it really is and flowing with change had for me become a way of controlling my inner world.

The difference between controlling and simply watching becomes extremely subtle as one progresses in awareness. It can become a circle of awareness chasing itself like a dog chasing its own tail. I had become lost in this continual circle of self-chasing-self in an attempt to control my inner world, rather than just surrendering to whatever was happening in the moment, and I didn't know how to get out of the circle.

In addition to this, I had begun to identify myself with my practice. "I am a Vipassana meditator", "I have been doing this for twenty two years", "I have spent so much time in retreats and personal practice and dedicated so much energy to this practice..." There was altogether too much "I" in something that was meant to be reducing the amount of "I". My anger and feelings of being lost and empty at the thought of changing the practice were also good clues as to my attachment to it.

After a while I decided that my teacher was right—it was time to change. Teachers are helpful in this way—not as dictators to tell us what is True, but as guides to help us see what we may otherwise miss.

The moral of the story here is that even mindfulness needs to be practiced with mindfulness. Any practice is just that—a practice. It is a stepping stone and not a destination. Ultimately, all practice is unnecessary.

Keep this in mind both when choosing a new practice and when deciding that it is time to let go.

Part 5: Intention

So far in this chapter, I have talked about truth, thoughts, attention, and awareness. As I hope you are beginning to understand (or perhaps already know), the human mind/body/spirit system is extremely complex, subtle, and powerful. The reason for the lengthy discussion of these parts and functions of mind is that these are the controlling and governing factors that can be used either to make our lives beautiful and noble or base, ugly, and mean. We have this choice, regardless of our external circumstances, and it is up to us to choose. Understanding some of the levels of mind and how they work can help us understand how to recognize these choices and how to choose in ways that promote more peace of mind and well-being for ourselves and others.

To recap, then, truth is not an absolute but a process. We progress from relatively smaller and more divisive truths to relatively larger and more inclusive truths as we progress in understanding ourselves and this universe in which we live. Thoughts are the words and pictures that are constantly running through most people's minds. Sometimes there is silence in the mind, but for most people this silence is quite rare. Thoughts are nearly always there—though they may be mainly words, mainly pictures, or mainly sounds, depending on the person. Thoughts, however, are not identity.

If we were to compare the levels of the mind with a computer, thoughts would be like the user interface of the operating system. They are the advertising messages flashing on your computer browser, the little instruction boxes, text on the pages, videos and music from YouTube and the like. Just like what can be found when randomly browsing the internet, thoughts can jump from topic to topic randomly and quickly and can contain useful information or completely useless information. They can be directed and purposeful, as when using a search engine to learn about a specific topic, for instance, and they can be random and without much purpose, as when clicking aimlessly on whatever happens to catch your eye on a page.

Where thoughts are the text and information on the screen, *attention* is the amount of focus and energy that the user puts into the information on the screen. While sitting at the computer and surfing the net, a person can be completely focused on what he is doing, or barely focused at all, paying more attention to what is going on in the room behind her or thinking about the argument she had with her boyfriend the day before. Attention is a measure of the focus put toward what is happening right now and how much of a person's resources are involved in what is happening in the present moment.

Awareness, on the other hand, is the global ability to look in on what you are doing and consciously notice it. *Attention* is like the tightness of the beam of a searchlight. A tight beam puts a bright light on a small space. A wider beam puts less light on a larger space. *Awareness*, however, is like the person holding the searchlight and adjusting its width according to the situation. Attention creates intensity. Awareness creates wisdom.

I sometimes think of awareness as *the wise watcher*—a part of me that keeps track of patterns, notices when things don't make sense, and uses each situation to learn more about who I am and how I work.

Intention is a fourth important aspect of consciousness. To use the computer analogy again, *awareness* represents the computer user, *attention* is the focus of the user and *intention* is the choice of software that the user is using. Thoughts are what happens on the screen and can come from a variety of places, including random connections with the internet. If the user intends to write a story, he would do best to choose word processing software. If she intends to work with graphics, a different program is needed. The program helps to define and enable the act of creation that comes about from our awareness and attention. Just as the kind of program defines and shapes what we can create with a computer, an *intention* helps to define what we will create in our lives.

Another helpful analogy for intention is the idea of a compass. A compass can point in any direction, but you can use it to set a specific course for a specific location. As the terrain changes, the compass keeps you going where you had intended, rather than wandering in circles or getting lost. Again, intention provides the direction, definition, and shape for what you want to do.

The idea of intention becomes more important the farther into the paradigm of fields you travel. Since a field is based on information, a field that is conscious of itself (such as, for instance, you) is affected by its own intentions. In many very real ways, the intention is a determining parameter that defines the shape and content of an experience. This means that if a person intends to find a problem, he is much more likely to find it than if he intends to find that everything is OK. A person who intends to dislike another person is likely to be successful. Intending to like this same person could also prove to be successful. Intention sets up filters for what we see and experience so that we can then fulfill the intention that we have set up.

Since who we are is a composite that includes what we do and what we experience, intention not only shapes and defines what we can do but also who we are and what we are capable of doing or experiencing. Without an intention, one is open to a great deal of randomness and chaos. With an unsuitable intention, good opportunities can become very unpleasant or even dangerous situations.

It is therefore important to be careful when setting intentions, and to understand how they work. It is also important to remember that intentions can be physically useful, but can also actually be detrimental to living in an awakened state. Intentions are powerful when you want to create or manifest what you desire in your life. They are also powerful reinforcers of the *me* and therefore tend to help in the creation of resistance to experiencing life simply as it is.

There is nothing wrong with using intention for consciously manifesting goals and desires. As with any tool, however, intention also has drawbacks. When it is used to try to get what you want, intention can become a blockage to gratitude, acceptance, and surrender and it can also reinforce an egoic sense of entitlement. All of these things are contrary to flow and will ultimately cause dis-ease mentally, physically, emotionally or spiritually. Intention should therefore be used with care, especially when directed toward material gain. Intending trust, gratitude, acceptance and blessing toward others is ultimately more life-giving than intending to acquire a new BMW, or a million dollars, or a beautiful partner. Paradoxically, it is when we are no longer in a state of wanting something that it more often becomes available to us.

With this in mind, here are some rules that can help you to set intentions, should you decide that you want to do so.

Rule of "The Present"

Intentions work best if they have already happened. Though this sounds like a paradox, it is actually a very important part of the way intention works. For instance, if you would like to have more money in your life, you could set the intention "*I will make more money*". However, a much more powerful and effective way of saying the same thing would be: "*I experience gratitude for the abundance that is in my life*". The first intention starts out with an idea of lack or not enough in the present and aims at fixing the lack by getting more in the future. This intention is likely to backfire and simply bring more of the lack, since lack is literally what is being asked for. By saying "I will make more money" it is understood that what I have now is not enough. The intention really says "not enough now, more later". This will create "not enough now" for as long as you wish to continue it. "Later" never comes, because it is always "later".

The second intention acknowledges that I already have what I desire in the present. As I continuously re-affirm this in my life, my physical reality and perceptual experience will both change to become in alignment with the intention. *More* happens—not in an unreachable future but in the only place that it can be experienced—the present moment.

There is a Zen Buddhist story of a young monk who asks his teacher how to obtain a staff like his teacher carries. The staff symbolizes great learning and is a kind of symbol of rank and power within the order of monks. The old monk replies "If you have one staff, I give you more. If you have no staff, even what you have I take away."

This story applies to the rule of *The Present*. Once we acknowledge that we already have something, then we will find that we get more of it.

Rule of "The Universal"

Another important rule of intention is to aim for universals rather than specifics. For instance, you may wish to have a better relationship with your spouse, and so you set an intention such as "*I want my relationship with (spouse's name) to be more harmonious and loving*". This intention breaks the rule of the present as well as the rule of the universal because it wishes for something better in the future (rule of the present), and it wishes for a specific feeling with a specific person (rule of the universal).

A more powerful way of stating this would be to say "*I experience well-being and fulfillment in all my relationships*" In this intention you already have at least some of what you want, and you enable it to become more fully realized. You also do not set unnecessary limits. Why not feel great about the way you relate to everyone?

Rule of "Self"

The third rule of intention is that it should be stated so that you are its point of action. If your intention requires the cooperation of someone else, it is much less likely to be effective. The example above also demonstrates this rule. The first statement, "*I want my relationship with (spouse's name) to be more harmonious and loving*" assumes some cooperation and similar desire from your spouse. Hopefully, this will be present. However, it is possible that your spouse already feels fulfilled, doesn't want the same things you do, or whatever. It is best to remember that what you are working toward is a sense of well-being and fulfillment for yourself—so state it this way: Your well-being does not have to depend on anyone else.

When you say, "I experience well-being and fulfillment in all of my relationships," you acknowledge your own boundaries and your ability to be whole and complete within them. Relationship begins with a sense of wholeness on the inside, and you can only really affect and change what happens within your own boundary. If you set an intention that depends on someone else, it is very important to be sure that you and this other person both understand the intention clearly and that you agree on what you want to achieve. Generally, it is more effective to set intentions that focus on what you can do from within your own boundary, and that gives others the freedom to do what is best for them.

Chapter 11
Through the looking glass—Concepts and practices for awakening

The concepts of living within, and as part of, a universal field, and of perceiving everything as a mirror, are ideas that can seem paradoxical. As expressed in verse forty-one of the Tao Te Ching, the way forward can seem like retreat and the easy way seems hard. The intellectual mind has difficulties grasping the twists and turns of concepts like living from the inside-out, or as a holographic flow within a universal field, and can churn in confusion and incomprehension forever if allowed to do so.

> When a superior person hears of the Tao,
> She diligently puts it into practice.
> When an average person hears of the Tao,
> he believes half of it, and doubts the other half.
> When a foolish person hears of the Tao,
> he laughs out loud at the very idea.
> If he didn't laugh,
> it wouldn't be the Tao.
>
> Thus it is said:
> The brightness of the Tao seems like darkness,
> the advancement of the Tao seems like retreat,

the level path seems rough,
the superior path seems empty,
the pure seems to be tarnished,
and true virtue doesn't seem to be enough.
The virtue of caution seems like coward-
ice,
the pure seems to be polluted,
the true square seems to have no corners,
the best vessels take the most time to
finish,
the greatest sounds cannot be heard,
and the greatest image has no form.

The Tao hides in the unnamed,
Yet it alone nourishes and
completes all things.

Lao Tsu. 41st verse of the Tao Te Ching.
Translation by J.H. McDonald[22]

If you have come this far, you have already seen many exercises, tools, and concepts all built around the idea that we are moving into a period in the development of the human species where we are growing into a new way of understanding the world around us. The tools that you have seen so far include practices touching into the different aspects that are a part of each of us: physical, mental, energetic, and multidimensional or spiritual.

The tools listed in this chapter are further examples of ways in which you can work with these levels of your own being to improve the quality, depth, and breadth of your life experience. It is not necessary to use or practice all of them. Pick and choose among them to find what seems to fit best in your life right now. Come back often to see if it is time to try a new tool or if you are still good with the ones you have.

---

22 *Tao Te Ching, by Lao Tzu, Complete Online Text. A translation for the public domain by J.H. McDonald. 1996. Retrived from: http://www.wright-house.com/religions/taoism/tao-te-ching. html#41*

As you are reading, and as you are going about your day to day tasks, try to keep in mind that what you feel is equally important—or perhaps more important than what you think. The mind can be a tyrant that denies anything it cannot understand. Letting go of what we think we know can be a frightening thing but also a very freeing and rewarding one. Though it may seem paradoxical, the more we can release, the more we truly have.

In a hologram, each part of the image carries the entire image. A holographic plate can be shattered into tiny pieces, and each piece will still carry the entire image, though the resolution may be diminished. The reason this is possible is that a hologram is an image of a wave pattern, and it is the pattern that carries the image. As you bring the Awakening into your life, and as you read the rest of this book, try to look at yourself and the world around you with the idea of the holograph in mind. You are the wave pattern that is also the holographic wave pattern of the universe. You represent the whole.

This universe is also a wave pattern with similarities to a hologram. As you set your intention for what you want to learn and what you want to accomplish, you will find it anywhere you look and in anything you do. Everything is connected, everything is ultimately one and we are a part of the great dance. It doesn't matter where you are, what you do, or what circumstances surround you—the great wisdom of the universe is available to you.

Part 1: Forgiveness

The weak can never forgive. Forgiveness is the attribute of the strong.

Mahatma Gandhi

To forgive is to set a prisoner free and discover that the prisoner was you.

Lewis B. Smedes

Forgiveness is, contrary to most people's understanding, not something that is done to or for someone else. Forgiveness is an action of love toward self, a service rendered to oneself in order to reduce suffering and anxiety.

From the traditional western viewpoint, forgiveness tends to be a gift bestowed on an often undeserving person. "This person has done something wrong, has harmed me, but through my charity and superior spirit, I have given this person the gift of forgiveness." Generally, this form of forgiveness comes with quite a few strings and is accompanied by a "holier than thou" feeling on the part of the person doing the forgiving. This type of forgiveness makes sense from many points of view. However, it is not terribly useful.

From the perspective of energy, forgiveness is an extremely useful and necessary gift that I can give myself. It has very little to do with the person from whom I have perceived harm and everything to do with my own state of mind and health. In order to understand forgiveness, we need to first return to the definition of the universal field:

> The universal field is a matrix of information that includes all forms within the four known dimensions of time and space (and likely much that goes beyond these dimensions). Within the Field, information is activated and made manifest by an activating force that we refer to as energy. This force exists as vibrational waves which can also condense into what we perceive as solid matter. However, nothing is truly solid. All that exists within the Field is in a constant state of change, and energy is in constant motion.

Energy is also polarized into negative and positive charges. This polarization and interplay of opposites is found at all levels throughout the Field and is a fundamental characteristic—at least within the physical universe.

A human, from the field perspective, is a complex formation of vibrational frequencies operating within the context of the greater field. The energy that keeps these frequencies coherent and in place must be constantly flowing, and all manifestations of the frequencies—physical, mental, energetic, spiritual—are constantly changing vibrational phenomena. For all life forms, the flow of energy into, through, and out of the system is essential. Without the flow, life is no longer possible. This is important when considering the idea of forgiveness because lack of forgiveness—holding on to hatred, victimization and other feelings of contraction—is also a violation of flow and therefore a blockage of life energy.

The idea of flow is a fundamental and basic property of natural systems on all levels of complexity and scales. An example of the study of flow in systems from the scientific world comes from Ilya Prigogine, a Nobel Prize winning chemist who won his Nobel Prize in chemistry (1977) for his work with what he calls dissipative structures. In thermodynamics, a dissipative structure is a thermodynamic system that creates unexpected order or structure when energy is flowing through it. The order, or structure, is present only when there is a constant supply of energy that is moving through the system. When the energy stops, the system "dies" i.e. the structure that was developed dissolves.

One example of this kind of system is called a Bénard cell. In a Bénard cell, a thin layer of a viscous fluid is heated from below. The heat causes molecules from the bottom to rise to the surface where they dissipate heat and sink to the bottom again, are reheated and rise to the surface, etc. What would be expected with this is that there would simply be random movement—like a pot of boiling water. What actually happens is the formation of a honeycomb-like pattern of convection cells. Billions of atoms in a previously random and chaotic arrangement spontaneously organize themselves into a complex and stable structure. This same kind of arrangement can also be seen in columnar formations (called jointing) created when lava cools in a specific way.

Human social systems can also be seen as systems of flow, and flow dynamics is a very useful tool for analyzing where a system is healthy and where it isn't. A government, for instance, that collects taxes from its citizens and then redistributes this money wisely back into the country maintains a healthy system of flow and the country thrives. When individuals in the government begin to collect too much power, direct money into personal accounts and engage in corrupt deals with large corporations, the flow is blocked and the country begins to become unhealthy. The point, whether we are talking about a government, a company, a family, an individual or even a thermodynamic system like the Bénard cell is that wherever flow is blocked, the system becomes unhealthy.

There is a maxim from Chinese medicine that states "Where there is pain, there is no flow, and where there is flow, there is no pain." Flow is fundamental to health in a living system because flow is the basis on which the system is built. Any blockage in the flow eventually results in pain.

A traumatic violation perpetrated by one person on another is a definite blockage of flow for both people involved, and it results in pain. If flow was understood, the perpetrator would not commit the act in the first place just from the standpoint of self-respect and self-love. However, lacking self-love, a person then finds a need to attack someone else. The second person is then wounded in some way and flow is blocked for this person as well. If the second person really understood flow, then he would have enough self-love to let the wound heal as quickly as possible and to re-establish his own flow. He would not waste time and energy on revenge or identifying with victimhood, or in other ways prolonging the pain.

The most common response to attack, however, is to congeal or constellate, around the pain caused by the attack. This response is like the tightening of a muscle around a wound. The muscle goes into contraction as a way of trying to protect the wound from movement and further trauma. In the short term, this can be a good strategy. However, if it continues for very long it cuts off the blood supply and causes a hardened knot that never really heals. This is also what happens when a person is unable to forgive. The body, mind, and energy system constellate [23]around the pain, harden and become identified with it. In an unconscious and implicit agreement, the person who was attacked agrees to continue to give energy to the wound—and therefore to the attacker—by remaining tied to the pain.

Coming back to forgiveness, <u>forgiveness is a conscious choice</u> to transform a fear-based emotion, feeling, memory, or event into a love-based experience. This conscious choice removes the contractive blockage to flow caused by the negative emotions and invites greater energy, health, and well-being into one's own body—regardless of the effect or lack of effect that it has on the person you perceive to have hurt you. Not forgiving is like agreeing to chain yourself to eternal payment of your energy to the person who hurt you, block part of your own life energy, and suffer as much as possible in the hopes of eventually causing your attacker to suffer as you did. Forgiveness is realizing that punishing and hurting yourself is not going to hurt your attacker and that you can give yourself the gift of freedom, health, and prosperity instead.

If someone offers you a hot coal, you have some choices of what you do with it. If they force it into your hands and it burns you, then you are burned and that can't be changed. However, once the attacker goes away, you have a choice of continuing to hold the coal, or letting it go so that your body can heal. Many people continue to hold the coal for a long time, burning themselves more deeply with their refusal to let go.

The power of forgiveness should not be underestimated. It is based on a fundamental principle of life that is itself founded in basic laws of nature: Negative emotions block flow and this causes more sickness and pain. Positive emotions promote flow, and this causes greater health and well-being. All it takes to be free is a choice that should be quite simple: "Do I really want to hold myself bonded in pain to this person who I have perceived to have wronged me, or do I want to set myself free?" Really, when seen in this way, the choice should not be terribly difficult.

---

23 To constellate is to gather, or cause to gather, into a group. In this context, constellate refers to a psychological tendency for trauma, pain, or grief to become points of identification, gathering a sense of self and purpose around a central wound. People who seem to live for revenge or who fixate on punishment are good examples of this. It is possible to constellate around anything though—victimization, poor health, addiction, etc.

Exercises for Practicing Forgiveness

1. Forgiving the people you have difficulties with

For this, and other exercises in this book, it may be helpful for you to read the exercise out loud into the voice recorder on your phone or other recording device. Then find a quiet place, relax, close your eyes, and let your own voice guide you.

To begin, become aware of your breath. Take several deep breaths, breathing in fully and then allowing the air to fall out of your body, releasing as much as you can. Do this at least five times. On each inhalation, be thankful for the gift of life that the air brings to you. On each exhalation, release any tension that you feel in your body. In the stillness between each breath, stop a few seconds and allow your awareness to touch your body. Try to notice at least one physical sensation somewhere in your body each time.

Now think of all of the people that you know, standing in an area in front of you. Divide the area into two sides and arrange your image of these people so that the ones for whom you have positive feelings are on one side and those for whom you have negative feelings are on the other.

Say thank you to the people you like or feel positively about and allow them to leave. From the people who are left, choose the one person who seems most prominent or who you feel most ready to forgive right now.

As the others leave, watch as this person comes into the center of your attention. As this person stands in front of you, locate the place in your body where you have not forgiven him or her. You can do this simply by setting your intention to be aware of it and not listening to any doubt you may have of your own abilities. Focus on this part of your body and on the feeling of the emotional and energetic block that is located there. What does it feel like physically? Is it hot or warm or cool? Is it heavy or light? Is it solid, hard, spiky, earthy, soft, liquid, vibrating, tingling? Does it have a colour, a sound, a smell? Just allow your mind to be clear and notice whatever sensations arise for you.

Continue to breathe deeply and just notice the sensation of not forgiving this person. Allow it in your awareness as you would allow a hurt and frightened child. Without judgment, see if you can breathe into this feeling and simply acknowledge its presence. Allow your thoughts to be as they are, without editing them and without following them. Allow the images and words of all the hurt that you believe this person has caused you to arise in you and to transform into the next thought or feeling naturally. You don't have to interfere. These thoughts and feelings are changing on their own. Stay with this as long as you wish.

Perhaps you will notice feelings of release and expansion as old feelings surface and dissolve. Perhaps you will feel deeper anger and contraction as your mind tries to cling to old injustice and pain. Whatever happens in this time, simply breathe and know that it is changing. It is already gone. It is already OK. There is nothing left to do. Just breathe.

If you find your mind becoming stuck in a particular line of thought, it may help to remember that there are only two choices—to expand or to contract. Remember also what you have learned about your connection within the universal field and the mirror effect of what you see. This person is ultimately a part of yourself, a reflection of some part of you. Ask yourself: *Do I want to continue to be bound to this person in pain, or do I want to set myself free?*

Continue to breathe this way. Like a loving parent comforting a small child, allow yourself to feel your own love and your courage for facing your fear-based feelings. What is past is past, what is done is done. Now is the time to make new choices. Now is the time to be free.

When you are ready, open your eyes and look slowly around the room where you are sitting. Try to see each object in the room without judgment, releasing it from your past assumptions and recognizing it as an object of mystery, something new to you and beyond understanding. Let go of the tyranny of the past and allow yourself to be free in this moment.

If you wish, it can be helpful to journal about your experience. It is also helpful to repeat this exercise often.

2. Forgiving oneself.

Often, once we have removed the first layer of anger or fear by forgiving someone else, we will find that another layer rises to the surface and we have a choice to face—or to deny—an aspect of shame, guilt, judgment, or hatred that we have held against ourselves. Acknowledging these feelings and beliefs is the most important thing. Look on them as you would look on a newborn child, with no judgement and with no intent for them to be or do anything at all. See them. Only that. Don't judge or fix or change or alter anything at all about yourself, and also don't hold on to what you were. This moment is totally new, you are totally new and you are and have always been, already OK. Relax into the stillness that has no dependency on thought or feeling in any way. You are already there.

3. Forgiveness in extreme situations

There are extreme situations where forgiveness seems impossible. How can one forgive the rape and murder of a child? How can one forgive atrocities such as those committed in Uganda or Somalia during the genocides or the torture and death of millions of Jews during the Second World War? Human beings cause horrendous pain for each other, and there are acts that seem so heinous, so evil and atrocious that nothing could ever redeem the perpetrator or bring any form of comfort or resolution to the victim(s).

Forgiveness may be a nice idea, but in some instances it can feel almost insulting to suggest that it is possible at all.

There are no easy ways to answer this question. In the end, forgiveness is a personal journey and something that cannot be forced. However, if you are faced with a situation in which you must struggle with this kind of forgiveness, here are a few things to consider:

You have been presented with a huge challenge with which you must choose how you will perceive yourself and your reality. Do you choose to see the world from the objective/material viewpoint from the *outside in* or do you choose to see the world from what I have been calling the awakened viewpoint from the *inside out*? This choice determines if you believe that *what happens* is what matters most or that your *perception* of what happens is what matters most.

In the former case, the event must determine your feelings and reactions, and you have little choice but to be hurt. In addition, you are a powerless victim—the evil that was done is "out there", and retribution is the logical reaction.

In the latter case, you still cannot change what has happened, but you do have the power to change how it affects you. You can realize that nothing is more important than your own state of mind and your own right and ability to choose that state of mind. You can also consider the meaning of what has happened from a larger perspective.

You have also been presented with a very challenging test of love vs. hate—but not in the way you may expect. This is not about loving or hating what has been done, or even about loving or hating the person or people responsible. This choice is about loving or hating yourself. Will you choose to love yourself enough to release yourself from the pain of hatred and desire for retribution, or will you condemn yourself with the chains of your hatred?

Remember, forgiveness is not about condoning or even accepting evil or atrocity. There are times when a person can be forgiven but where strong action must still be taken to keep further harm from happening. Forgiveness is not about choosing what consequence a perpetrator must or must not suffer. Forgiveness is about freeing yourself from the pain and chains that are a result of negative attachment.

This is a very personal choice and one that does not have a *right* answer. There are consequences for any choice and any action that is taken. The important point here is that it is worthwhile looking carefully and truthfully at the consequences before choosing. In the end, every choice is between love and fear. To which of these do you want to give your power and your energy?

Part 2: Integrity: the basis of self-worth

*Perhaps the surest test of an individual's integrity is his refusal
to do or say anything that would damage his self-respect.*

Thomas S. Monson

A building has integrity just like a man. And just as seldom.

Ayn Rand

Integrity is an essential tool for operation in the new paradigm. Engineers
use the term "structural integrity" to refer to the strength and resilience of
a building or machine. The structural integrity of an airplane, for instance,
refers to its ability to hold together under conditions of stress and high
structural strain while in flight. An airplane with compromised structural
integrity is unsafe to fly.

On a similar note, a bridge or building must have structural integrity
in order to withstand day-to-day use and also to be prepared for adverse
situations such as severe weather or earthquakes. Buildings that are hastily
built and use low quality materials tend to have low structural integrity.
These kinds of buildings manage to function as long as everything is good.
However, they may collapse and kill many people when an earthquake
happens (as has happened in many places over the past few years, including
China and Haiti).

Structural integrity, then, is the ability of a structure to maintain its shape
and ability to function in the face of challenge. Buildings and machines with
structural integrity hold together under stress, withstand attack, maintain
their shape under pressure, and continue to fulfill their function even under
severe and difficult conditions.

These qualities and abilities are also desirable, and necessary, for humans.
This is especially true as we move deeper into our awakening and become
more aware of the changing nature of our energy-based selves. In order to
continue to flex and flow even with the stresses that shake and bend us,
we need a source of inner flexibility, calmness, and strength that can carry

us through the storm. Integrity is what provides this support, strength, and suppleness.

Developing integrity is a life-long practice that involves continually honing our ability to discern which kinds of choices increase our strength and which kinds of choices decrease our strength. Fortunately, discernment is not difficult, and the basic choice is very simple.

Every choice that can be made, however complex it may seem to be, can be simplified into one of two basic possibilities. One possibility involves practicing contraction, is based on fear, and results in strengthening mental pathways for weakness, stress, fear, self-delusion, and ultimately self-disgust. The other possibility involves practicing expansion, is based on love, and results in strengthening mental pathways for resilience, strength, calm, security, self-knowledge, and ultimately self-awareness and self-love. All this happens minute by minute as we practice either expansion or contraction in every choice we make, every moment of every day.

Here is an example of how this works. John (a hypothetical person) is out too late one night, sleeps in, and arrives at work late for a morning meeting. As he enters the room he apologizes saying that he was held up in traffic. Later that day, he has another meeting with a small work group. Each person in the group had a task to complete, and today was the day to put them together for the final draft. John hasn't finished his part of the work because he put it off for too long and then went to a concert last night when a friend invited him on the spur of the moment (This is also why he slept in). He blames the boss and the project, complains that he had the most difficult part, and drums up support in the group for the fact that the boss is a slave driver with expectations that are far too high. How can he expect people to keep up with these kinds of demands?

After work, John stops off at the bar for a drink with some co-workers and ends up staying for several more drinks. When he finally gets home, he remembers that he promised to help a friend after work. He knows she really needs his help and will be angry that he didn't even call. Rather than telling her the truth—that he forgot and went drinking with some friends, he apologizes saying he was tied up at work and just couldn't get away.

John's pattern for decision making in this example is shaped around expediency. He will take the easy route wherever possible, will make up excuses to cover up for lack of responsibility, and will blame others or use complaints and negativity to cover up when he hasn't done his job well. Moreover, John is willing to break a promise to a friend and then lie to make it seem like he had no choice. Each of these decisions involves a small contraction—in each case, John is making himself, and his world, just a little bit smaller, a little bit tighter, a little bit more unsafe. He isn't brave enough to tell his boss the truth. He isn't secure enough to take responsibility for letting his work group down. He readily forgets commitments and therefore is practicing the inability to trust or be trusted. He is too insecure to tell his friend the truth when he stands her up and breaks a promise.

Each of these decisions is relatively small. However, the cumulative effect is very large. As was discussed in the section about "The World as Our Mirror", there is a direct relationship, or internal reflection, for everything that we do and see outside of us. Our sense of self is a fluid creation, interacting with and being shaped by each of our choices and actions. By taking the expedient route, procrastinating, and not taking responsibility for his own actions, John is building a sense of self that will apply these same principles inside as well as outside. He is building a sense of self that lacks integrity and the strength and sense of inner well-being that goes with it. He is also building an environment in which people will learn to not trust him. In a negative spiral, his actions will create an expectation in others that he will let them down. They will reflect this expectation back to him, which will cause him to complain, blame, and avoid even more, and the spiral will continue to turn.

If we press the rewind button on John's day and go back to the start, here is what it could look like with some integrity inserted:

John sleeps in one morning and is late for work and a meeting. He enters quietly and later talks to his boss to explain that he had a chance to go to a concert last night and that he probably shouldn't have gone. He takes responsibility for having made a bad choice and apologizes for being badly prepared for the meeting.

Later that day he has a meeting with his work group. Again he is unprepared and not ready. Again, he takes responsibility for some recent poor choices and insists on doing the extra work needed to complete the project on his own. He makes a commitment to get it done within two days.

After work, a friend asks John to come to the bar for a drink. John feels tired, and it's been a difficult day. He'd really like to go, but he remembers that he promised to help a friend who is moving. She needs help with some heavy lifting and can't do it on her own. He says "no thank you" to the bar and goes to help his friend. When he gets home, John is tired, but he goes to work right away in order to meet his commitment to his work group. Finally, before he goes to bed he double checks his alarm for the next day.

This example involves integrity that is tied to a certain set of values and a certain work ethic. It is one way that integrity can be applied but not the only way.

A second way of applying integrity in this example is for John to realize as he rushes late into work that he doesn't value what he is doing very much. Looking very honestly at what is important to him, he realizes that he doesn't want to do the work he is doing. He decides to look honestly at his life and what he really wants and needs and begins to take steps to change his way of making a living. Perhaps this also involves letting go of many things and living more simply. Perhaps it simply means changing jobs. However, it means being honest and looking courageously at difficult inner truths.

It also still means being honest and keeping commitments with friends— or deciding not to make commitments in the first place.

In either of these cases, John has shown himself that he is capable of taking responsibility for his own actions, that he will tell the truth and acknowledge truth, and that he is trustworthy inwardly and outwardly.

In the first example, John shows himself that he is unable to be true to anyone, including himself. In the second example, he is secure enough to talk frankly to his boss and tell the truth. In talking to his boss this way, he also shows his boss that he's human, he makes mistakes, and he can be trusted. He does this again with his work group, proving to himself that he is strong enough inside to admit when he has let someone down and to make amends. When he turns down the invitation to the bar and keeps his promise to his friend, he shows himself that he can be trusted and that he can do what he thinks is right, even when it is difficult.

In the third example, John began to trust himself to be true to his inner sense of direction and intuition. Ideally, he would still do everything that he did in the second example, but he would also look deeply into who he is and take steps to change his situation if it is not supporting his values.

In both of the last two examples, his choice of action expanded his sense of confidence in himself, ability to trust himself and others, and belief in his own integrity and strength. These actions also affected the people and environment around him, creating a positive spiral of support as other people recognized John's strength of character and reflected it back to him.

Though this example may seem to be a bit obvious and simplistic, it is not always easy to see how we chip away at our own sense of self, and the idea of practicing integrity is not as common as one might think. Over the last few years I have asked hundreds of kids, mostly aged six to thirteen, what they think integrity means. I was surprised to discover that almost none of them had ever heard of the word, or of the concept. As I talked to more kids about it, I found that not only do kids not know about the concept of integrity, but many parents also do not practice or teach it.

This is really too bad because integrity is essential to a child's sense of self-esteem as well as a child's ability to withstand peer pressure, say "no" to drugs and dangerous situations, be trustworthy and honest, and a host of other important developmental tasks. Growing up without integrity is like building a bridge without the structural steel that reinforces the cement. It might still look like a bridge, but it could fall apart at any moment. The same is true for a sense of self that is not strengthened with integrity. It can look like a sense of self, but it can also fall apart at any minute.

The first Noble Truth of Buddhism essentially says that life is difficult, and that this fact is unavoidable because it is a result of change—which is also unavoidable. It goes on to say that we suffer because we struggle with this difficulty. The more we struggle, avoid, deny, and run from the difficulties we face, the more we run from the truth of who we are and the truth of our own reality. Learning to face the difficulties takes practice, and this is why we need to practice facing each small difficulty as it arises, moment by moment, each and every day. As we build our strength and ability to stay balanced under the pressures of the small difficulties, it is like reinforcing our basic structure. Like a building that has been reinforced to withstand an earthquake, practicing integrity reinforces our inner foundations so that they can withstand the bigger shocks and trials of life when they come. As a by-product, it also builds a stronger sense of peace, well-being, comfort, and joy. When we come from a place of inner strength, there is much less to worry about.

Integrity is a practice. All of us have some integrity, and all of us have room for further improvements. The best explanation of how to practice integrity that I have found is in the book *The Four Agreements* by Don Miguel Ruiz.[24]In this book the author suggests that we should make four agreements with ourselves that will help us to become stronger in who we are and to develop a greater sense of personal freedom. These agreements are as follows:

- Be Impeccable with your word
- Don't take anything personally
- Don't make assumptions
- Always do your best

I would add: *Do what you think is right, even (and especially) when it is difficult.*

I would highly recommend this book, as the explanation given for how to use these agreements is very helpful. However, you do not have to read the book in order to get started. Any time you keep one of these agreements, you build yourself up just a little bit more, and you take a step toward a greater sense of well-being and freedom in your ability to be who you are.

Integrity is something that can be practiced anytime and anywhere. It is never too late to start, and every time you keep an agreement, you add to your ability to be true to yourself and others. Give yourself this gift. Practice

24 (Ruiz, 2001)

challenging yourself and meeting the challenges, and practice keeping the agreements.

As you practice, you will also be giving the gift of integrity to others. This is even more important if you have children. Children do what they see far more readily than what they are told. If parents keep these agreements with their children and model how to use these agreements in daily life, they will be giving an invaluable gift to their children. Self-esteem can be taught, and it can be learned. Both learning and teaching happen when you make yourself a living example of integrity in action.

Part 3: Gratitude is a gate

Gratitude is a state of mind that works like a switch in an electric circuit—it opens or closes our ability to receive.

Todd Blattner

Gratitude, like many of the so-called "virtues," is generally misunderstood. Often, gratitude is associated with guilt and is surrounded by lots of *shoulds* as in "I should feel grateful for the gift I was given" or "you should be grateful that you have enough to eat—think of all of the children in the world who don't have any food at all."

Gratitude is something that often feels like something we are supposed to do, but it does not seem to have a great deal of personal benefit. It can feel somewhat grudging and forced and like something that requires extra work and effort. However, there are also times when most people experience spontaneous and real gratitude, and at these times gratitude can feel surprisingly good.

When I was staying with my teacher in Thailand, I was sitting and eating during the morning lecture, as was the custom at that place. The teacher often also accepted gifts at this time, which were given to him by visitors and people from surrounding communities. These gifts were generally food or donations of money or supplies, which he then used to support all the monks and laypeople that lived with him. We were given a meal once a day, and it was generally a fairly unexciting meal—enough to sustain but not a banquet to savour by any means. In this context, food, and especially tasty food, had a different level of preciousness attached to it than it does when there is always plenty of any kind of food that one wants.

As I was finishing my meal, the teacher singled me out and gave me several very plump, juicy, ripe bananas that had been given to him for his breakfast. At that time and place, in that context, the gift and the way that it was given hit me directly in the heart and I started to cry. It felt like a weight being lifted from me, and a flood of relief washed over me. The feelings were not due to hunger—I wasn't hungry—and they weren't due to lack in any way. The gift was a sharing of abundance in a very generous and loving way. Gratitude was natural and spontaneous, and it felt like releasing a dam or opening a gate. A part of me that had been hardened and guarded was opened, and energy was flowing again.

Giving and receiving are really two parts of the same action working together in a way similar to the flow of electricity. Electricity needs a positive and a negative pole in order to flow. Flick a switch, and electricity moves from one pole to the other because there is a circuit. Without the circuit, there is no flow.

In the case of giving and receiving, love is the energy—the electricity in this analogy. It needs to flow, and it requires the two poles of giving and of receiving. Without both poles, there is no circuit and love does not flow as easily (unlike electricity, love can be given even if it is not well received. It is initially more difficult to do this however). Both giving and receiving are therefore necessary; they are equal, and they are fundamentally the same action. By receiving I give and by giving I receive. By giving the bananas to me, the teacher opened the circuit of his own heart and received the benefit of the love that flowed through his system. I received the physical food of the bananas and the energy food of the love. My openness to receiving allowed a strong flow so that both of us were able to experience more and to become opened further. Because of this strong flow, I was able to experience a feeling of gratitude that went beyond my habitual guilt-based feelings and simply opened to spontaneous emotion.

Gratitude is like the switch that opens the circuit and turns on the light. As gratitude grows, it increases the circuit's ability to carry the current of love—the current of giving and receiving—and therefore allows an opening to greater flow. Far from being a guilt-based reaction to being given something, gratitude is the switch that opens the circuit of giving and receiving and is therefore an energetic key to abundance.

Contrary to the apparent truth of the physical world around us, we are swimming in, and part of, a field of universal potential in which our own attitudes and beliefs affect what is made manifest in our lives. Abundance, therefore, begins with the intention of gratitude for whatever exists in this present moment. However small or large this present abundance is perceived to be, cultivating gratitude is like learning to open a valve. It may be rusted nearly closed and difficult to turn, but eventually it will open wider and as it does, more energy begins to flow. Abundance is the result of being open, and gratitude is the gate or valve that allows this openness to happen. Feeling gratitude for what exists in this moment allows abundance to grow and build so that future moments will be able to contain even more.

A caveat to all this is that giving and receiving don't work if there are expectations attached to them. It is very common, perhaps normal, for a gift to come with an obligation attached. In the "I'll scratch your back, you scratch my back" kind of exchange, a gift or a service is given with the expectation that it will be paid back at a later date. This is totally against the principle of giving and receiving since it implies obligation and indebtedness. Gratitude, in this situation, becomes an acknowledgment of debt, and giving becomes a way to manipulate people or to store up favours for a future time when they will be called in.

On the energetic level, giving with expectation of return creates, and is created by, a belief system in which there is scarcity and we must compete and win. Giving is therefore a calculated strategy where I will give something of my own, or in the case of energy, I will give a part of the limited energy resources that I possess in order to bind you to me and obligate you to return what I have given with interest at a future time.

The apparent reality that surrounds us fits with this belief system. Darwin's observations of survival of the fittest and most of the immediate physical evidence that can be seen, felt, or experienced backs up the old-world paradigm that giving must be used as a survival strategy because there is not enough to go around.

On the physical level, it is undeniably true that there is scarcity, lack, and competition and that survival is often very difficult. On the deeper level of energy, however, there are different principles at work, and these principles do affect how we experience our world and what we create in each moment as our future arises around us.

While I may be poor, for instance, and have barely enough to eat, my experience of this situation will be very different if I suffer through it with anger, fear, and bitterness or if I cultivate a deep sense of gratitude for what I have. The way that I experience the present will then affect each of the moments that follow, each tiny choice directing me one way or another. Within the universal field, my choices, actions, thoughts, feelings, and intentions will all be working together to guide me toward the focus of my deep beliefs. If I deeply believe that anger is justified, I will focus on the reality of anger and more situations that confirm the need for anger will come into my awareness. If I deeply believe in lack, I will create more opportunity to live in the experience of lack, and if I cultivate a deep sense of gratitude, I will invite greater peace and abundance into my life.

When I was conducting anger management groups, there was an occasion where a man who didn't think he should have to be in the group verbally attacked me. I was able to listen to his concerns and to help him direct his anger in a more useful direction so that he could calm down. By the end of the course, this man had learned enough about his own belief systems to understand how he had been hurting himself and others with his anger and how he could start to make some changes. His external reality had not changed, but his perception of this reality had changed. He was not as angry, and he did not allow his perceptions to justify his anger as often. With his change in belief and perception, his reality began to change. He began coming to the course willingly, and at the end he even strongly suggested that anger management should be a mandatory course for all high school students.

Although he did not change his entire life or completely change his habit of anger, this man was able to go below the surface of his experience just far enough to see that he was hurting himself, and this allowed him to make some changes in his life. He was still affected by the same stresses and the same apparently out-of-control situations, but he had learned to see them (and himself) a little bit differently, and this allowed him to choose different ways of acting in some situations. As he changed his responses, the people around him also began to see him differently and to react to him differently. From the perspective of the universal field, his learning on the psychological level began to change how he interacted with all that was around him and to attract more positive experiences into his life. He began to interact and co-create his personal world in a less violent way.

Generally, beliefs about abundance and prosperity, giving, receiving, and worthiness, are farther below the surface than anger. Anger is not really even an emotion on its own but simply a reaction to deeper movements of energy—but the principle is the same. If you can go deeply enough to find the root belief and allow this belief to change, it will also begin to make changes in the reality that you perceive and in the future that you co-create within the universal field.

In the objective/material worldview, Darwin's survival of the fittest concept is a deeply held belief and a widely-noted observation that confirms the necessity for struggle in a world where resources are limited and living things must compete with each other in order to obtain the necessities of living. In this worldview, giving is a calculated act used to bind and manipulate in hopes of building a bank account for future use, and gratitude is an admission of indebtedness. There is a great deal of truth and usefulness in this way of seeing the world—observation of apparent physical reality confirms it and practice of this sort of giving seems to work well for many people.

It takes an act of will, and of trust perhaps, to take a step out of this way of seeing the world and into the deeper perspective of energy and the Field. Once this step has been made, very little initially appears to be different on the physical level, but one's internal experience begins to change:

- The action of giving becomes more joyful and more free.

- Receiving becomes an opportunity to open to abundance and worthiness

- Both giving and receiving result in greater abundance.

- A greater sense of peace, wellness, and wholeness develops, and daily struggles become less stressful.

From the awakened perspective, it is understood that energy and intention come before physical reality. In other words, *abundance is caused by gratitude*—rather than gratitude being a result of abundance. When this is understood, it becomes natural to place more attention on cultivating gratitude for the abundance that is already present in one's life. It becomes obvious that this attitude is what allows abundance to grow.

Of course, results of this practice will vary. Some people are naturally able to access deeper levels of the mind/body/energy system or have fewer inhibiting belief systems. There is also a connection with the inertia or *karma* of past actions. Sometimes it can take a while to climb out of a hole that has been a long time in the digging.

However, change will happen, and many levels will begin to work together. Gratitude is the gate to abundance and the opening through which love and peace flow. Cultivating it in your life will bear fruit—sometimes sooner and sometimes later—but the fruit will always be there.

Exercises for cultivating gratitude

1. Count your blessings

When I was a child my grandmother would often tell me to "Count your blessings Todd". I didn't pay a lot of attention at the time, but as I've grown older, I have begun to understand what she was trying to tell me. There is never a situation in which there is nothing to be thankful for, and there is never a situation in which being thankful will not be helpful in some way.

2. Paying attention

Practice being thankful by remembering to notice. Thank the sun for shining, the grass for being green, the flower that poked out of the cement and brightened your day, people who made it possible for food to be on your table, or for you to have clothes to wear. You name it, you can be thankful for it.

3. Gratitude in unexpected places

When I traveled in India, I found that beggars had a much different status from street people here. They were considered by many to provide an essential service—the opportunity to reduce one's sense of pride and ego by practicing generosity. So... consider being thankful to the next street person you see for providing you with this same opportunity—and consider other situations or people which you would normally find to be annoying. Can you say "thank you" to them as well?

BLATTNER UNWORLDLY

4. Gratitude to your higher self

This exercise is based on practices developed by Tom Kenyon[25]:

Hold your hands as high above your head as you can, turn your fingers inward and touch them together. The place where they touch is an energetic chakra point and a connection point with the part of you that is more directly connected with the Field. It is kind of a dimensional portal point. Get an idea in your mind's eye of where this point is.

Focus on your heart for a few moments or on the area in your chest where your heart is located. While you are doing this, think of one or more things that you are grateful for. If you can't think of anything, start with something really basic—like "I'm grateful that I woke up this morning", or "I'm grateful that I have air to breathe and I'm able to breathe it". There is always something worth being thankful for, even in very difficult times.

If you can feel the sensations of this gratitude, great. If not, just imagine it.

Now send this gratitude to your higher self—the part of you that is more connected and in tune with the Field—by sending this feeling and/or intention of gratitude to the place above your head that you marked earlier with your fingers.

---

25 Www.tomkenyon.com Tom Kenyon also offers a wealth of information about energy and living with the changes that are happening in our world. Much of his information is channeled from a group of beings that he calls The Hathors. Tom's website is a good mind expanding experience for skeptics because he writes from a slightly skeptical perspective himself.

Try not to have any expectations. Just focus on this point and send gratitude. Doing this opens a channel. Sooner or later, you will begin to experience the energy flowing back to you. You will also notice that painful, difficult, or intense emotions will change more quickly, and you will not need to stay miserable as long.

5. Gratitude meditation

Meditation has many forms and many purposes. One form of meditation, called *mantra* meditation, uses repetition of a word or phrase as a way to focus the mind. Words have their own vibrational power—some words more than others. Repeating a word builds the vibration of that word or phrase in your energy system, so if you are using a word that has a high or useful vibration, it can help to calm, heal, and strengthen your energy field.

Mantra meditation has limitations in that repetition of a single word can be something like creating a shield or force field. Since you are actively creating a particular vibration with the mantra, this vibration tends to drown out awareness of everything else that is happening, and it can become a hard shell if practiced too often and too much. The shell can stay with you, even when you are not meditating, and act as a protection on one hand, but as a filter and resistance to the flow of what IS on the other. Like any form of belief, if it becomes too rigid and too solid, it loses its helpfulness and becomes a blockage in the energy system instead.

However, if practiced with awareness of its limitations, mantra meditation can provide a relatively fast way to focus the mind and to increase awareness of particular concepts and their related vibration. Meditation on gratitude is one example of using mantra meditation in this way.

Meditation on gratitude can eventually be something that is practiced any time and any place. However, initially it is helpful to set aside some time where you can be alone, undisturbed, and quiet.

It may be helpful to read this meditation out loud (slowly and calmly) to a recording device and then play it back to yourself.

Sit in a comfortable position but not so comfortable that you are likely to fall asleep. Cross legged on a cushion, kneeling with a meditation stool, or sitting in a straight backed chair are all possibilities. Close your eyes and begin to repeat "Thank you" over and over again. You can say the words silently in your mind or out loud, whichever feels better to you.

Notice what happens in your mind and body—you may feel resistance, feel silly, angry, sad, happy, irritated, or restless—whatever you feel, just notice it without judgment and keep repeating "Thank you" to whatever comes up.

Say "Thank you" to whatever you feel or think no matter if it seems good or bad or pleasant or unpleasant. You are saying "Thank you" to being alive in this moment, being able to experience whatever you are experiencing. You are saying "Thank you" to yourself for the magical beautiful being of energy that you are, and through your connection to the field, you are saying "Thank you" to all that lives and all that exists and all that is beyond living and existing.

Continue to say "Thank you" and allow your mind to be open, free, and unrestricted. Allow the gate of gratitude to open within you, simply by saying "Thank you" to everything that you feel, knowing that no matter if it is good or bad, pleasant or unpleasant, painful or enjoyable, it will change. Say "Thank you", let go, and say "Thank you" again...

Once you become comfortable with this meditation, it can become a very helpful part of each day. Remembering to say "Thank you" a few times when you wake up, when you eat, when you are feeling upset, when you are standing in a line or stuck in traffic—any occasion at all—will begin to create positive change in your life.

Gratitude for couples

Gratitude is an excellent way for couples to increase their level of intimacy with each other, appreciation for each other, and quality of life together. It is also a very helpful way of increasing sexual enjoyment and sensuality in a relationship.

There are many ways of practicing gratitude as a couple. The two exercises below are based on saying thank you through touch:

1. Massage

If you and/or your partner enjoy physical touch, massage is an excellent way to practice and communicate gratitude. There are many books available about massage and if you are interested in this form of communication and heightened experience with your partner I would recommend making use of more resources than I can provide here. However, here are a few principles to get you started:

Remember that intention and energy precede action. When you are giving or receiving massage, try to keep your mind from wandering too much. Use it as an opportunity for meditation—you can use the *Thank you* mantra to help you focus, or you can try to simply focus on the changing physical sensations of the touch.

Try to feel your fingers touching your partner. Feel your partner's skin and the muscles beneath it so that you become aware of where the muscles are loose and pliable and where they are tight or hard. When you find hard, tight places, try squeezing or gently pinching between your thumb and fingers. Hold and gently increase the pressure until you feel a slight movement or relaxation of the muscle. Release the tension, move a little bit, and repeat the action.

Practice with using different ways of rubbing, always remembering to keep your awareness on what you are feeling. Try squeezing with your thumb and fingers, rubbing with the heal of your hand, gently scratching with your fingernails, rubbing very lightly and gently, and then pressing harder and digging in a bit. Talk to your partner to see what he or she likes, and use your own feelings. Remember what feels good for you and then try it on your partner.

Learning new techniques can be helpful, but the most important thing to remember is to use the massage as a meditation of gratitude. As you are massaging, or being massaged, keep returning your mind to gratitude and to the physical sensation. Try not to analyze or think too much. Follow your feelings and allow your hands to guide you.

2. Energy massage

Between the pelvis and the upper chest there are four major chakras or energy centers. The first, or root chakra is located at the base of the spine and is associated with survival, grounding, deep connection with the physical earth and physical self and the elemental quality of earth. Connection with this chakra enhances security, foundation, and physical well-being.

The second chakra is located in the abdomen, near the belly button, and is associated with relationship, connection to self and others, sexuality and sexual connection, feeling, sensation, movement, and the physical qualities of water. Connection with this chakra reduces insecurity and anxiety, increases body awareness, and enhances ability to relate through feelings with one's self and others. It also enhances ability to experience sexual fulfillment.

The third chakra, located at the solar plexus, is associated with ego-identity, power, metabolism, will, and autonomy. Connection with this chakra's positive qualities enhances energy, digestion, effectiveness, assertiveness, self-efficacy, and non-dominating power.

The fourth chakra, located in the center of the chest at the level of the heart, is associated with love, social identity, and self-acceptance. It is the center of the seven chakra system and is the integrator of opposites: mind and body, male and female, persona and shadow, ego and unity. A healthy connection with the heart chakra allows deep integration of our psychological parts and pieces and centering our emotions and thoughts on our own authenticity. It also encourages feelings of compassion, peace, and love toward self and others.

With these chakras and their meanings in mind, massage of the trunk of the body can be a very healing and opening experience for both the person doing the massage and the person receiving it. These energy centers can be massaged from either the front or the back—the back is the best place to start as it is less sensitive and also tends to be more generally ignored. As you get more comfortable, move to the front.

Techniques for back massage include squeezing, gentle pinching between thumb and bent forefinger (this works well for the band of muscles on either side of the spine), rubbing with the heel of the hand in a clockwise circular motion, gentle tapping with fingers, etc. Again, try not to think too much and allow your own body sensations and hands to guide you. Also—talk to your partner. Find out what feels good.

Massage of the stomach and chest is more delicate and so be careful to start out gently. Stay in communication with your partner to find out what is comfortable for him or her. Some techniques include gently rubbing the palm of your hand in a clockwise circular motion around the abdomen; using a gentle side-to-side kneading motion, like kneading bread while working your way from the base of the abdomen to the solar plexus and back again, pushing in on one side and pulling back on the other; using the heal of the hand to rub in small circles over specific areas; gently pushing up under the ribs with your fingers (careful here—this can be quite sensitive for many people, so be very gentle), and rubbing in a circular motion over the solar plexus.

Again, remember to use this as an opportunity for meditation, constantly bringing your mind back to focus on the qualities of the chakra area you are massaging and on experiencing what your hands and body are feeling. The person giving the massage receives as much or more healing as the person who is receiving it, so remember to be open to both giving and receiving energy from your partner, no matter whether you are the person giving or receiving the massage. You don't have to feel the energy but be open to it. You may be surprised by feelings of heat, tingling, vibration or other sensations. Just remain open to the experience.

A good way to end this massage is to place your hands on your partner's abdomen and gently vibrate your hands so that your partner is gently shaken back and forth for a few minutes. Focus on feeling your hands and allowing healing and loving energy to move between you. After vibrating your hands in this way for a few minutes, stop and just hold your hands in place without moving for a minute or so, then gently and slowly lift them away. Focus on gratitude, being thankful for this opportunity to touch and be touched by another person.

Part 4: Joyfulness

We hold these truths to be self-evident, that all men are created equal, that they are endowed by their Creator with certain unalienable Rights, that among these are Life, Liberty and the pursuit of Happiness.

Declaration of Independence, United States of America

Joyfulness is a state of being to be chosen, not an object to be chased. Joyfulness is an internal choice; it has no relationship to what we own, where we are, or who we are with.

Todd Blattner

When the founding fathers of the United States wrote the Declaration of Independence, they made an unfortunate mistake when they decided to use the wording "*pursuit* of Happiness". This mistake was due to a misunderstanding of the meaning and source of happiness.

Happiness is actually just a lesser state of joy, and it is not something that can be obtained or pursued. The wording of this statement has helped to create a culture and a dream that has spread throughout the world. This dream, unfortunately, involves the misunderstanding that if one only looks hard enough, fights hard enough, or pursues ardently enough, happiness will come. Happiness is a commodity of sorts, chased with the intent of capture. What one does with happiness once it has been captured is unclear, but one assumes that it will be treated in the same way as other commodities—locked up somewhere so it isn't stolen or perhaps traded for something else.

All this makes quite good sense from the objective/material point of view. After all, from this perspective, everything that we need comes from *out there*—somewhere outside of ourselves. Happiness is therefore something that must be obtained, and as it seems to be in short supply, it makes sense that we must have to look for it rather ardently. Those who pursue with enough vigour will win happiness for themselves.

This is a good dream, and one that has fired the imagination of many people who have come from places where one is not allowed to even aspire to happiness or to freedom. However, from the point of view of energy, it is a dream that is a bit sad and very wasteful. From this perspective, the pursuit of happiness is a dream that is based on a serious misunderstanding and one that brings a great deal of misfortune into the world.

To understand why this is so, it is important to remember that from the point of view of the Field, our fundamental level of existence is based on the flow of energy through an informational matrix. This flow is the basis for the life force and, indeed, the basis of everything that exists in this universe.

The universe has a very simple way of communicating to us about its nature. We experience joy and love when we experience flow, and we experience suffering when we block the flow. It is therefore very easy to become aware of what we are doing. If we're suffering, we are working against the universe and trying to block the flow of energy that we are receiving. To the extent that we are experiencing joy, we are open to the flow.

The state of being open to flow or blocking flow has absolutely nothing to do with anything that we have, anything that we do, or anything that we search or strive for. The only thing that affects openness to flow is what we do with our choices and intention, regardless of what we have or don't have.

Unfortunately, this simple and handy system is only simple and handy when understood from the viewpoint of the Field and of the energy perspective. When seen from the point of view of the objective/material worldview, this same principle can get quite twisted and confusing—but we'll come to that in a bit.

When we experience an emotion, the physical reality of this emotion is a set of biochemical reactions in our body that produce sensations that are recognized by our brain. The brain recognizes a familiar combination of sensations and associates this combined feeling with other similar feelings from the past in order to determine if it is a *good* or *bad* thing. For instance, some people feel a set of sensations that involves heightened energy, tension in the stomach, heart beating faster, etc. and experience it as anxiety. Others experience this same set of sensations but interpret it as excitement. Others interpret it as fear. Our bodies do not actually have a very wide range of physical responses to choose from. It is the associations and judgments that we make in our minds that make the biggest difference in how we experience what we feel.

Emotions can be compared to the strings on a guitar. There are not very many strings, but depending on the skill of the musician, there can be quite a lot of variation in the sounds that are made. In the same way, there are not very many basic emotions, but there can be a huge variation in experience of these emotions, depending on the skill and awareness level of the person experiencing them.

Staying with the music analogy, musical notes can be grouped into octaves, and the same note can be played in different octaves. The note "C" for instance, can be played as a low "C" on the left-hand side of a piano keyboard, a middle "C" in the middle, and a high "C" on the right-hand side (with a couple of other "C's" in between as well). Each of these notes is still a "C", but it is played at a different pitch and has a different sound and feel.

Emotions also work this way. Sadness, for instance, can be played as abject misery sadness, grief sadness, melancholy or nostalgic sadness, fond sadness, joyful sadness, or transcendent sadness. Each of these emotional experiences is based on the same set of basic physical conditions, but each one is experienced through a different level of perception, and each carries a different tone or vibration. Transcendent sadness is a state of inviting a huge amount of flow and feeling the sadness moving inside as a nearly euphoric sensation of gratitude and love. Although the external appearance may still look like sadness with tears and sobs, the internal experience can be pleasurable or even ecstatic. This experience transcends ego and opens the doorway of the spirit. If one is able to resist attempting to cling to anything and to maintain one's openness, this kind of sadness quickly transitions to a state of joy that is not tinged by sadness at all. When there is flow, things happen much more quickly.

Abject misery sadness, on the other hand, is a state of clinging desperately to something and refusing to let go. It invites pain; it revels in the ego's ability to reject, rebel, and withstand the pain. This kind of sadness justifies grudges and anger, supports divisive belief systems, and in the paradoxical way of the ego, strengthens the ego's position. Abject misery sadness says: "Look at me in my misery. I am so strong to withstand it. I am so right in my beliefs

Helen

about the evil that I see. I am justified in violence or in lack of integrity. It is the way of the world, and it has made me this way."

When we see the world from the viewpoint of a separate, lonely, and disconnected individual, struggling to survive in an uncaring world, the clear and simple signals of pleasure when energy flows and suffering when it is blocked become twisted and misinterpreted. From this separated and lonely viewpoint, flow is an enemy because it entails change, uncertainty, and expansion. If we have invested a lot of energy into building strong walls of belief around ourselves, change and expansion are not wanted. The power of flow, which in truth will heal us, is seen as the enemy, and when change begins to happen, it feels uncomfortable or painful because it must break through all the rigid resistance we have built. Flow is an enemy to security when security is based on the resistance to change we have built.

Back to the music analogy: misery can be thought of as a particular emotional key. Misery has a low rate of vibration and of awareness. Misery also contains a large degree of resistance. It is thick, heavy, resistant to change, and stubborn when clinging to what it knows. Misery creates blockages and does whatever it can to resist clear flow. Anger, fear, love, sadness, hate, happiness—all can be played at this vibrational level, and all will have the basic qualities of misery. Even happiness and love will come out with qualities of misery vibrating through them. From this place of understanding, happiness, expansiveness, freedom of expression, and belief—all can be interpreted as threatening or dangerous and experienced with discomfort and pain.

Joy is another emotional key, located several vibrational octaves above misery. It isn't the highest octave, but it is much more fun and much more energetic than misery. Joy involves a higher and finer vibration that feels more pleasurable. It is open to change, does not cling to things, and promotes release and energetic flow. When in the joy octave, any emotion, even sadness or anger, has properties of joy vibrating within it. Sadness can be quite pleasurable, and the positive changes that can come about from the cleansing power of sadness happen much more quickly and readily. A person who can experience most of her emotions from within the joy octave will tend to learn more quickly, move through difficulties with more ease, feel less stress, get sick less often, and generally enjoy life a lot more. The joy octave is much more fun to live in than the misery octave.

We all have a choice, however, and for their own reasons, many people choose misery or anger or other related octaves as the tone through which most of their emotions are played. As they focus on the octave of their choice, they train their body/mind system to produce more of this tone, they align themselves with people who create or induce the same tone, and they create situations that appear to make the tone necessary.

It is very important to understand that joy, or happiness for that matter, are not *things* that can be pursued, chased, captured, or otherwise held on to. They are vibrational states, or tones, and conditions of flow. Joy is natural to our existence, as is love. As Rumi says, "Your task is not to seek for love, but merely to seek and find all the barriers that you have built against it." The good news is that everything we need to be joyful is already inside us.

Unfortunately, there is also some bad news. Misery is a lot easier, and misery tends to be the default—the place we go when we are too tired, run down, or angry to do something else. Misery is much easier to deal with because it is a lower energy state. It is easier to balance, slower and heavier. Also, misery is something that one does not worry about losing. Joy, on the other hand, is quite a high energy state. It is more difficult to contain—it wants to explode out in exuberance, and this is not always appreciated by others around us. Joy tends to be giddy and lack a sense of the serious nature of things, which can upset those who are trying to stay miserable, as well as sometimes seem a bit irresponsible or impractical. Joy does need grounding—too much of it and one feels a bit like floating away. It takes some practice to be joyful and remain balanced and focused.

Although almost all people say that they want to be happy, many are quite terrified when they actually experience joy, unless it is only for a short time. This is because of the nature of joy to promote flow of energy and letting go. The ego part of our identity is constructed mainly from the blocks and restrictions to the more freely flowing energy that we had when we came to the world as babies. This ego part wants things to remain the way it is, and wants the blockages to remain solid. Its existence depends on them. However, joyfulness opens up the flood gates, releases blockages, and lets energy flow again. This is very threatening to the ego, and many people can't tolerate it at all; joy can actually be painful to many people. Some people have cut themselves off so thoroughly from their ability to feel the flowing release of joy that they will go to great lengths to kill it in other people as well. In these cases, joy has become something evil that must be stomped out. It carries with it much too much freedom, too little respect for tradition, and too much threat to the well-being of the ego.

It is important to assess honestly where you stand in your ability to accept and contain joy. If you are like most people, at least in North America, you will probably find that your capacity for joy is quite low. Don't despair! It's never too late to start accepting more joy into your life. I've listed a few suggestions for starters below—but don't stop here. Be creative, clever, and expansive; invent, research and practice your own joy-building adventures!

Suggestions for adventures in joy-building

1. Are you enjoying this?

There is a story about a monk who was always very happy. Many people would come to him with questions and this was a bit curious as he always gave the same answer. Perhaps it was the way that he gave the answer that was important. At any rate, people would come to him to tell him of their misery, their sickness, their misfortune, their loss or injustice that had happened, and he would listen carefully. When they had finished speaking he would look at them with deep compassion and ask them sincerely "And are you enjoying this, dear?"

This monk had come to a point of acceptance in life where he experienced all of life as a great adventure and place of play. All the drama, misery, and misfortune that we put into our lives is, from a larger perspective, just a great and magnificent game. "Are you enjoying the game dear" is a great question to ask yourself next time you are embroiled in a deep and troubling life drama. It helps to remove some of the seriousness and self-importance of it all and remind us that there is a bigger picture to all of what we do.

2. Stop!

Another short story about monks comes from my stay in Thailand. One old monk would come up to me repeatedly through the day, stop in front of me, point at my face and yell: "STAAAAAAAAWWWWWPPPPP". Then he'd go away laughing. I was a bit offended at first. Later I realized he was telling me to remember to get out of my self-centered musings, dramas, perceptions—everything. Just stop. What's left over in the silence when you do?

4. St. Germain's Violet Flame

St. Germain is said to have helped to make the violet flame of transmutation available to anyone who would like to use it. This flame transmutes lower vibrations and difficult karma and helps to transform the reality of your entire multidimensional lifeline. In the here and now, it helps to dissolve heavy issues like anger, grief, or emotional dramas—like which dress to wear for that big date.

This is one of those things that you'll just have to decide to believe in or not as you see fit. It is not just for people who believe in Christian saints, and it has really nothing at all to do with religion in any way. It works just as well if you think of it as a visualization that works on the psychological level or if you think of it as an actual fire that works on an energetic level. Either way, it's pretty simple to use.

Ask St. Germain for help and call in the violet flame. Visualize the flame burning all around, in and through you with a purifying light. Let it transfrom whatever is holding you back, holding you down, or blocking you from experiencing joy. Don't get too serious about it. Just call it in, give it permission to work with you, and let it go. Notice what you feel.

Note: It can be helpful to call in protection when you do this. (Remember, either believe or don't here.) We live in a universe where opposites attract. Bringing in greater light can also attract more darkness, especially if you believe strongly in the good/evil polarization. If you use the flame, also ask for protection from someone like Archangel Michael or a saint or god from your own religious background. Just say something like, "Archangel Michael please protect me and surround me with a dome of light"—or make it up for yourself. There are lots of internet sites that will help you with wording your request or explain this further. Some seem a bit far out there for us skeptics—so prepare to be open-minded.

The point here is to realize that you are always working within your own beliefs. If there is something in you that believes you are less than joyful, then this something is a mistaken belief. There are many ways to talk to this belief and help it to change. If the violet flame is helpful for you, then use it. If it isn't, then don't get too serious about it. Let it go, and try other things that are more acceptable to your current beliefs.

5. Say "*YES!*"

Think about all the things that you are likely to say "No" to. Consider the following categories: money, sex, helping others, accepting help from others, giving yourself a gift, giving a gift to someone else, etc.

Over a period of one week, carry a pen and a piece of paper in your pocket at all times. Each time you notice yourself saying "No" to something, make a note of it. Try to become aware of what your body does when you say "No". Where do you feel it? How would you describe the physical sensation of the "No" reaction in your body? Getting a strong conscious awareness of this reaction is important because you will be able to use it to recognize your limits, your automatic "No's", and also to recognize when saying "No" is necessary. The body awareness is the first step.

At the end of the week, look over the list of what you have said "No" to. Do you recognize any patterns? What kinds of things do you say "No" to most? How often do you think the "No" was a conscious decision made in your own best interest, and how often was it simply a habitual reaction limiting your experience?

Next week, try saying "Yes!" more often. Notice what you feel and what happens[26].

Here is a list of other possibilities:

- Join a laughing yoga class

- Practice laughing—by yourself or with a friend. Set a timer and laugh uproariously for no reason for 30 seconds. Work up to a minute or two. This has the side-benefit of burning more calories than jogging, being a very good abdominal exercise, and creating endorphins that improve your mood. It also decreases stress and strengthens your immune system.

- Give yourself permission to be happy for no reason at least once today.

- Have an adventure—talk to a stranger, sit down and chat with a street person, go to a new restaurant, quit your job and travel in Peru for six months—big or little, adventures are good for your brain and good at breaking us out of fixed ways of thinking and acting.

- Practice sneaking up on people. Sometimes they won't like it much, but find people who don't mind. It can be a great awareness practice as well as fun to arrange with someone to try to sneak up on each other often. Then you get the fun of sneaking and the awareness practice (and fun) of always being aware of where your sneak-partner might be jumping out at you. (Some people don't find

26 "Yes Man" is a 2008 movie starring Jim Carrey that takes a comedic and informative look at saying "Yes!" to life. It is a good movie to watch if you are thinking about trying this exercise.

this very amusing—if you're one of them then do something different)

- Smile a lot.

- Play music or sing. If you can't sing, try it in the shower for a while. Don't let lack of ability get you down.

- Climb a tree and sit in it.

- Lay in the grass in the sunshine.

- Play with a young child. (Be sure you don't have an agenda, don't have to accomplish anything, and don't have to worry about time, logic, or morality. Just crash toy cars, build block castles and knock 'em down again, and put the wrong kinds of clothes on dolls...)

- Next time you are taking yourself seriously, don't.

- Consider, from time to time, the possibility that you are a being of light and energy pretending for a time to be this body that you are wearing and that you are here in order to have fun and to learn a few things. What if this was true? Are you enjoying it, dear?

- Dance. It doesn't matter if you dance by yourself in your living room or in a ballroom or on a beach or in the forest or around a fire—just dance.

- Do something nice for someone for no reason and with no intention of it being returned.

- Wear really brightly coloured clothing from time to time—or all the time.

- Make up your own joyful activities...

* * *

Remember that:

- Joy is available at any moment, regardless of the circumstances in which we find ourselves.

- Joy is not something to chase but to attune to.

- Our capacity to experience joy is not governed by what we own, how much money we have, or any other physical or material criteria.

- Our capacity to experience joy depends completely on our inner strength, integrity, and capacity to accept the high energy feelings without losing ourselves in longing or in the fear of loss.

Truly, we do not fear misery and suffering nearly as much as we fear happiness or joy. But this is changing...

Chapter 12
Using negative emotions as allies

The world is a mirror, teaching me who I am. I grow and expand by accepting and loving every part of my being. Any event or emotion is therefore an opportunity to look closely in the mirror, see what I do not presently accept, and practice forgiveness.

Emotions, from the energetic perspective, represent vibrational frequencies. Of course, emotions happen on the mental and physical levels as well, with all of the many thoughts, feelings and chemical and electrical reactions and messages that are involved. However, the concept of emotion as a vibrational frequency can simplify understanding of all of the other manifestations of emotion, and so it is a useful concept to explore.

In the first place, in order to understand how to use emotions, we need to know what the goal is. Do we want to create drama and turmoil? This can be enjoyable at times, and many people are somewhat addicted to it. Look at the popularity of soap operas or violent movies or horror flicks—or love stories or comedies. Emotion is exciting and fun, and that's OK; there's nothing wrong with enjoying one's own feelings.

It is also important not simply to repress feelings. Many people have learned that the only alternative to excessive emotion is flat emotion. They simply stuff it down inside, stiffen the ol' upper lip and move through life as if they don't feel a thing—which sometimes becomes true if they practice hard enough. Experiencing emotions is part of being human, and repressing or burying them doesn't help.

However, there are times when emotions seem to become too much in charge of our lives or when we spend too much time in negative emotions that are uncomfortable and unpleasant—both for ourselves and for the people around us. In these situations, it is helpful to have some tools with which to take charge of the unruly emotional forces and channel them in directions that are in our better interests.

In other sections of this book I have discussed the difference between the objective/material way of seeing the world and what I have been calling the awakened way of seeing the world. In the former, the principle focus is on objects *outside* the mind/body system; in the latter, the focus is more balanced but directed to the *inside* of the mind/body system. We have a choice of which perspective to take, and our perspective then governs how we act. Looking outside, we believe that if we have a problem or unwanted emotion, we have to fix or change someone or something outside ourselves. Looking inside, we can understand the concept of the mirror and direct our energy to working with what is within us.

Helen

The trick is to come back, over and again, to the understanding that every choice with which we are faced ultimately can be seen as a choice between love (expansion) or fear (contraction). I can choose to perceive that I have been attacked and must defend myself from this outside attacking force. I can also choose to understand that I have looked into a mirror that has helped me to see more deeply into my own soul.

If I have been attacked, of course I must fight back and defend myself. In order to be externally strong, I must be able to overpower the outside forces that threaten me. This automatically involves fear, contraction, defense, and then often counter-attack.

If I perceive the world from the inside-out, however, then attack is a mistaken perception. If I perceive attack, it is a strong demand for me to look into the mirror and to accept that I am not seeing something that is *other* than myself. Everything I see is a part of myself and I cannot hate it without also hating myself. I can't cast it out without casting out part of myself. If I wish to be forgiven, I must forgive what I see and experience as well.

My choice of perception determines my subsequent action (to fight or to forgive)—and also defines what it means to be *strong*. From the objective/material perspective, I am tiny, vulnerable and threatened. Strength requires violence, attack, and force. From the energy perspective, I am a being of light and energy, experiencing a physical existence. Everything that exists is a part of me, as I am part of everything that exists. Strength is found in maintaining my connection with the source of my being at all times, despite the many temptations to become a part of the continuing drama of attack and counter attack.

If you remember that it is your choice how you perceive a given situation or emotion, you will be well on your way to using whatever situation (or emotion) you are in as grist for the mill in your own path to freedom and self-mastery. You also, of course, have the choice of using every situation (and emotion) as a way of inflaming the drama and angst in your life. Either choice is valid, but it is helpful to know that there is a choice.

There is also a further step in all of this, when the mind becomes willing to give up its ideas of supremacy and centrality. The mind wants to believe that it has choices, that it is in charge, and that there are things it can do. This is natural and OK. It is also useful to remember, however, the quote from Rumi with which this book started: "Out beyond ideas of wrongdoing and rightdoing, there is a field. I'll meet you there."

Out beyond the judgments and choices of the cognitive mind, there is the Field—the ground in which there is no need for choice or intended action in any direction. Here, in this place that is everywhere and also nowhere, that contains everything and also nothing, that is beyond mind and also the source of mind, in this place that is not a place, there is nothing else that needs doing. In all cases, in this field, out beyond wrongdoing and rightdoing, you are already home.

Part 1: Awakened anxiety

Worry is a thin stream of fear trickling through the mind. If encouraged, it cuts a channel into which all other thoughts are drained.

Arthur Somers Roche

Any emotion is, on a physical level, a set of sensations that is caused by the action of a variety of electrical signals and chemical messengers and processes throughout the body. These sensations inform our conscious mind that something is going on and the conscious mind decides what it is and how to react to it. When this system is mainly unconscious, it is a closed loop. In the case of anxiety, each time a trigger event happens, the limbic system reacts by sending out electrical and chemical anxiety signals. The anxiety signals activate a variety of processes in the body; these processes produce reactions which cause physical sensations; these physical sensations are transferred to the brain via nerve signals, and the signals are interpreted as a complex that is recognized consciously as anxiety.

To this point, everything has been unconscious. However, now the conscious mind is aware of what is going on and has an opportunity to get involved in the action. Generally, it gets caught up in the flood of sensations and gets involved by creating anxious thoughts. These anxious thoughts are a further triggering event so that the limbic system continues to send anxiety signals, and the whole process loops on itself, increasing in strength with each loop.

The more this loop is practiced, the stronger it gets. The neural pathways involved with the reaction become strong, well connected, and very sensitive. Moreover, since the mind works on associations, the number of triggers begins to grow. When other stressful events happen while the anxiety reaction is happening, they can be connected as new triggers. Events or situations that are vaguely similar to trigger events can also be added in, so that the number of possible anxiety triggers continues to grow. Not only do we get better at being anxious the more we practice it, but we also get better at being anxious about a wider variety of things.

On an energetic level, anxiety carries its own vibrational frequency which is very close to fear. This frequency is broadcast on the "fear station"—the collective experience of the fear vibration—and can be quite a powerful signal. It helps to increase the likelihood that people nearby will also feel anxious, and it adds to the general strength of the anxiety vibrational signal throughout the world.[27] It also attracts events, people, and situations that will create more anxiety.

I grew up on a ranch and so have spent quite a lot of time with animals. The best way to get seriously hurt while riding a horse, dealing with an angry dog, facing down a cow that wants to run over you, or other situations with animals is to feel and show fear and anxiety. Animals sense this and it is a strong signal to attack or to become anxious themselves. In the wild, a scared animal is a weakened animal and therefore more likely to be easy game for predators. Our human world is not so far removed from this. Unfortunately, feeling anxious and/or fearful will tend to attract bullies and/or people who sense an opportunity to take advantage of you.

Obviously, this is not a happy situation. The more anxiety one has, the more anxiety one is likely to get, and the process will continue indefinitely. This is a spiral trap, one that leads to greater suffering and one which can seem to have no way out. Thankfully, however, the same situations that hurt us can also heal us, if used correctly.

The first step in changing the direction of this spiral is simply the awareness that it exists. Here is the sequence:

Trigger → electrical and chemical messages → sensations → recognition of sensations as anxiety → anxious thoughts → feedback to repeat and increase the effect of the trigger → more electrical and chemical messages → and so on.

---

27 Since we are all connected in the Field, our actions and feelings are not limited to our own locality. Effects appear to be stronger in close proximity, but the mindset that one holds does contribute to the mind state of the entire mass consciousness. Choosing fear adds to the strength of the fear frequency in the world. Choosing love adds to the strength of the love frequency.

If I am aware of this sequence, I can begin to watch it as it happens in my own body and to recognize some of the triggers, sensations, and thoughts. If my conscious mind recognizes that it is repeating anxiety reactions, these reactions will automatically begin to diminish.

When I recognize the sensations, I have more choices of what to do with them. From the awakened viewpoint, the first and most important thing to do is to acknowledge the feelings and say "thank you" to them. This has exactly the same effect as picking up a small child who has just skinned her knee, giving her a hug, and letting her know she's safe. She can be crying uncontrollably one second and happy and laughing the next. The skinned knee is all better because it has been kissed and accepted. This same principle works when applied to the feelings inside. Saying "thank you" and giving these feelings love and acceptance just as they are is a very powerful way of allowing them to do what is natural—change to something else.

While you are saying "thank you" it can be helpful to calm your body by intentionally breathing deeply into your lower abdomen. This can be a challenge for some people—I have found that many of the children with whom I work have forgotten how to breathe deeply and think it's strange that I ask them to do this. They expand their chests or lift their shoulders or scrunch up their faces and perform all sorts of strange antics that have nothing to do with natural breathing.

It is natural to breathe deeply into a relaxed belly, and this in turn sends signals to the autonomic nervous system telling your body that all is OK and it can relax. If you have problems with this, try lying down on your back on a firm surface. Put your hands on your stomach and then just relax and breathe normally. Place your attention on your hands and feel them lift slightly when you breathe in, then fall slightly as you breathe out. Once you get the feel of it, you can try making the breath deeper for a few breaths, then go back to automatic relaxed breathing. This is a very good exercise to practice when you go to bed at night as it helps to clear out the tensions and worries of the day and prepare your mind and body for sleep.

Back to anxiety again, you may find that your mind is busy and fixated on all of the things that you are worried or anxious about. In this case it can be very helpful to use the "T chart" mentioned in chapter ten in the exercise for working with self-talk. Write down all the anxious or worried thoughts on the left, and change them to more helpful thoughts on the right. Practice catching the worried thoughts as they appear in your mind and replacing them with more helpful, calming thoughts.

On the energetic level, it can be very helpful to practice with your boundary and grounding. Use a string, as described in the section on boundary, or just imagine the line where you know it to be. Know that you are shielded inside the sphere marked at this boundary edge and that who you are is safe. Own and take responsibility for the feelings, desires, thoughts, and sensations that you experience inside this circle, and know that all that is needed for these experiences to change is for you to stop believing in them.

Once you have a boundary, there are many ways to practice grounding. One way is to imagine yourself as a tree with a strong but flexible trunk. Your roots of golden light extend out from the base of your spine and the bottoms of your feet and reach down into the ground to the center of the earth. When you breathe in, you can imagine breathing in the quality that you need in the moment—perhaps calmness or courage, and when you breathe out, imagine the energy of the breath flowing down through your roots and into the ground, carrying tension and anxiety with it.

I also find it very helpful to practice Ho'oponopono at these times. Simply repeating *"I'm sorry, please forgive me, thank you, I love you"* can be very calming and helpful.

Although there are many things that you can do that can help to calm your mind and body, don't get stuck in these things. They are only tools to use if your mind or body are too upset to be able to do nothing at all to fix the situation. However, *the most important thing that you can do is nothing at all*. Just welcome the feelings, say thank you, and let them change.

It is the nature of emotion to change. This anxiety will change as well. It is OK to let go.

Part 2: Awakened anger

If a small thing has the power to make you angry, does that not indicate something about your size?

Sydney J. Harris

Anger is one of the sinews of the soul.

Thomas Fuller

From the perspective of the objective/material view of the world, anger is generally understood as something that happens *to* me, caused by something external to me and requiring that I do something. It is an explosive feeling, directed outwardly, focused on the difference between *me* and *them*, emphasizing how I am alone and separate, and demanding that someone or something outside me change, hurt, or pay so that I can feel better.

From a psychological perspective, anger is a feeling that is based on fear and centered in powerlessness. As the quotation by Sydney Harris suggests, the more fear and smallness we carry inside, the more easily and quickly our anger will come out. Smallness is not a judgment here. Smallness is simply a mistake in understanding that causes us to feel that we are not adequate enough, strong enough, or safe enough. This mistake in understanding is perfectly logical and rational based on the objective/material worldview. In this worldview, we are small, fragile, separate, meaningless beings striving to out-compete each other long enough to pass on our genetic information to offspring, find what pleasure and happiness we can, and die. Feeling a *lack* of smallness is actually irrational from this point of view.

However, the feeling of smallness is generally buried deep in the subconscious and is not felt on a conscious level. A person does not usually say, "I'm feeling small and frightened, so I'm going to kick you in the head until I feel better." An angry person just feels an explosiveness inside that is searching for an outlet. This can actually add to the terror felt down deep inside, because along with the feeling of being powerless against outside forces, there is often a feeling of being powerless against these strong feelings inside. This can be an extremely uncomfortable and frightening feeling, and a person in this situation needs to find relief.

The less we believe in our ability to manage what happens from the inside-out, the more we have to control it from the outside-in. Anger is the result of feeling frightened and powerless and believing that the only way to get rid of these feelings is to demonstrate power by controlling people or things outside of us. If I can have an effect *out there,* it will demonstrate that I am not powerless. If I destroy something or someone out there or cause them to hurt badly enough, I will be able to keep my own inner fears buried a bit longer. If I can hurt you, I have power over you. If I can control you, I have power over you. If I have power over you, maybe I can believe for a little bit longer that I have power over my own fears as well.

There is another side to anger though. In the second quotation at the beginning of this section, Thomas Fuller calls anger the "sinew of the soul". To many people, anger is what provides them with the strength and motivation to act. It is literally like a sinew—a tough connecting tissue that holds things together. Many people build their sense of self around the toughness that anger gives them. Rather than feeling uncomfortable and tormented by the feeling of anger, these people feel empowered and strengthened by it. For people in this situation, anger is a tonic or elixir of life that gives them their strength. They will therefore nurture their anger, hold tightly to what they hate, and be excited by the prospect of a strong enemy. Forgiveness is an alien and difficult idea, because to forgive is to give up one's own source of strength. Why would I forgive you when I can hate you and be empowered by my hate? Why would I forgive you when I can fight with you and take your power from you? At an even deeper level, how can I forgive you when it is the anger which seems to be the only thing that has allowed me to survive?

This situation may sound extreme, but it is actually very common. Many children grow up in situations where the loss, neglect, or lack of safety around them gives them no reason to believe in anything but the power of their own anger and its ability to keep them safe. Anger as source of strength is also found in relationships on every level—relationships between a husband and wife, between one group and another, one race and another, one country and another. This is a dance that has been going on between humans for as long as humans have existed and, though misdirected, it does actually have some usefulness—at least from the perspective of the objective/material worldview.

In a world of competition and survival of the fittest, anger as a source of strength is actually a very good strategy. If I am able to control and direct my anger into a prolonged hatred, I am able to use the energy and strong motivation that my anger generates in a way that can be helpful to myself. I can use it for competition, for being better than others, and for justifying the ruthless behaviour needed in order to take what I want from someone else. If I am able to control and direct my anger, I am also in a much stronger position than a person who does not have this control and simply explodes when the pressure builds up too much.

Another very useful thing about holding onto anger and hatred is that it can be used as a point of stasis in a world where everything is changing. As long as I can hold my anger tightly to my heart, I am able to know something that is constant and solid. I give the anger my energy, my love and my trust, and I build my sense of who I am around the wrong that I think has been done to me. I repeat and rehearse the list of wrongs in my head over and over, giving them strength and reality, and I turn the powers of my creative perception to proving how bad this person or situation is. Of course, I will find continuing evidence to support my beliefs and to further justify my feelings. The very small and frightened part of me, deep down in the core of my being, is now very well hidden and tucked away so that it's voice cannot be heard. I have a cause, a purpose, and an identity, and I can use it like an anchor against the shifting winds and tides of the changing world around me. So long as I have this anger or this hate, I have myself.

This story is enacted in most action movies in one way or another. The hero meets with a villain, and the two provide each other with the opportunity to see the parts of self that they have disowned, but miss it and hate each other instead. They also provide each other with huge amounts of motivation for violent action, justification for doing things that they probably otherwise wouldn't, and a strong sense of purpose in their lives. This story is also the story of most people who are fighting for a cause of one sort or another, especially those who make their fight violent. It is the same story for suicide bombers, terrorists, drug traffickers, and those who fight against them, and for dictators, corrupt generals, and corrupt policemen, and those who hate them. In one way or another, most of us have a side we stand on—and this is necessary. However, the degree to which we use this standing on a side to define who we are and the degree to which we cling to our anger and hatred defines the degree to which we are hurting ourselves as well. ✓

From the perspective of the Field, however, anger is just energy that wants to move. It is not positive or negative—it's just an action potential that can be used in a variety of ways. However, just like fear and anxiety, anger is also broadcast on an energetic level, and its vibrations can quickly infect other people, especially if they are nearby.

An example of this comes from a young boy in first grade who came to see me often. He was quite artistic and intelligent, and though he was a bit hyperactive, he was generally cooperative and pleasant to be around. He had difficulties getting along with other children his own age, however, and he really hated being told what to do. His reaction to disagreements was to jump very quickly into anger, to yell, and sometimes to strike out as well. One day he and I and another child—a little girl—were putting some boxes of Lego away. The little girl didn't want to put the box away in the way he thought she should and he started to yell at her. As he did so, I experienced a very sharp and powerful energy jolt in my solar plexus and found myself ✓ feeling an instant jolt of anger as well. The episode was over quickly, and the two worked out their problem with each other, but it was a very good lesson for me about the power of anger to transfer itself from one person to another on an energetic/vibrational level as well as via vocal and behavioural signals.

Anger can easily be seen as something that is done *to* me, and this is the general belief fostered by the objective/material worldview. However, it is more helpful to remember the concept of boundaries and to take responsibility for whatever is inside our own boundaries. From this perspective, anger can be *suggested* from the outside, but the choice of how to act always remains with the individual on the inside of his or her own boundary.

If I choose to see a person outside as being the cause of my anger, I will base my actions on the need to change, fix, or get rid of this person. This will involve either manipulation or violence perpetrated against someone else and, as has been discussed earlier, will act like a contraction in my own mind/body/spirit system. I cannot harm another without giving evidence to myself of my own smallness, my own fragility, my own susceptibility to being harmed in the same way by others. I have treated this other person as an expendable object; the deep core of my being knows that what I believe of others must also be true for myself. This is a thought that my conscious mind cannot admit into the light of its knowing. I therefore must expend ever increasing energy to keep this knowledge locked into the darkness, and I must also exert increasing energy to prove my strength in the outer world. I must acquire more power, more hatred, more anger, more money, more control. Once started, it is never enough. As my sense of self contracts within me, I must constantly attempt to prove my greatness in the outside world and acquire more power in order to protect the fragile self inside. This is a story that can be seen in many lives.

There is another, even more subtle way that anger can be used in a contractive way. When one person judges another person or situation in the world *out there* to be bad and then tries to fix it working from a base of anger, the work that they do will be coloured with the emotional vibration that is at the base of their actions. An ostensibly peaceful demonstration that is full of angry people is likely to erupt in violence. An angry activist for the rights of animals or for saving the fresh water or trees or whales is likely to find him or herself in angry and confrontational situations which often damage his or her cause more than help it. A revolutionary soldier fighting to end the corruption and torture of a dictator almost always (history has shown) ends up with a new kind of corrupt government still practicing torture. A husband or wife who tries to fix or change the things that anger him or her about his wife or her husband ends up with an angry and resistant partner. When a person attempts to change something *out there* with a base emotion of anger, and/or with the intention of manipulating or controlling in order to get something in return, eventually it will backfire.

Using anger and hatred in these ways is more useful, it is true, than the chaotic and uncontrolled explosions of people who have not yet learned to direct the energy of their anger at all. However, there is a much more skilled, beneficial, and efficient way to use this energy. This more skilled use of anger begins with the choice of expansion and rests on changing one's perspective of what anger is and what it means.

From an awakened perspective, the energy of anger is a gift given by a friend. Remember, the world I see outside myself is a mirror showing me what I believe and who I am. When I meet a situation or person that gives me the opportunity for anger, I have met an opportunity to see *what I think I am not* in this instant of time. This is something I have disowned, repressed or been unable to forgive. This is a very useful and important thing for me to know, as it gives me a chance to love and accept more of who I am and to build my internal strength.

Also, from the awakened perspective, anger is something that happens *through* me and not *to* me. It happens within the space of my own boundary and is therefore something over which I have power of choice. Like the energy of a fire in a wood stove, the anger I feel can be contained and directed for useful purposes, or like a can of gas thrown on the floor, my anger can have the potential to create an explosion that will burn down the house.

Before we go to the practical part of this discussion and learn how to contain, direct, and transmute anger, I think that it is important to say that people who use this skill are not necessarily pacifists, nor are they pushovers. There are two stories that help to explain this.

The first story comes from the Bhagavad Gita, one of the principle texts of the Hindu Religion. This text tells the story of Arjuna, a young prince who is being advised and tutored by the god Krishna. In the beginning of the story, two armies are lined up about to join in battle. Arjuna is leading one of them, and many of his family members are on the other side. Arjuna sees the futility of this, understands that despite all the anger and disagreement, it is still family that he is fighting, and he wants to stop. It doesn't seem worth it to him anymore.

Surprisingly, Krishna advises against this. Instead of walking away or giving up, Krishna tells Arjuna to fight—but to fight in a very skillful way. From the perspective of the Hindu religion, "The Atman, the indwelling Godhead, is the only reality. This body is simply an appearance; its existence, its destruction, are alike illusory."[28] From the absolute perspective, therefore, it makes no difference if he fights or does not fight. It is all illusion anyway.

On the physical level, however, the battle is upon him. It has evolved from his past actions and is a reflection of who he believes himself to be in this moment.

> "At any given moment in time, we are what we are; and we have to accept the consequences of being ourselves. Only through this acceptance can we begin to evolve further. ... Arjuna is bound to act, but he is still free to make his choice between two different ways of performing the action. In general, mankind almost always acts with attachment; that is to say, with fear and desire. Desire for a certain result and fear that this result will not be obtained. ...But there is another way of performing action, and this is without fear and without desire. ... Freed from fear and desire, he (an individual) offers everything he does as a sacrament of devotion to his duty."[29]

The battle will happen with or without Arjuna, but the role he has chosen, and the role that has been given to him, is to be a warrior and to be part of the battle. Knowing this, he must fight, but he must fight with the non-attached devotion that does not fight enemies with anger but performs a duty out of love.

The second story comes from a Taoist perspective. A powerful general of many armies hears of the existence of a great holy man and sage who lives on a mountain top. The general goes to see the holy man and becomes angered by something the holy man has told him. In a rage, he shouts "Old man, do you have any idea how powerful I am? Do you not know that I could kill you without blinking an eye?"

To this the sage calmly replies "General, do *you* have any idea how powerful *I* am? Do you not know that I could *let* you kill me without blinking an

---

28 From The Bhagavad Gita, translated by Swami Prabhavananda and Christopher Isherwood (1987. p. 176)

29 (Ibid. pp. 177, 178)

eye?" The general, helped by the presence of the sage, instantly understands this and bows down to the holy man, pledging to learn from him.

What the general has understood here is that power over the outside, illusory world is ultimately worth nothing at all. Power over the internal world, and power to rise so far above the illusion of it all as to let someone kill you without any hate, fear, anger, regret or attachment of any kind is a very powerful mastery. As one begins to understand the nature of fear, it becomes clear that the lust for power and the desire to kill are both attempts to run away from the fear of dying. There is no worldly power that can overcome death, but there is a possibility of self-mastery that will take us beyond it. The general realized that the holy man had achieved this mastery and that his power was much greater than the general's own.

In both these stories there is the potential for anger, violence, and death. The two "heroes" chose very different ways of acting in the physical world, but both were practicing the same skill. Externally, the action taken by one looked like violence and the action taken by the other looked like pacifism. Internally, however, they were both practicing the skill of containing, directing, and transmuting the energy of their anger, hate, or fear so that it could be used for their own expansion and growth.

A third story, not so profound, but from my own experience, comes from an anger management class. In one of the group sessions there had been quite a bit of anger expressed by several of the participants. Thankfully, my cofacilitator and I were able to redirect the anger and come to a positive resolution by the end of the session. After the class, one of the participants stopped me to say "Wow, if I could learn to communicate like that, I wouldn't have to be afraid anymore." This was particularly significant because this man was a very large, muscular body builder who probably outweighed me by at least eighty pounds. His experience, however, was that there is always someone bigger or stronger or tougher. The possibility that there was a way to manage anger that did not involve violence was a revelation to him and one that gave him hope.

* * *

Anger is something which manifests on many levels—physically, verbally, psychologically, emotionally, and energetically. It can therefore be addressed by working from any of these levels. However, it is helpful to work from more than one level at once whenever possible. There are many excellent programs which provide detailed steps for working with anger, and it is beyond the scope of this book to provide a full program of this sort. However, I will discuss some basic principles, and some things to look for in anger management programs, should you choose to join one[30].

Here are some steps in learning to manage anger:

Realize and admit that there are situations where your anger is a problem or where you do not manage it skillfully.

In order to change something, it is necessary to first realize that it is a problem. When I was facilitating anger management classes, men would sometimes come with no recognition that they had an issue at all. "I came because my wife made me", or "I came because the court made me". "I don't have a problem. If people would stop being such jerks when I'm around, I wouldn't get so angry".

If anger is getting me what I want and I don't mind the harm it causes to others, it is not worth my effort to change anything. I need to understand that my way of using anger is harming myself and to care that it is harming others before I will be motivated to learn new ways of working with it.

Recognize that it is possible to take responsibility for your own emotions.

This is a very difficult thing for many people. With all strong emotion, but especially with anger, we are conditioned to believe that it is something that is outside of our control. Many people experience emotion as something that happens *to* them, and as something that they have no way of modifying, changing, or managing.

---

30 Voluntary anger management groups are available in most cities and the support of a discussion group is very helpful and highly recommended when attempting to overcome an anger problem. A Google search for "anger management support", including your city name will generally come up with a variety of suggestions.

It is helpful to realize that emotion does not happen *to* us, but *through* us. Although it originates at subconscious levels and does often bypass conscious control, it is also possible to modify the flow of emotion as it moves through us, to re-focus and direct it, and to use the energy of emotion in more positive ways. Changing the belief that emotion happens TO me to the understanding that it happens THROUGH me is a big step that empowers me to begin to take charge of my life more successfully.

Take full responsibility for your own emotions.

This requires a strong declaration that "the buck stops here." It requires an end to blame and the realization that your choices and your choices alone are responsible for your behaviour, regardless of what provocation you may perceive.

This is possibly the most difficult step for many people. In anger management sessions, one of the most common complaints is "It wasn't my fault! She made me do it—she knows how angry I get when she yells at me like that; what did she expect! She had it coming!" Or "What was I supposed to do? He was calling me down in front of my kid. I'm not going to just stand there like a wimp and do nothing!" —or a hundred other excuses.

These same kinds of excuses are heard on the schoolyard all the time and from kids who get sent to me for counselling. "He called me a name; she was bugging me; he looked at me funny; she hit me first; he took my ball; she stole my swing; he tripped me when we were playing soccer". People of all ages seem to be quite good at finding reasons to blame others for their anger or for their violent actions.

Taking responsibility requires returning to the idea of boundaries, remembering that I am responsible for what my hands, feet, mouth, and body do, and that there is no excuse whatsoever to blame anyone else for my choices. This can be extremely difficult, but it is also a necessary step. Without it, someone else will always be responsible, and I will always be giving my power away. However, if I begin to take responsibility, I also begin to build my own integrity and personal strength. By owning my emotions, I take back my power, my self-respect, and my sense of control in my own life.

Though it may not seem this way initially, the reward is well worth the pain and effort required to achieve it.

Become aware of what anger feels like in your body.

The preceding steps are like the foundation of a house. They can seem to take a long time and it doesn't look like very much is really happening. However, they literally lay the groundwork on which the rest of the steps rest. Without establishing the first steps in a strong way, it is likely that the next parts of the building will fall down.

Once the foundation is set, however, it is often amazing how fast the walls go up and the roof goes on. Something really seems to be happening and almost overnight there is something that looks like a house. The same is true for the step of body awareness.

As has been discussed earlier in this book, emotions arise in the subconscious mind as a conditioned (programmed from earlier experience) response to the way in which we perceive events that are happening around us. The subconscious mind sends electrical and chemical signals to the body which create sensations that we feel and recognize as a particular emotion. This process is a bit like a freight train starting down the tracks. It takes it some time to get going, but once it's going it is really hard to stop. In the same way, the feedback loop of electrical and chemical signals, sensations in the body, recognition of sensations, dislike for these sensations, attempts to get rid of the perceived cause of the sensations, more uncomfortable sensations, and so on, starts a freight train of physiological reactions that is difficult to stop. If I wait too long, it will simply overpower me, and there will be nothing I can consciously do to stop it. The blow-up will happen, and I will be left to pick up the pieces once my conscious mind is returned to me.

In order to recognize anger, or any strong emotion, before it gets too strong and overpowers me, it is necessary to learn how to track the body signals that tell me that the emotion is coming on. When I talk to elementary students about this, I often use the image of a thermometer. I ask them to colour the thermometer in zones marked for "safe", "warning", "danger" and "explosion". For each zone, they write down physical sensations that they can feel in their bodies when they are in this zone. This then gives them a chart of warning signs to use so that they can catch anger while it is still in the "safe" or "warning" zones and easily re-directed, rather than waiting until they are in the danger zone, or even worse, letting it go past danger and into the uncontrolled explosion.

For adults, I sometimes draw a diagram that looks like a wave instead of the thermometer image. This is because all emotions come in waves—they start out small, build to a peak, and then fall away. Like waves, emotions also repeat themselves, especially if they are practiced (repeated over and over). Anger waves, for instance, tend to become larger, more violent, and more frequent as time goes on if a person does not take responsibility for the emotion and learn how to calm the "waves".

It is useful to note that the anger wave exists on many levels. It is a psychological wave of increased negative thinking, a physical wave of increased adrenalin, cortisol, and other fight or flight reaction chemicals, and an emotional wave that also includes the vibrational frequency of the emotion on an energetic level. The wave can be dampened—meaning that its size and strength can be decreased—by working with any of these levels. However, the physical level is generally the easiest place to start.

The diagram below shows a wave that could represent anger or any other strong emotion. In this diagram, the wave builds relatively slowly in the tension building phase. The acute release phase is where the blow-up occurs. People with severe anger problems can black out, not remember what happens during this time, and have no control of their actions. It is essential, therefore, to recognize the rising anger wave before it

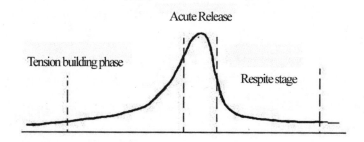

gets to this point and to change its direction while there is still an ability to do so. Body signals that warn of anger can be placed along the tension building phase, located at the positions where they seem to occur. Like the anger thermometer, this gives a map that shows a series of warning signs. Each warning sign is like an exit from a highway—it gives the possibility of choosing a different path instead of repeating the old pattern of building tension → explosion → guilt → start over.

Learn new ways of thinking that defuse angry thoughts.

On the psychological level, changing the anger wave requires becoming aware of the thoughts or *self-talk* that is present in one's mind. If I am paying attention to my body signals, I will be warned that I am getting angry when I start to feel, for instance, my stomach tightening and my jaw clenching. This is a signal to pay attention to my thoughts. If I recognize the anger soon enough, I will be able to take myself to a quiet place where I can write down all the negative thoughts that run through my head. If not, I may have to go through the anger cycle again. However, I can at least begin to note and remember the kinds of thoughts that repeat in my mind. When I am calm again, I can write them down.

Once some negative thoughts are collected, write them on a "T" chart. On the left-hand side of the chart put the heading "Unhelpful" and on the right-hand side, put the heading "Helpful". Write the negative thoughts on the "unhelpful" side, then go through the list and find a way to turn each unhelpful thought into a helpful one. For instance, "It's her fault" could become "I am responsible for my own actions". "I can't help it" could become "My emotions belong to me and I can be in charge of them". "I'm worthless" could become "I can learn to like myself", etc.

Practice changing your thoughts in all sorts of situations. Whenever you notice an unhelpful thought, practice finding a more helpful replacement right away. This practice will help to keep the anger wave from building.

Learn new behaviours to use as creative outlets for the energy that is generated by anger

Behaviours are the results of thoughts and emotions. However, they can also be a way to influence thoughts and emotions. It is therefore very important and helpful to learn new ways of expressing yourself and new things to do when you feel yourself becoming angry. Activities like jogging, working out, hiking, walking the dog or walking in a park or forest, sitting by the water, reading a book, any sort of sport, yoga, meditation, aikido, art, music, or any creative activity are all excellent ways to use the energy of anger in a positive way. Any activity that is not destructive or harmful to others and that you enjoy is a possible replacement activity to use when you get angry. Make a list of things you like to do or things that help you to feel calm. Use it when you first begin to notice your anger signals!

See anger as energy

As you become more aware of your body and mind, and as you expand and awaken your perception, you will also become more aware of yourself as an energetic being. This awareness can help to speed up change and to give you new tools to work with. One of these tools is to look at what happens within you and around you from the perspective of *energy* and *flow*. If you feel attacked by someone, try consciously changing your perception from that of being attacked to that of being offered energy. What is the feeling or flavour of the energy being offered to you? Where do you feel the energy in your body and how does it affect you? Do you have to accept it, or can you let it go? Does it feel caught, dammed up, or stifled? Where in your body do you feel that the flow of this energy is blocked?

It can be helpful to visualize yourself as a cloud or air or something that can easily let objects pass through it. Allow the energy to pass through you without having the need to hold on to it, accept it, or claim it as your own. This energy is a gift. You have a choice of accepting it or of saying an internal "no thank you" and letting it pass through you without sticking.

If you feel the energy of anger in yourself, consider it as a gift of extra power and motivation. Like being given an extra tank of fuel or charging a battery, you now have more energy to work with. To what positive project or activity can you direct it?

Ultimately, everything is vibration, and it is your interpretation that gives meaning to what you feel. As you begin to experience this reality, you will find that any strong emotion can be dissolved and powdered into a finer and smoother vibration. What was painful and stuck at one level of understanding can be pleasant and flowing at another.

* * *

From the viewpoint of the Awakening, there is really no such thing as *anger*. There is only energy and the choices that we make about how we perceive and experience the energy. Anger requires the perception that we have been wronged in some way, and it requires judgment of our current situation as bad and wrong.

Ultimately, the only skill that is necessary is the skill of letting go. This means letting go of the perception that we don't like a given situation, letting go of the belief that we must be right, letting go of deep belief that we are small, helpless, and meaningless. It also means letting go of the belief that our ideas of how life *should* be are more important than the truth of what actually *is*.

When we practice these things, we can also begin to see the world as perfect and OK just as it is, regardless of how it appears. This does not mean that we no longer need to take action—Arjuna chose to fight even when he realized that he didn't hate the people he was fighting. It simply means that we are able to act without the driving insanity of anger taking away our intelligence.

Let go. The world is OK as it is. You are OK as you are. Eventually you will come full circle and "grok" this truth for yourself.

Part 3: Awakened fear

What we fear comes to pass more speedily than what we hope.

Publilius Syrus -*Moral Sayings* (1st century B.C.)

I must not fear. Fear is the mind-killer. Fear is the little-death that brings total obliteration. I will face my fear. I will permit it to pass over me and through me. And when it has gone past I will turn the inner eye to see its path. Where the fear has gone there will be nothing. Only I will remain.

Frank Herbert, *Dune*—Bene Gesserit Litany Against Fear

Fear is a base emotion, the foundation of all other negative emotions, feelings and actions and as such it is also ubiquitous. It can be found everywhere, in anything, by anyone and it is always there, lurking in the shadows, waiting for its moment.

Fear comes in many guises. It can infiltrate any experience, turning the smell of a rose into sickly sweet warning or the wonder of love into a death's head of loss. It projects shadows, dancing like demons through the mind and takes even the sweetest of experiences into a sickening spiral of gathering shadow, loss of faith and trust. It saps courage, wilts integrity, and seems to force desperate, stupid, and vicious actions in a fruitless attempt to escape from something nameless and formless, stalking just out of vision's reach.

Fear is cold damp tremors in the night, the taste of tin and smell of cold sweat. It is death just around the corner, and it is expected pain. It is belief in loss in every form, and it is the companion of both strong desire and of possession of what was desired. Fear sees threat in every face and situation, builds strongholds and barricades, loves guns and weapons of all sorts. Fear cannot trust, cannot love, cannot let go. It sees the world as a single message: *Something bad is going to happen. Soon...*

Fear looks like a riot in the street, a man with a gun, a torture chamber, a child listening to her parents' drunken fighting. It looks like an insurance company, a homeland security alarm level code (it's code orange today or maybe chartreuse), a snowflake in a darkened stormy sky. Fear looks like child soldiers, global warming, and economic failure. It looks like competition and not enough to go around, dwindling resources, a bill with no money to pay it, a foreclosure, a fire. Fear is sown in our subconscious in visions of Hell, demons, and dark forces. Deep in its bowels, fear is a black existential void, still and cold and lonely, infinite emptiness paradoxically filled with infinite indefinable threat and imminent pain.

Conversely, fear can even look like sunshine, or a butterfly, a stranger's smile, an offer of friendship, or possible new love. Fear can be in all of these things because fear is not a thing. Fear is a perspective—addictive, exciting, spine tingling, or depressing, bonding and horribly sticky, insistent, uncompromising, full-on yell in the face demanding, attention grabbing and ruthless—but nothing.

On the conscious level, fear is like a pair of glasses with a particular colour. Put on the glasses and the world is coloured the same tint as their lenses. Take them off, and the world goes back to being its own colours again. On the conscious level, this is all there is to fear—and both meanings of this sentence are intended. On the conscious level, fear is a choice, a perceptual filter, and a matter of trust. Choose love, choose to see beauty, choose to trust in the creative perfection of this moment, and fear will have no hold and no existence. Just as darkness is a "no-thing" that cannot exist when there is light, fear cannot exist where there is love, trust, and presence.

On a physical/emotional/energetic level, fear is a vibrational tone that underlies perception and controls the direction of imagination. A vivid example of this came to me with a very frightened child one morning. This child arrived in my office completely spooked. He was pale and shaky and in obvious distress. It eventually came out that he had been experiencing paranormal attacks that could have been straight out of the *Paranormal Activity* [31] movies. He had watched these movies in the past and they had made such an impression on him that he started experiencing the ideas in his own life. He told me through shaky tears of being drug from his bed, pulled down the stairs, haunted by dark shadows that slammed doors and broke things and

---

31 Paramount Pictures (2007). Written and directed by Orin Peli. There are now sequels, *Paranormal Activity 2, 3, and 4.*

*what kind
of listener?*

other harrowing experiences. Whether his experience was "real" or not in a scientifically verifiable way is debatable. However, in his own mind the fear, images, and experiences were real, and this is all that mattered for him. No amount of telling him his experience was unreal would change how he felt or what he believed, and neither would it help him.

This boy's father had killed himself when the boy was very young and the boy had a large complex of feelings associated with his father including feelings of abandonment and rejection, responsibility and guilt, yearning and anger. Although I didn't mention his father while we were talking, I did give the boy validation in the form of my belief in his belief of his experience along with validation that whatever had happened before, in this moment he was safe. I also went into my own inner experience and asked for help[32]. We talked a little bit about Harry Potter and the making of a patronus.[33]

As the boy continued to relate his experience his fear began to subside and he became less focused on the fearful images. As the ending of his story came nearer it felt as if the heavy weight was lifting and there were figurative rays of light poking into the images. Suddenly the story changed completely and he said that he had seen a bright light that looked, he thought, like his father. The gestalt of the image transferred to me as well so that I could also see and feel this light, shining through the darkness of the fear and turning it all into a dream that was already fading. After this, we talked a bit more and then he said he felt much better and left. I will never know if what this boy

---

32 This is another part of awakened belief. In the objective/material worldview we are alone and unable to connect to sources of help or information that are beyond our regular five senses. A growing number of people experience very real subjective validation that this kind of help is available, however, and they regularly connect with their own perceptions of God, Buddha, Angels, Ascended Masters, Higher Self, or whatever fits for them. From the point of view of the Awakening, form is not fixed within the Field, and truth depends on the flexibility and openness of the mind in question. Help can come to us in whatever form is most likely to work within the beliefs and values to which we currently cling. Again, the reality of this begins with a choice to allow the help to exist for you, or not.

33 A *patronus* is a protection charm generated to ward off the wraithlike dementors from the *Harry Potter* stories that suck out life and joy and thrive on fear. A patronus is made by thinking of a deeply happy/loving experience and projecting this feeling into the charm, which appears as a holographic animal. Harry's patronus appeared as a stag, the same animal as his dead father's patronus.

told me is true and if he really did experience what he said he experienced. It is likely that investigation of the physical facts would indicate that there was no way to physically validate or verify the experience and that it was "all in his head"—although he had apparently experienced these events along with his sister and so the memories were possibly in more than one head. In any case, the objective reality was highly questionable, but the subjective reality was very real. For the boy, the subjective reality is all that mattered.

This is the case with fear in all forms, and the principle can be taken through all levels of experience. Ultimately, fear is a subjective phenomenon, dependent on belief. To the extent that we believe in lack, pain, cruelty, loss, and death, we will experience fear.

Belief in Hell, demons, psychic attack, dark magic, and the many ways in which evil and darkness are practiced and worshiped creates particularly thorny issues with fear. The Field will manifest any belief that we ask of it, and since all these beliefs are so strongly held in our group consciousness, it is likely that they do exist in some form and some reality. Certainly they exist as subjective experience for some people, and for some of these people the reality is terrifying in a way that is beyond imagining.

The way out is not simple when one is stuck within this kind of belief and subjective experience. This experience is based on a fundamental feeling of loss of power, where a higher source has literally condemned one to damnation, justified by one's own choices and actions. In the face of not only God's judgment, but my own, how can there be escape? How can the tiny and worthless bit of slime that is the conception of self in this position resist in the awesome, and paradoxically compelling, face of the power of shadow and demons from the deep?

It is into this tragedy of forgetfulness of our true nature that the great teachers of our past have stepped. The Buddha offered the Eight-fold Noble Path as a way to focus on rebuilding our strength and belief in whom we are. Jesus offered his teachings of love, the evidence of his lack of death, and the promise that he is always with us. Lao Tzu offered the Tao and understanding of the flow and balance of light and dark in the yin and yang. Each teacher, in his or her own way has offered the same thing. Each has offered a way to see light in the darkness and to alter our subjective experience from one of fear to one of reconnection with the source—however we conceive of it—and with who and what we truly are.

In the Awakening, we can choose to see ourselves in the position of powerless wretch, judged and condemned by God, or we can begin to understand how deeply we judge ourselves and begin to practice forgiveness. Stepping out of the fear requires letting go of belief in our smallness and powerlessness, stepping out of belief that we are judged, and remembering that darkness has no existence other than as the absence of light.

Like the boy when his images became centered on the bright light rather than the dark terrors, we can choose to put importance on reacting to the evidence given us by our five senses and conditioning or to put our attention on letting go and relaxing into the light that dispels the fear.

In this letting go, it is important to understand that light and dark or fear and love are not opposites at war with each other. Darkness is an absence of light. From the perspective of the Awakening, there is no such thing as fear, or death. Fear is a result of forgetfulness of who we truly are and what this game of life is all about. This forgetfulness is deep and persistent, but it is not an ultimate reality. Just as forgetting where your keys are does not mean that they have ceased to exist, forgetting who we truly are does not mean that experience beyond our five senses and mind does not exist.

There is no way to show that the experience of the boy in the example is real, and there is no way to prove that there is anything beyond the body's six (five senses and conscious mind) organs of perception. The extent to which we experience fear, or to which we experience well-being in any situation, becomes a function of our choice of belief and the amount of faith we put into our choice. The conceptual framework of the Field and the Awakening are not a final definition or an offer of the one and only Truth. They simply provide a larger and more flexible framework for understanding which can help to move beyond the smallness and fearfulness that has been present in human belief systems for so long.

* * *

Fear is, of course, a physical phenomenon as well as a psychological and spiritual one. On the physical level, fear is mediated by the amygdala in the brain and the HPA axis (Hypothalamus, Pituitary, Adrenal system)—that mediates the fight or flight response. Fear is a result of perception of threat in this system, based on past experience and trauma. Since most people currently living on the planet have been conditioned in a trauma and fear-based worldview, fear is therefore a prevalent reaction.

On the more extreme (but still extremely common) side of things, fear reactions are hardwired in physical brain developmental changes that can begin early in pregnancy and continue as a child develops. These changes are brought about by exposure to violence and/or neglect in the family, bullying and other traumatic experiences at school and in the community, traumatic loss, abuse and accident, war and natural catastrophe and the daily "slings and arrows" of normal experience. All these things build a catalogue of experience that is associated with danger in one way or another and is therefore shunted to the amygdala for immediate action rather than to the prefrontal cortex for further processing. Understanding is therefore bypassed, and the thinking mind is most often relegated to rationalizing why it behaved so irrationally.

When it receives the danger signal, the amygdala then sends out signals via the HPA axis to the entire body to be ready and on the alert for the *something bad* that is likely to happen at any moment. In much the same way that the United States Homeland Security used colour codes to signal its terrorism alarm levels, the amygdala sends out messages to the body warning that something is amiss. It often does not know quite what this something is, but a threat has been perceived, and the system must be alerted.

In the case of trauma, large areas of experience become associated with threat, and the amygdala can become hyperactive. Children who have experienced trauma at a young age become hardwired to expect threat at any moment. Their experience is one of constant checking—"Am I safe? Am I liked?" They live on the edge of subconscious panic, constantly checking their surroundings, perceiving danger everywhere. They will often display symptoms of attention deficit disorder (ADD), oppositional defiant disorder (ODD), moderate to severe behaviour issues, and learning difficulties—all because their brains are so busy attempting to determine the level of threat and over-reacting to the stimuli around them. Their amygdalae are set on a hair-pin trigger, and their body-mind system is in a constant state of hyper-arousal, ready to react.

It is interesting to compare patterns on different levels and to see how similar patterns keep reappearing and repeating themselves. The terrorist attacks of 9/11 were a traumatic event for the United States that sparked a series of fear reactions that continues to this day. These fear reactions were not different in form and function from those of a child subjected to trauma. The nation reacted with initial fear and anger and lashed out in retaliation. It systematized its fear reactions into defensive barriers and programs in the form of Homeland Security and the War on Terror; it produced and maintained a permanent alert level warning system (like the amygdala and HPA axis) which reminded everyone to be constantly wary and afraid, and it re-directed huge quantities of its resources towards perceiving, discovering, and killing real and imagined threats somewhere *out there*. It even invented its own "axis"—George Bush's "Axis of Evil"—danger and evil lurking somewhere out there waiting to pounce the moment Americans let down their vigilance.

In doing all these things, the United States began to be seen by many other countries as a bully, self-absorbed and self-destructive. It also started a chain of events, particularly the war in Iraq, which have hastened its own economic demise and, as is typical of fear-based action, virtually destroyed any remaining world belief in the integrity or altruism of the American system. In its search to find security after trauma, the United States has sabotaged its own integrity and power and helped to bring about even greater fear, trauma, and despair for its own citizens as well as for many, many others throughout the world.

On the school yard with a bully or in the world of international politics, fear and its patterns are the same.

On a level above the chemical/physical level but still below the level of consciousness, fear is a meme. A *meme* is a viral idea that is spread from mind to mind by contagion. Like viruses, memes transmit themselves from one person to another, replicate in the host, and are then passed on to other

people. Memes can be small things—like a new fad in the fashion world—
or relatively larger things like an entire religion and all the thinking and
background that goes along with it. Memes are everywhere—they carry and
transmit the customs of a culture, pass on family traditions and rules, and
carry the information that helps citizens of a country to identify themselves
as different from other countries[34].

Although fear is one meme among many, fear is also a base or foundational meme from which many others are built. Without fear, there would be
no need for a war on terror or for all the systems of defence and offense that
have come from it, nor for the levels of control that have been instated or the
degree of monetary imbalance that has resulted. In the same way, without
fear there would be no bullies, no victims, no need for defensiveness, and no
waste of the resources consumed in the production of these defences.

As is taught by the martial art of Aikido, strength and security are found
in joining, redirecting, and releasing incoming energy rather than perceiving
it as attack. Fear-based action is an extremely unskilled way of reacting to
the world, based on the knee-jerk function of evolutionarily ancient animal
alarm systems.

On an energetic level, fear has a specific vibratory signature or tone within
the Field. It is a particularly compelling and strangely attractive tone, and it is
highly contagious. If you have ever been close to someone who is very afraid,
you will have experienced how difficult it is to not become afraid yourself.

When people become afraid, they generate the fear frequency, and this
frequency is transmitted to the Field in a similar fashion to radio being transmitted to a listening area. Every person within the transmission radius of
the fearful person has a "radio" receiver and can receive the fear frequency.
As these people receive the fear, they begin to experience it themselves and
broadcast it further. When one person perceives fear, therefore, it creates a

---

34 Don Beck and Christopher Cohen's book *Spiral Dynamics: Mastering Values, Leadership and
Change* (1996) provides an excellent in-depth discussion of memes as the transmitters of
worldviews and cultural belief systems. It also provides a framework for understanding the
development of worldview belief systems as a progression in levels of complexity and maturity that happens on both the levels of ontology (individual development) and phylogeny
(development of the species).

contagion effect that both passes the experience of fear to others and increases the strength of the fear vibration within the Field.

An easy-to-see example of this is in mob behaviour, when otherwise reasonable people become violent, terrified, or euphoric together. The vibrational tone of each person's individual field joins with the others around it and creates a resonance within the larger field of the group. Individual fields then become overwhelmed by the group field vibration, and people do things that they would normally completely reject. Alcohol or drugs, of course, greatly enhance the mob effect, as they further lower the conscious mind's ability to think individually and to resist the group influence.

At this time in human history, there is an especially virulent transmission of the meme of fear along with all the emotions and actions that go along with it. The meme of fear is broadcast daily, from minute to minute by media that knows that excitement sells. It is supported by governments that know it is easier to control a population that is afraid, and by businesses that understand that fear provides great opportunities in advertising and marketing. If you choose to look at the information that is available from media and advertising around you, it is not hard to find the subtle (and often not so subtle) ways in which fear is spread around.

The presence of a strong meme for fear is not necessarily good or bad. From the objective/material worldview, fear can actually be a rather useful thing, as it is a strong motivator, provides group and cultural cohesion against an outside threat (real or imagined), and keeps people in a state of arousal and excitement. This is a great thing for promoting consumption and consumerism, which keeps our economy running and our jobs going. It also helps to remove personal responsibility for actions (self-defence justifies almost anything), and strongly supports the efforts of the part of the human mind that does not want to understand itself. Although most of these results of fear do not contribute to individual happiness or security, some of them do contribute to the gross national product and certainly to making some very wealthy people increasingly wealthier. To be fair, most of us benefit from fear-based systems in that they are what we are used to and what support our way of living.

As discussed above, when we are afraid, control is shunted away from the more advanced parts of our mind, particularly the prefrontal cortex, and given to the more instinctual part of our mind in steps mediated particularly by the amygdala and HPA axis. This change in locus of control hijacks the conscious mind, which then directs all of its energy toward manufacturing justifications for what are basically instinctual fear reactions.

The result of this is a situation where people see provocation everywhere and react to the provocation with strong anger or self-protection reactions—justified of course, by the provocation. Since provocation and attack create an atmosphere of fear, and fear breeds more contraction and protectionism as well as attack, fear results in continually increasing levels of violence, insecurity, and destruction. Again, the example of the reaction of the United States to the 9/11 terrorist attacks is an excellent illustration of this principle.

The idea that fear and violence beget more fear and violence is not new and doesn't require the concept of energy fields to be explained. However, as explained earlier in this book, the conceptual framework of the Field does help to explain why the most common approach to stopping the cycle of fear and violence (namely, fighting against it) doesn't work.

To review, in the conceptual framework of a field, the field itself is completely neutral and flexible. It provides the possibility matrix from which anything can be created, just as a lump of clay provides the matrix for the creation of any shape that can be imagined by the artist. The Field reacts to intention as the clay reacts to an artist's hands, bringing thought into physical form.

Since the Field is neutral, it doesn't distinguish between negative and positive energy or intention and is equally able to manifest either one. Any intention directed toward attack or defence, therefore, creates more fear because both these intentions are based on fear. The energy of these actions in effect tells the Field "I believe strongly in fear. It exists in my world. Please help me to see what I believe in". The Field does exactly this, creating more situations in which to feel, create, or fight fear for as long as we continue to request it.

Fighting fear with fear, or fighting fear at all for that matter, doesn't work. Fighting fear is like panicking in the darkness, floundering in a pitch black room and screaming at the images conjured within one's own mind. Fighting fear is projecting demons on the walls and into the eyes of everyone around us, pointing out groups with differences for distrust and persecution, perceiving the world through filters of paranoia and distrust, and believing in our own smallness and lack of worth. It is a useless, damaging, self-destructive behaviour—but it is also one of the most common behaviours we engage in.

This is the insanity that can be seen all around us in the world—the insanity and addictive self-destructiveness that is a part of the human heritage and that is wreaking havoc with the world.

Fortunately, in the Awakening, growing numbers of people are becoming aware of their own fear-based insanity and learning to observe it. Approaching fear can seem like a frightening step backwards at first. It can be experienced as a setback after seemingly conquering the worst of anger, grief, or depression, or it can become a complication for any of these. Fear is always underneath these emotions, and so it can raise its head at any time—often it is strongest just when it seems that the others have been finally vanquished.

Coming out of fear is not complicated, except that the mind makes it so. Coming out of fear is as simple as flicking a switch to turn on a light in the darkness or changing a pair of glasses to see through a different-colour lens. However, the difficulty lies in the location of the fear reaction deep in the subconscious mind and below the level of conscious control. Making the change is simple. Reaching the depth of mind needed in order to make the change is not quite as easy. Reaching these depths of mind is something that requires time, patience, and disappointingly to many skeptics, faith.

The world is either a fearful place or it isn't. There is attack, danger, and threat offered everywhere, or there is love and well-being. At the very base of perception and emotional reaction there are no gray areas, and there is no half-way point. We can consciously mediate and moderate, cover up feelings with learned responses, and consciously redirect our emotions before they get out of hand—and this is all good. However, it does not change the condition at the very base of all feelings that is a simple and automatic decision between fear and love. The job of reaching the place inside where this automatic decision is made can be long and difficult—especially for people who have suffered from trauma as small children. However, it is not impossible, and it begins with faith.

As related earlier in this book, there is a story in Zen Buddhist tradition about a young man who sees an old monk carrying the staff that symbolizes leadership and accomplishment in his tradition. The young man wants a staff too and asks how he can get one. The old monk replies "If you have a staff, I will give you another. If you don't have a staff, I will take it away".

This paradoxical situation is true in many cases in life. If you have money, it is easier to get more, and if you don't, it is easy to lose what you have. It is true for love, for friendship, for trust and for faith. It is also true for fear. If you have fear, you will receive more. If you don't have fear, you will continue to receive less.

This is a paradox that can't be solved by thought or logic. In fact, in order to solve this paradox, one must go completely against the rational and scientific way of thinking in a way that is likely to make most skeptics want to throw this book away. I know it made me feel that way. However, stepping out of fear requires making a choice and then living that choice every moment regardless of evidence to the contrary delivered to you by your senses.

So what is this choice? It is the same choice that has been discussed throughout this book, over and over in many ways, and it is the same choice that is at the base of the Awakening. When you hit the bottom of fear and you know that there is nowhere left to run; when you have tried all of the distractions and games and you realize that no matter what you do you can no longer hide from yourself, then you have to choose.

In the deepest, darkest crevices of who you are, are you worthy of love? Are you worthy of well-being? Despite fears of weakness, loneliness, worthlessness, powerlessness, ugliness, guilt, desire, or pain, are you worthy? Despite all evidence that may be to the contrary, are you worthy?

The answer, of course, is "Yes!"—but in their heart of hearts 99.99% of people on this planet do not truly believe it. This is the step of faith, the great leap of trust that becomes a thousand little leaps, moment by moment, every day, for the rest of your life. Choose worthiness and act from that worthiness.

One small action at a time, as you choose, so you will create and so you will begin to see. As you choose worthiness for yourself, you also choose worthiness for the world. This is a choice for forgiveness—forgiveness despite all evidence against it.

This is the faith that is called for by religions, though its purpose is often lost in the dogma and control that comes when people give their power to others. If you are a believer in a particular faith, this is the time to ask for help and to establish your own personal connection with your God. If you are not a believer in religion, it is still time for you to ask for help and establish your own personal connection—be it with your higher self, the ascended masters, a particular god or goddess, the archangels, guardian angels, or simply with the Field, it doesn't matter. What does matter is that it is time to make the choice of worthiness and then, despite all evidence to the contrary, to continue to give the gift of this choice to yourself and to the world around you over and over and over, every moment and every day for the rest of your life.

This can sound rather heavy and grim and so it is also important to remember to be light about it. Worthiness is about not taking yourself so seriously, letting go of things that come to you, good or bad, and cultivating lightness of spirit. A great way to start is to smile.

Exercises for letting go of fear

1. Hug yourself.

I worked as a teacher in an adult education center for First Nations people for several years and was privileged to be able to help organize and host a POWWOW on the reserve. At that time an old woman who called herself "Grandma Grizzly" took it upon herself to tutor me in some of the spiritual traditions of the people and to help me to understand the culture so that I would make fewer mistakes.

One of the simplest, best, and most useful gifts she gave me was when she told me to "Put your left hand on your right shoulder and your right hand on your left shoulder. Put your head on your arms and give yourself a hug. Remember that even in the worst of times, you can always be there for yourself—and, if you want, know that I am there hugging you too."

I've used this so many times in the years since I met her, and I always remember her when I do. She had traveled many difficult and traumatic paths and she had come through it all still able to give the gift of her love. Her gift is still with me, and I would like to pass it on to you. I'm sure she would be glad.

2. I don't have to believe in this!!!!! I don't have to give my attention to this!!!

Remember this each time fear invades your perceptions of yourself, your experience, or the world around you. Watch for that feeling of "Something bad is going to happen" and remember that you do not have to give it your attention. Thoughts are not to be believed at the best of times. Certainly do not believe them when they are filled with fear. **3. Simplify, and live with less.**

Practice letting go and learn to live with less. Try not buying that new pair of shoes or not going on the expensive holiday. Look for ways to simplify your life in every way—things, people, activities... how can your life become simpler? Having less means living in a lighter way, having less to protect, less to support, and less to fear.

4. Relax.

My teacher in Thailand constantly reminded all of us to relax, let go, let it be. There is no need to put *self* into the fear and turmoil. It will happen without you, and it will end without you. Everything that has a beginning has an ending. This fear will end without you doing anything to end it. Let go. Relax your mind. Realize that you don't understand and that is OK. Just be, release, and relax. Everything is already OK.

5. Use affirmations.

Affirmations are very helpful, especially when waking up and before sleeping, but at any time when you are struggling as well. Make up your own helpful affirmations so that they fit your beliefs and come from your own inner wisdom. Here are some that I like to use when I feel afraid are:

I am a being of light and love. I came from the light, and I am returning to the light. All is well.

This is not a crisis. I am safe. It is already OK.

6. Ask for help!

Help is available all around. Talk to friends, see a counsellor or minister, priest or rabbi. Better yet, make your own connections and call on Jesus, Buddha, God, Allah, the Ascended Masters, the Archangels, your Higher Self or whomever or whatever you believe in. Call in the light, allow it to surround you and relax into its presence. Even if it seems like simply an exercise in positive psychology, try it. You may be surprised at the results.

7. Lighten up. Let go of stuff. Don't get too serious or take yourself too seriously.

I was for a while slightly addicted to a television show called *The Big Bang Theory*. The characters in the show were constantly having interpersonal problems that in real life would be quite long lasting and relationship destroying. However, in the show there was always a handy scene change or episode change, and when you came back, the problem was gone, and they were on to the next thing.

I think that this is a great way to be. We all could use that little scene or episode change that lets us just let go of whatever happened a moment ago and remembers that everything is OK. We're here for fun, friendship, and adventure. Don't get hung up on the drama.

8. **Smile.** It's hard to be afraid or overly serious when you're smiling.

9. **Cultivate virtues.**

Many wise teachers have taught about virtues for a reason. When we practice them, we feel better and are less afraid. The Golden Rule, the Eight-fold Noble Path, the teachings of the masters— these teachings have been around for thousands of years because they are helpful.

Most of the exercises in this book are also about getting over fear, as is the Awakening in general. Each time you choose to act from your own wholeness and worthiness, you take a small step out of fear and into love.

Have courage. Remember your wholeness. Keep taking steps.

Part 4: Awakened grief

*When you are sorrowful look again in your heart, and you shall see
that in truth you are weeping for that which has been your delight.*

Kahlil Gibran

*As long as I can I will look at this world for both of us. As
long as I can I will laugh with the birds, I will sing with
the flowers, I will pray to the stars, for both of us.*

Sascha

In my job as a counsellor for children I periodically am called to a school
to help when there has been a death of a classmate or of someone who is
connected with the school. When addressing a group of children, I always
caution them not to judge the responses of others. Some people respond to
grief with tears and sadness, some people's first response is anger, and some
initially feel nothing at all. Some people respond to death or loss with giddy
laughter and silliness, some become quiet and withdrawn, and others want
to talk about it.

Each person's response is a product of his or her present understanding
of death and loss as well as his or her particular physiology and the way in
which his or her body processes information. It is also strongly linked to
all other memories of loss that a person has experienced and tends to be
compounded by this. Sometimes a child who has no connection at all with
the person who has died will have a very strong grief reaction, and other children will get upset about it. "What's your problem?—you didn't even know
him...". However, death opens the door to all our memories and harrows the
fields of our fears, bringing up all related thoughts and anxieties that have
been lurking in our subconscious. Children, or adults, who react strongly
to a death have generally had a loss of their own or deep fears of such a loss.

I have found many of these different kinds of reactions in myself as well,
so the first part of this chapter is the story of my own experience with grief
and depression. My experience is not special, different, or remarkable in any

233

way. However, as I am quite familiar with it, it seemed a good way to discuss various ideas and concepts connected with grief. Also, though the details are different in all of our stories, the feelings are the same. We all have to walk the path of grief at one point or another. It can help to see that our feelings are shared by others—and that no matter how bad it seems right now, this too will pass!

As you read this first section, then, please remember that the details of the story aren't really important. Just look for times when you feel a connection in yourself—when your own feelings are touched or when you find something that helps to explain a feeling or experience you have had. Finding connections like this are generally soothing and expanding, and they are an important part of dealing with both grief and depression. It helps to know that your story is both unique and also something that is shared by others.

If nothing seems really to resonate, don't worry about it. Just skip to part two and leave the stories out. And so—on with the story...

The first significant death I remember was when my Aunt died of cancer. I was fourteen and I remember being sad, but not really understanding very much. My sadness was not very deep or long lived, even though I had been quite close to her.

My grandfather died when I was about seventeen. I was very close to him and had spent time staying with him and helping him work his farm in central Washington State. He was diagnosed with pancreatic cancer, and I remember visiting him and being shocked at how this strong and healthy man had diminished. Only a year earlier I had difficulties keeping up with him stacking eighty pound hay bales in the hot summer heat. He was in his early seventies then, and I was sixteen. Now he was stooped and thin, wracked with pain and nausea. This time the sadness sunk in more deeply. I also felt fearful though—fearful of what was happening to my grandfather and of all of the unknowns of death and the frailty of the body. Rather than cherish my last moments with my grandfather, I found myself wanting to get away. Later, at his funeral, the tears came and I was able to feel my sorrow.

In contrast to this, when my other grandfather died he had been failing in health for a while and didn't seem to me to be very happy in his life. He had a stroke and went into a coma. I went to the hospital to visit him with my family and remember feeling a strong sense of joyful freedom for him. I couldn't explain this feeling and felt guilty about it at the time. As I stood by his hospital bed, I reached out to touch him and felt the strongest sensation of energy flowing that I have yet experienced. It felt like a strong flow of electricity, but cool, passing from my hand to his body. It surprised me, and I pulled my hand away quickly. I don't know if there was any connection, but a short time later he woke up and was able to say goodbye to my grandmother.

In each situation of death, I found differing reactions and differing degrees of attachment, but my reactions to death tended toward a greater sense of peace and acceptance as I got older. My experience with meditation, study of philosophy, religion, and psychology, and my experiences with energy and momentary connections with what I now think of as the Field all convinced me that death was not an ending and not something to be sad about. It was sad to say goodbye, but the actual passing on seemed to me to be more a graduation than a termination—something that could even be celebrated.

None of this study and experience prepared me, however, for the death of my wife, Joy. When she died, I found the gap between what I believed I knew and what I really understood to be huge. In fact, before I began to feel better, I went through a protracted time of total confusion in which I didn't believe in anything anymore. I felt lost in a trackless fog where nothing I had known before made any sense and where there was nothing solid to hold onto. All my pompous philosophizing was lost in the moist world of emotion, and all my study and learning seemed to be ludicrously tiny and inadequate. She was gone, and for a while it felt like most of me was also gone—mired in a tortured swamp of emotion and loss.

While wandering in this swamp of emotion, I decided I would go to a place I had found a few years earlier in Thailand and stay with the monks there. Perhaps a bit egotistically, I thought I could go spend some time being quiet and looking directly at the emotions and then I'd come back all fixed up and ready to get on with things.

I got much more than I bargained for in my time at the temple. I became a Buddhist monk for two months and learned a great deal about what it is like to live that way. I found it to be, in a way, a practice for dying—to be a monk is to let go of the attachments that normally gives us a sense of security or identity. House, car, job, money, relatives, friends, country, language, food, entertainment, comfort—all of these people and things may or may not be in one's life again. As a monk I realized that there was no control, and intentionally gave up control of any of these things. Just as in dying, everything—including my hair and clothes—was left behind and there was nothing left of what used to give meaning and identity to my life.

To be a monk, for me at least, was an opportunity to confront the emptiness and meaninglessness that hide in the deep wells of fear that lurk in my (and I believe everyone's) subconscious and to learn to look more closely at my *self* stripped of all the embellishments, objects, and relationships that generally give meaning and definition to who I am. It was also a total cultural immersion in which almost nothing of my own previous experience in life meant anything or had any corollaries. I ate different food, slept on a wooden bed with no padding, wore monk's clothing, lived without air conditioning in a climate completely opposite to the coolness of Northern British Columbia where I had lived all of my life. The language, customs and culture, beliefs and philosophy were all very different from what I had known before.

At the temple I was taught not to *do*, not to strive, not to focus, not to try. Most of what is valued in Western society was thought to be highly unhelpful there. All our busy-ness, trying, striving, intending, manifesting, focusing, creating, building—to the monks these things are just empty running about that results in greater fear, tension, and suffering. Even grief was seen in a completely opposite manner. While in Western culture grief is seen as inevitable and necessary, at the temple it was simply an ego attachment that was best dealt with by simply letting go.

While I was in this environment and had the support of the monks and my teacher there, I did find that I was able to "let go". I began to think about Joy less and to feel less bereft and desolate. The panicky fears and the deep anguish grew less intense, and I felt like I was coming to a place of greater peace with the situation. Perhaps, if I had stayed there, this would have continued and I really would have just "let go".

I had gone to the temple with the intention of staying only one month but ended up staying nearly three months. However, I had a limited leave of absence from work, and I was not ready to confront my fears of permanently letting go of my job, house, and security. I felt that I had to return home, and so I left the monkhood[35] and returned to my home in Canada.

Upon returning home, I found I had been deluding myself in thinking that I could get away from my feelings by going away. Returning home was extremely difficult for me, as it compounded a deep sense of reverse culture shock and uncertainty about how to reconcile the diametrically-opposed lifestyles of the monk and the "normal" Western person, while also hitting me with memories and reminders of Joy and all that was no longer in my life. I returned to my empty house, to her clothes and belongings, to the places we had been, and reminders of what we had shared together. My return brought with it the experience of grief as something that has its own mind, its own time, its own rhythm, and its own pace, and I was thrown back into the emotional swamp that I had left to begin with.

During this time I suffered from various physical issues that would mysteriously come and go. The left side of my face had a worrying numbness, my body ached and hurt often, my left leg and hip began to be troubled by sciatica, my head felt pressured, and an inexplicable fear lurked just below the surface waiting to jump out at me whenever my guard was down. Seeing things that had belonged to Joy or going to places we had visited together brought an involuntary feeling of loneliness and loss that panged itself into my stomach and chest with a strong physical force.

In addition, my mind gradually lost the clarity I had felt while at the temple in Thailand. While there, I had experienced an increasing feeling of being in touch with my mind and body and even a tantalizing closeness to other dimensions and beings that had previously been beyond my perception. Feelings and desires passed through my system more quickly, my body felt healthier and lighter, and I felt less stuck in my emotions. When I

---

35 It should be explained here that, in Thailand, becoming a monk is not considered to necessarily be a lifetime commitment. Many people become monks for a week, a month or a few months at some point in their lives. It is considered to be an action of great spiritual merit both for the men who become monks and for their families and friends who support them.

returned home, this clarity and easy flow of feelings slowly faded away, and I experienced a profound sense of loss of touch with myself that helped to propel me into a deeper depression.

I felt a lack of energy that made going to work each morning into a huge challenge; each morning required what seemed like an epic battle in order to get myself to move and leave the safety of my bed. I felt stuck, unable to choose what to do with myself or my life. I was afraid to leave my job as a counsellor with the school district but also afraid I would be unable to continue it. I went to work each day with a feeling of overload and came home feeling heavier and more unable to return the next day. It seemed like life was piling more and more upon me, and I was going to break down and be unable to cope.

This was also probably the most fearful and painful time of my life so far. When I was with Joy I was full of certainty. I knew we were meant to be together, we could handle whatever came, and I was able to be sure and solid in my sense of who I was. Our love for each other was all that was needed and because of it there was plenty of extra to give to others as well. Even during her sickness, there was never a question for me of sacrifice or difficulty in caring for her. It was such a privilege just to be with her that it did not seem to be a hardship at all. She was so courageous—how could I do less?

However, after she was gone, all these feelings of courage, optimism, and hope were dashed to the ground and seemed to be irretrievably buried. I was cyclically angry at being left behind, despondent, and sad. I wanted to cry but couldn't, and then would be blindsided by tears or sobs unexpectedly. My perception of the world was gray and hopeless. I could not make a choice about anything—even choosing what to cook for supper (or to have supper at all) was overwhelming at times, and I lost interest in most of what I had previously loved. I felt I had very little energy left over after work and would come home to be alone, then pace restlessly around the house or waste time watching YouTube videos or aimlessly surfing about on the internet. I tried to write but often found myself unable to come up with anything to say. I felt like a hypocrite, writing about all these "awakened" practices and not living them.

My desire was to get on with life and to live what I had been taught at the temple—"just let go". Letting go, however, seemed to be something that required a state of mind that I was unable to achieve any longer—a clarity that I had lost after leaving the protected environment in which I had learned it. Along with my despondency about being alone, a kind of panic began to build that I was slipping into a state of suffering from which I would be unable to return. My body and mind seemed to be conspiring to hold me in a state of fear, contraction, regret, and sadness that was totally anathema to what I believed and to how I wanted to live. I could see myself stuck in what amounted to a selfish longing for more of what I could not have and lack of gratitude for the precious gifts of Joy's presence in the time that we did have. I could see myself violating my own beliefs and principles, and yet there didn't seem to be anything I could do to change it.

I found that after the first couple of months, people were not as ready to hear my story and problems anymore. All my friends and family were still polite about it, but it became obvious that I had complained too much, talked about my feelings of loss too much, and repeated the same fears about the same circular inabilities to make decisions, and they were tired of hearing about it—or felt it was no longer helpful to enable my depression. I was told by five different people on seven separate occasions that I should look into antidepressant use, though I stubbornly refused to do so. I am not sure if this was an egotistical rebellion against the use of drugs or if it was a good choice. I felt highly incompetent in everything having to do with choice making.

During this time my outer world and inner world became quite different, so much so that I began to worry secretly about creating a personality split at some point. Outside I was returning to the "same Todd" that people had known before and keeping up an appearance of being reasonably together. Inside, I felt like I was falling apart and continually raking the pieces together, adding more glue to make it look like I was a whole person. I was worried about my mind state and the lack of depth it seemed to have. From a mind that had been so clear at the temple that I could reach into any emotion and simply let it pass away into a clean emptiness, I was now stuck with a mind that spent most of its time singing inane little ditties to itself and bouncing randomly among unhelpful thoughts. Rather than a kind of mental Teflon like I had experienced at the temple, now I had mental Velcro. Emotions and thoughts—especially negative ones—along with the physical sensations in the body that were their corollaries, stuck immediately and would not move on.

I had been home for about four months when the strain of all of this finally became too much for my body. I had not been really sick for several years, and so it came as a shock to come down with an illness. Not only did I become sick, but it wouldn't go away. For weeks it came and went. I would feel OK for a few days, then have flu symptoms or cold symptoms. It made the fatigue worse so that there were some days where I hardly got up at all and many others where I would have been much happier not to. In my previous mind state, even physical ailments would generally slide away easily. It simply took going to the depth of mind at which the ailment resided and letting it go. At that time, though, my mind was stuck on the surface like a buoy on the water, and I couldn't touch the depths that were in turmoil within my consciousness. This, of course, only added to the despair I felt.

I had a two-week holiday for spring break and decided to visit some friends who had a cabin in the woods that I could stay in. The cabin was a rough log cabin, built by hand some thirty years earlier, located a ten minute hike from their house through the snow. It had electricity and a small wood/gas cook stove but no running water. It looked like I felt—sagging into the soil, roof covered in moss and leaking slightly, hunkered into a small clearing both protected and darkened by the forest of spruce and cedar. I had come both seeking and fearing solitude, and now I had it.

Not only did I have solitude, but I had my illness as well. When I arrived, I felt weak and tired, and even the short walk to the cabin seemed difficult. My first night I felt very alone and though I did not mind being alone in the woods before this, I felt afraid.

I had decided to seek this solitude to try to face the feelings I had been running from—the feelings of loneliness, loss, and fear and the choice that had been hanging over my head for months. I felt I needed to decide if I was going to let go of my house and job and all of what previously defined my sense of self and security and return to the temple in Thailand or try to stay where I was and hope that time would eventually bring a solution to the problems I was facing.

Joy's death, and its direct connection to my stay at the temple in Thailand, had caused a kind of perceptual break for me. I had lost my ability to see myself as having very much control over what happened to me in life and had a fear of being simply a pawn in a game. I didn't believe in the world as it was portrayed by my culture—the objective/material viewpoint—but I was unable to experience subtler levels of the Field as I had in the past. It felt like stumbling around in a dark maze with no idea of where it was leading, what I was doing there, or how to change my fate in any way. I felt like a game piece, directed by somebody else, simply doomed to suffer.

I became rather fixated on the first noble truth of Buddhism during this time. It seemed like suffering was, indeed, the only truth of life. I was less optimistic about the possibility of escape than most Buddhists though and found myself being alternatively afraid that life does carry on after physical death, dooming us to the endless cycle of suffering, and that it doesn't, ending instead in nothingness. Either way, I mostly saw suffering and meaninglessness.

In fact, any way I looked at it, it came down to the idea that there was no meaning or purpose to anything and no real choices either. As I looked around me through my gray and dismal perspective I saw my parents aging and struggling more with health problems, my brother and his family struggling, my friends struggling, people all around me hitting their walls, leaving their partners, dying of cancer or struggling with illness, all of us heading for death through a series of experiences over which we had little or no control. What's more, I saw all of us heading for loss—the lucky ones were the partners who managed to die first I thought as I looked sadly at elderly couples and young lovers alike. My mood was very black, sad, pessimistic, and contrary to everything I believed in.

Depression is like this. As a complication or adjunct to grieving or as a condition on its own, depression is a voice from the darkness telling us that what we thought was true no longer works for us. Depression robs us of our faculties, paints gray ashes on our world, and takes away hope. It drains away energy and initiative, derides optimism, and both scorns and fears cheerfulness. While wrapped in its dark cloak, the desire to continue living can grow faint, and sometimes the main barrier to suicide is that one lacks the energy to do it.

I can't say if my friends and family who recommended antidepressants were correct or not. Many who suggested their use had been helped themselves by the medication, had experienced depression, had recovered, and had been able to eventually stop using the medication. In their experience, the medication was a helpful tool.

GARDEN

For some people, depression can become an endless bog that traps them for years, or even a lifetime. From the depths of this bog of listless gray, medication can be a ray of light and hope and it can be a useful choice. However, depression does also have a function and a purpose. In the middle ages in Europe there was often a place in the garden hidden deep in shadow and gloom that was reserved for depression and melancholy. *Saturn's garden* is a place to feel damp and cool emotions, settle into the moss and gloom, lose one's self in the fog, and let go. It is a humbling time and a time of reshaping where the images of self, desires, and beliefs that we have held can be unmade like so much potter's clay, then lumped and smashed together so that they can be reworked and shaped again.

There is very little place or time for Saturn's garden in today's world. Perhaps the young people who take on the Goth style help to keep it alive, though most don't understand why they are so fascinated with darkness and death. Our modern busy-ness does not leave any time for melancholy, however, and perhaps this is why there is such prevalence of antidepressants. Most of us don't know how, or aren't able, to find a refuge in which to experience and honour the feelings of depression and allow them to do their subtle work.

I was fortunate to be able to find a refuge and stay there, though the time was short. The cabin in the woods became my Walden for a week—a place to allow the feelings to be, without expectations, and to be refreshed by the solitude and by nature. It helped, though I think I needed time in the order of months, rather than just a week, really to honour and use the depression as a time in Saturn's garden and to allow the healing that it could bring.

My week in the woods saved me from antidepressants but still left me with uncertainty about what to do with my life or how to change it so that I could live more fully within my beliefs. I still felt like a hypocrite, living one way and preaching another, and I was still caught between two worlds. From the perspective of Western psychology, I was experiencing a reasonably normal grief pattern, of which depression is an important part. From the perspective of what I had been taught by the monks at the temple, I had lost my clarity of mind and was staying stuck in ego-driven clinging and desire rather than just letting go and being free.

Looking back at this time, I can see how both the perspective of the monks and the Western perspective are correct. Ajahn Brahm,[36] an English monk who studied many years in Thailand, has much to say about grief. He describes his observations of people in the village where he lived and how grief was not something that was a part of their lives. They loved each other and cared for each other as much as anywhere else, but they understood the principle of change, and they did not spend time in suffering over loss that was out of their control. For people in this village and by extension, Ajahn Brahm suggests, most of the people brought up in the Thai culture, grief is an unnecessary and basically self-indulgent emotion. Long expressions of grief are not in alignment with an understanding of the true nature of life and the reality of change. How can one grieve over loss when one knows fully well that it is an inevitable part of being alive? How much better it is to give thanks for what was beautiful and continue into the future with an even deeper understanding of the nature of change. A person who truly understands the reality and meaning of change lives this life without fear and without anxiety or grief.

I, however, was not brought up in a culture where an understanding of the nature of change and its influence were a part of my heritage. Instead, I grew up in a culture that does everything it can to hold on to youth, deny death, deny loss, and hold on to security. In my culture, romantic love is

---

36 Ajahn Brahm currently resides in Australia, where he is the spiritual director of the Buddhist Society of Western Australia. He is an author of several books, as well as insightful lectures that can be found on YouTube. His home website can be found at: http://www.ajahnbrahm.org/index.php

idealized as the highest and best that one can attain, and most of the popular songs, movies, TV shows and magazines advertise the desirability and necessity of being in a good relationship with a beautiful (or handsome) partner.

Not to point blaming fingers only at my culture, my own nature seems to be strongly drawn toward being in a loving relationship as well as to holding on to what was good in the past. At the time, I still struggled with anxiety and searched for security, I looked at old photographs and reminders of good times that had gone by and I often saw my world through the sepia coloured glasses of the "good old days that are gone". I'm not particularly proud of this, but it is true nonetheless. Simply "letting go" and moving on didn't come easily for me.

Instead, I found myself sitting blankly and staring into the distance while memories and images ran through my mind and grief sludged through my heart and stomach. I caught myself picking up a remaining piece of her clothing and holding it to my face to try to recapture a hint of her smell or the softness of her touch. I tortured myself with memories of things we had done together, meals we had cooked, times we sat in the sunshine in our kitchen or worked in our garden, movies we'd watched, and trips and adventures we had enjoyed together. I wandered through the silence of my home and wallowed in how alone I was in the emptiness, in the space that her absence created. I longed for her touch—the soft and gentle strength of her hands, the smell of her hair, the comfort and security of her body next to mine, the warm openness of my heart when she was near. Despite all my training in how I ought to be dealing with these emotions, thoughts, and feelings, there was quite a long time where I didn't care. I wanted to just lose myself in the sadness.

In many ways, it felt like I had little choice. The feelings would come in waves and just overrun my defences. I could go to work and basically seem to function through the day acting on old programs, smiling when appropriate, then come home and feel like just a shell of a person, not really there. In the silent emptiness of my home, I would find myself crying or curled up in a ball on the bed or stumping about aimlessly, feeling lost and alone.

In my counselling with adults and children, I have often talked about the different stages of grief that are classic to Western psychotherapy. These stages begin with shock and denial and progress through anger, bargaining, depression, and finally acceptance. I found myself sliding in and out of these stages on a regular basis and wasn't particularly satisfied with them as an aid or explanation for how I felt. Sometimes I was angry, most of the time I was depressed or sad, once in a while I would feel a tentative tendril of acceptance or even joyfulness, and then it would go back into anger or sadness or depression. I have to admit that I did see a generalized progression where sadness, anger, and depression slowly gave way to longer periods of acceptance, but my experience was that all of these feelings got jumbled together as often as not and chased each other in circles.

There were other feelings to jumble into the mixture as well. Grief is seldom connected to a single issue or cause. It drags into service all the old tragedies and traumas as well. For some people it can include huge amounts of guilt because of what they did, did not do, or think they should have done. I spoke with a woman once who had completely fallen apart after the death of her child and who was unable to forgive herself. She felt she was in some way responsible for the death, and she became stuck in the vicious circle of grief reinforced by guilt. To her, grief was an accusing finger thrust in her face pointing out all of her faults and failures. Forgiveness is a powerful antidote, but it took a long time for her to begin to be able to use it.

As mentioned earlier, strong emotions have the ability to pull up feelings that are connected to all experiences that are even slightly related. Along with this tendency to act like magnets drawing out all similar past experiences, emotions also have addictive qualities, and once caught in the grip of one of them, it can be very difficult to let it go. This was certainly true for me at times. I found other people's ideas of what I should be feeling, how I could get over things, or what I could be doing to make myself feel better to be unhelpful at best and highly irritating at worst. A stubborn part of me didn't want to get better, and I especially didn't want to be told how to feel better by someone else who wasn't having my experience.

There is a kind of masochistic pleasure in wallowing in the depths of sorrow, and perhaps a real benefit as well. People much too quickly try to rid themselves of despair with medication or a forcefully cheery disposition. There is a fine line to walk between the repression of an emotion and attachment to it; the location of this line can only truly be known by the person who has the emotion.

While it is true that it is not beneficial to hold on to grief and/or depression and that it is detrimental to become identified with it, it is also true that it is often not helpful to try to make it go away with medication. The heavy cloak of grief brings a darkness and despair that, if heeded, can reach into the depths of our hearts and minds and speak to us of the truths of life. This whisper of deeper truths from the cool moist depths of Saturn's garden is also a place where awakening can begin.

* * *

As suggested at the beginning of the chapter, this first section has mainly been a story of my own, somewhat unawakened and ordinary experience of pain and loss. That is the point of this section, however. Grief is *ordinary*. Pain and loss are common, everyday experiences. Each and every person on this planet will experience loss, pain, and grief at some point in his or her life. Every person on this planet will experience the death of others and eventually his or her own death—and yet most of us fight the experience of grief, sorrow, pain, and death with all our might. We expend huge amounts of energy in denial of death or in struggle to avoid acknowledging it or accepting it. Awakening to grief, however, as well as to depression, begins by simply letting go of the struggle.

There is a story that was told to me by a Buddhist nun. This story begins with a man pushing his wife in a wheelchair. She is very ill, and it is feared that she will die. The woman asks the man to tell her the story about the Prince and his Wife. So, the man begins:

> "There was once a prince who married a beautiful princess. They were perfect for each other and loved each other dearly. They were never separated, did everything together, and never grew tired of each other's company. One day, however, they were traveling through a forest and a great snow storm came up. They were separated and lost. The woman found a cave to shelter in, but the snow was so heavy that it caused an avalanche and the cave was sealed

off. The prince searched frantically, but he was not able to find his wife in time.

Vowing never to forget her, he took her body home. Of course, this did not work for very long because she began to decay. Still he vowed to keep her bones forever and to honour her memory by never letting them go and taking them with him wherever he went.

Several years later he was traveling again, carrying his wife's bones with him in a bag. There was a rock slide from which he barely escaped, and he lost the bag carrying his wife's bones. When he finally found the bag again, all the bones were crushed and broken.

Still, he vowed he would keep her memory, and so he had what was left of the bones made into a powder, and he carried it in a bag around his neck, still vowing to keep her with him always.

cremation

Yet again, years later, he was traveling on a ship, and a great storm came up. In the storm, the string around his neck was broken and the bag was carried away by a large wave.

In desperation he screamed at the sky "I still have my memories, and I will always remember you my love. You will always be with me".

At that moment, in the midst of the storm, a glowing figure appeared and spoke to him. "What will happen, it asked, if you lose your memories. How will you hold onto her then?"

With this question the prince finally realized the truth—he could not hold onto her forever. She was already gone. He had to let go."

The story ends with the husband kneeling by an empty wheelchair and weeping. His wife is already gone. She came back to ask for the story to help him so that he could let her go.

When I was a Buddhist monk, I was taught repeatedly to *let go* and to see everything as *OK just the way it is*. These two ideas are not met with happiness by the rational mind or the ego because the mind is always trying to fix things and get itself out of situations which it deems to be uncomfortable. Living the truth of *everything is OK just the way it* is requires understanding that we only have two choices when it comes to what is already in existence. We can accept it, or we can struggle with it. The mind, especially when lost in a wailing and desperate sense of loss, is generally not interested in the idea that its desperation is unnecessary or that its loss is *OK*. How can something so horrible be OK?

The trick is to understand that the feeling has no effect on the situation. No matter how awful I feel, Joy—my wife and my love—is still dead. At a certain point in the process of my own grief, this statement metamorphosed from an angry and pain filled accusation hurled at God to a soft wisp of acceptance pulled like a silk ribbon from my chest. The anger, loneliness, and sadness still return. The acceptance isn't permanent—but it is there. It's a good start.

The gift of the wailing desperate intensity of strong feelings is that they demand attention. They scream "look at me" and in their forceful scream-ing they offer with great clarity the only choice that we truly have. We can choose to surrender into the feeling, offer it our thanks and blessing, and let it go, or we can choose to fight it, deny it, and try to get rid of it. The feeling is there—this is the truth of the moment, and is not negotiable or in any way under our control. Within this momentous truth, we can choose to bless the moment or to fight with it. As we choose, we receive the reflection of our choice. If we choose to fight, we get more and deeper pain. When we choose to accept, we begin to release ourselves from the obligation to feel hurt, and this is the doorway into a more awakened understanding. As U.G. Krishnamurti says "...the problem is that you think there is a problem".

It is this simple realization, found perhaps in the intensity of a pain that seems to be tearing one apart, which defines the Awakening in the emotion. We all know how to fight with reality, and indeed that is what most of us do most of the time. However, to awaken to the moment is to surrender to it, to step out of resistance and simply say "thank you" to whatever IS. Grief is simple and common. It is as deep as the deepest ocean, as wide as the widest sea, as wild as the greatest storm—and it is also simple, common, and every-day. It comes without our bidding, stays for a while, and—unless we cling tightly to it—eventually passes on its way again. While it is here, it is best to treat it as a friend, welcome it in, give it thanks, and always be ready to let it go.

With this in mind here are some suggestions for working with grief that I have found to be helpful. Some come from my own experience, some are helpful things others have told me; all are relatively simple and common. Perhaps that is why they help...

- Grief is like a physical wound. It hurts, it takes time to heal, and it heals by itself. You don't have to do any-thing—just give it time and love and be gentle with it.

- Grief happens in little pieces. Little bubbles rise up, often at unexpected moments, and burst. Don't get caught up in the emotion that they bring. Say thank you, and let them go.

- You may go numb for a while and it may feel like you can never love again, like you can't feel your heart, like you are more separate and alone than you've ever been. This can be very frightening. Don't worry and don't give these feelings your attention. Keep saying thank you. Keep going through the motions of being alive. Like the winter turning into spring, you will open and bloom again.

- Don't try to hurry or set a time-line on your grief, but don't hold on to it either. Let it come and go as it will, welcoming it with gentleness and forgiveness when it comes and releasing it with gratitude when it goes.

- Grief is physical as well as emotional and cognitive. Many, perhaps most, people experience real physical pain as part of the grieving process. Take care of your body, but don't become fixated on the pain. Eat well, exercise, get enough sleep, remind yourself that the pain is not forever. Let it go.

- Don't make hasty decisions –the old adage that you should not make major decisions for at least one year has a lot of wisdom in it. On the other hand, allow grief to break you out of old habits and open new doors. Grief is a deep connection with awareness of change and with a deeper understanding of where true value lies. Listen to its voice and let it take you into deeper connection with yourself and with what is important to you.

- Let go of the *things*. Give away clothing and belongings, take down the decorations in a child's room, change things in your house and your life. Like the prince in the story, you can vow to keep the person with you in the memory of things—but it will only bring further suffering. They need you to let them go—and though it does not seem like it, you need to let them go as well.

- Sometimes it may feel like you are losing your mind, going crazy, or falling apart. Remind yourself that "This is not a crisis. This is changing. I am OK". Many people experience these kinds of feelings. It is OK, it is not forever, this will also change.

- Allow yourself time to be alone, but don't completely lose touch with others. If you need to force yourself to go out and talk to a friend now and then, then force yourself. It's important.

- Walk a lot.

- Journal, write, draw, dance or perform your feelings and thoughts. Use whatever medium works for you and in which you feel comfortable, but express what you feel. Expression in these forms is a good way to be open and listen to your own inner voice as well as to ask for help. It is often surprising what answers you will find by simply being open and then writing—or expressing in some way—whatever comes into your mind.

- <u>Read.</u> There are many helpful books about grief. The one I personally found most helpful was suggested to me by a friend who said it "jumped out at her" from a library shelf. It is called *Seven Choices*[37] and is about one woman's path of recovery from loss through awareness of affirmative choices along the way. It also includes many people's stories of their own grief and recovery process and the author's research into the psychology of grieving.

- <u>Be in nature.</u> Be with animals and trees and let yourself feel their gentle nurturing energy. Let it in.

- Sit in the sun and soak it in.

- Honour yourself and your process and give yourself gentleness and gratitude.

- Smile, even though you don't want to.

- Notice little things and tiny moments of beauty or joy. A flower in a pavement crack, a warm ray of sun on a winter day, a stranger's smile, a shooting star, a sunset, a blade of grass in early spring... remind yourself in little ways of the beauty and continuity of life.

- Allow yourself to become simpler.

As I write this chapter, I know that grief is still a guest in my house, my body, and my mind. She has become gentler and her wailing voice has lost most of its strident insistency. Her voice and presence are still there though, a background whispered keening that sometimes troubles my sleep and floats up in bubbles of melancholy, loneliness, depression, or listlessness—but the intensity has diminished. She is a more silent and polite guest. Sometimes she even sits with me and comforts me.

Though it may seem like the most common and trite thing of all, perhaps it is also the most comforting, simple, and true in the end. Time does heal.

---

37 *Seven Choices: Finding Daylight after Loss Shatters Your World* by Elizabeth Harper Neeld (2003)

This will also change. It is OK to let go.

Chapter 13
Love

Perhaps all the dragons in our lives are princesses who are only waiting to see us act, just once, with beauty and courage. Perhaps everything that frightens us is, in its deepest essence, something helpless that wants our love.

Rainer Maria Rilke

True love begins when nothing is looked for in return

Antoine De Saint-Exupery

Love is unfortunately a very badly misunderstood concept. In the objective/material worldview, the single word *love* covers a range of emotions from lust to control and from compassion to unconditional positive regard. However, it is also *just* an emotion, and as such, it is based on a combination of biological and psychological factors.

We seem mostly to be confused about love. We fall in love and out of love. We are dependent on having a special other in our lives in order to experience love, and this special other must have very specific and particular qualities. Love is something that we receive from this person and give to this person, but is something that we do not generally give ourselves. Love is a commodity, something that is in short supply, something that must be found outside ourselves. In many different ways it is bought and sold, used as a source of power over others, and traded for loyalty, sex, money, gifts, favours, and a thousand other things. Love is lust, love is physical, love is an emotion, love is spiritual, love is pure, love is dirty, love is unconditional, love is control… Love is what we crave and cling to in a partner because we have forgotten how to give it to ourselves.

The extent to which our lives are centered on the search for love is so huge that it is seldom recognized. Like living on a round planet (such as the earth) but believing that it is flat because it is so big that it has the appearance of flatness, our lives are centered on the search for love but this search is so big that it appears to be just life. In the book *Eat, Pray, Love* Elizabeth Gilbert writes of a counsellor friend who worked with Cambodian refugees. Her friend expected the refugees to want to talk about horrifying experiences and trauma, but instead they mostly ended up talking about relationships, love, and their searches and struggles with both.

We go through life looking for love in everything we do and not under-standing that this is what we are doing. Many of us become so confused and lost that we give in to fear and live our lives inside an emotional fortress, finding fear and violence outside and protecting ourselves with more fear and violence. Now and then we find someone for whom we are able to open a small portal in our fortress. We let him or her in, expecting that love will hurt us because it has always done so in the past. Sure enough, this next person hurts us too, and yet another door is closed and another layer added to the walls of our castle/prison.

To see fear and violence in the world, and pain in love, is not an error. It is true that there is a tremendous amount of fear and violence in the world. It surrounds us constantly—in exactly the same way that we are bombarded by hundreds of thousands of radio waves from cell phones, radio stations, television transmissions, and other radio sources. The waves are there. It is a matter of our choice, however, and the equipment that we have with us, that determines what we tune into.

What many people don't understand, unfortunately, is that it is impos-sible to find love while tuning into fear, hate, and violence. We think we are fragile beings, threatened and lonely, insecure and overwhelmed, and we tune into the frequencies that accompany these beliefs. In the feedback loop that works between the Field and the mind, our deep unconscious beliefs filter and colour the information that is sifted out of the barrage of data that is constantly available to us. This mass of data is filtered to correspond with what we believe; we experience the world according to what we allow ourselves to perceive, and we use our experience to confirm our beliefs. This can become a very vicious circle indeed.

If we believe that there is violence and hatred in the world, we are not wrong. There is ample proof of this easily found anywhere we look. However, violence and hatred are only a part of what is happening, and they are based on a particular way of understanding who we are as individuals and as a race of beings. We are free to experience as much violence and hatred as we wish—but when we are ready to begin to change this experience, the change has to begin on the inside.

The world offers us raw data in quantities that we cannot hope to process. Our personal experience of this data depends on what we sort out from it, and this depends on what we believe. Therefore, belief comes before experience—always. Like the mustard seed,[38] we need to have faith in the power within us that can sprout through the hard outer shell and create life. When we know that we are filled with life and with love, we will see and experience these things around us as well.

We cannot find on the outside what we do not cultivate on the inside—quite the opposite in fact, we do find and see exactly what we focus on and cultivate inside ourselves. For this reason, the world that we see cannot be changed by acts of violence or even acts of goodness that come from the motivation of fixing what is wrong with things. Love is not found outside ourselves until we are able to connect with some part of our own love for self and others on the inside. This connection can then extend outward and begin to change the frequencies that we tune into (and therefore give our strength to). This is the way to change our experience, and this is the way to change the world. It can only happen like this, from the inside out, one person at a time, as one by one we awaken to a deeper truth and a deeper understanding of the nature of the Field of which we are a part.

---

38 "And Jesus said unto them, "Because of your unbelief: for verily I say unto you, If ye have faith as a grain of mustard seed, ye shall say unto this mountain, Remove hence to yonder place; and it shall remove; and nothing shall be impossible unto you." Matthew 17:20. (Holy Bible, King James Version)

This profound and subtle shift—the shift of understanding that what we see is a reflection of our own mind and that we are responsible for our own mind—is a central shift in the Awakening. As we realize that love starts with deep acceptance and forgiveness inside, and as we open our hearts to self-forgiveness and self-acceptance, we begin to see and experience forgiveness, acceptance, and love on the outside as well. As, one by one, we add our strength to the love frequency, we help to amplify this frequency so that it is more easily tuned into by others and more people are able to experience it, even if their ability to tune in is weak. One by one, we add our strength, and one by one, we help to make our own lives and the lives of those around us more peaceful, happy, and fulfilled.

As we awaken to the truth of our own mystery and beauty, and as we have the courage to look into the dark and hidden places of the soul and see the light, we also step into a new world. There is no need to leave the world or change the world or fix the world. All that is necessary is to forgive deeply and profoundly and release ourselves from the judgments with which we have condemned ourselves. When we accept ourselves, we can change the filters through which we judge and the world, and so forgive it as well. Forgiveness is always circular, beneficial inside and out.

Though the mind may scream that this is wrong, can't work, will be proven wrong by experience, and many other arguments, just accept the words, give them love, and practice kindness. Belief precedes experience. Therefore, contrary to what is expected in the objective/material worldview, if we practice love and forgiveness, they will become our experience.

While not denying or negating all the understanding that has come before, the energy paradigm offers a way of understanding love that is both simpler and larger than the previous way of seeing it. As in all cases where the concepts of the Field and of energy are applied, things become clearer, make more intuitive sense, and the range of possibilities also expands. Moving to this new understanding of love is an essential part of the Awakening.

The number of people who are choosing to love rather than to fear is growing rapidly in this world, though this does not appear to be so when listening to the cacophonous racket of the media. An essential choice for those who are awakening is which voice to listen to—the voice of fear as pushed and exploited by media and governments everywhere, or the voice of love which is quietly growing and swelling, one individual at a time, all around the world.

This choice is the first step in understanding love. In the paradigm of energy, love is simply an energy source and a vibrational frequency, and as such it can be accessed by anyone at any time, regardless of circumstances. As an energy source, love is a form of very subtle high frequency energy and it is the energy on which everything else in the universe is based. Kind of like the basic rectangular building block in a Lego set, love is a basic building block on which our universe is built. This is, however, not something that can be proven at this time, so it begins with a choice. What do you want to believe, and what do you want to promote?

In his book *Shantaram* novelist Gregory Roberts' main character speaks of being tortured and realizing, as he is chained to the wall and feeling the agony of the inflicted pain, that he is free—free to choose to hate the people who are doing this to him or not. Monks from Tibet who have been captured and tortured by the Chinese while being held in prison have said after being released that one of their fears in prison was losing compassion for their prison guards. Jesus offers perhaps the most compelling example of the choice between love and fear as he says "...Father, forgive them; for they know not what they do,"[39] even as he is hanging from the cross by nails through his wrists and ankles. These are all examples of extreme situations in which people realize that even in the extremity of pain and deprivation, they are free to choose between hatred (which is really fear) and love. This choice then determines their own experience—hatred increases the suffering and pain experienced, and love decreases it.

Most of us do not have to experience these extremes, thankfully. However, we are still given the opportunity each moment of every day to make the choice between love and fear, and this choice has a very real effect on our own well-being as well as the well-being of people around us and of our world as a whole.

---

39 Luke 23:34 (Holy Bible: King James Version)

As we navigate this physical reality, the choice between love and fear is both important and very real. However, at a deeper level, it is important to realize that *Love* is not even a choice and that even fear and hatred are simply love in another form. Just as a child can build Lego into whatever form he or she imagines, love can be shaped by our imagination into any form we choose. Even hatred, cruelty, pain, and fear spring from the ultimate source and are part of the Field that is activated by the energy of love.

This realization is extremely powerful if understood correctly. It does not mean that it is useful to continue to focus on hate or fear in our choices of thoughts and actions in this physical reality, but it does mean that there is nothing that we have to do to fix these things either. Like water poured over sugar, the understanding that everything is love dissolves the darkness and soothes the pangs of the deep wells of pain and fear. Even the darkest well and deepest pain is ultimately filled with love because there is nothing else. Rather than fight the darkness, all that is needed is the understanding that it truthfully does not exist. At the deepest level, the wells of terror and agony dissolve into a peaceful sigh of release. There is nothing more to do, nothing to fight, nothing to overcome, nothing to fear. Even the darkness is made of light, and as this realization seeps deeply into your soul, it will set you free.

Although at the ultimate level everything is love, at the level that we experience on a daily basis there are distinctions between experiences that are more pleasant and life giving and those that are more painful and life taking. At these less-than-absolute levels of perception, love is experienced as a higher vibration and is associated with actions that contain compassion, integrity, and kindness. From the energy perspective, love is an energy source that is both constantly in motion and constantly surrounding and a part of all things. Remember, choosing to focus on love is like tuning a radio to listen to a particular station. All the other stations are still out there on the airwaves, but the one that you experience is the one that you have chosen. It doesn't matter if people around you are listening to other stations, you can still make your own choice and tune your own radio.

As was discussed earlier, however, this radio has a two-way function. As you tune to the love station, it increases your energy, decreases your stress and fear, and increases your state of internal well-being. As your well-being increases this is broadcast back and spreads out around you, adding more well-being to the field. As more people play the love station, it increases its strength so that people who have had difficulties receiving the station before can tune into it. It is like this that the Awakening and the change of consciousness of our race will happen—not suddenly, but gradually as one person and then another awaken to the choice and start consciously choosing to love.

At first, the choice to love seems very difficult. What is love? How can I do it? Why don't I feel it? Like fish in an ocean, we are swimming in the energy of love—and the potential experience of love, but we are so accustomed to it that we don't realize it is there. We have become accustomed to thinking of love as mostly related to sex and almost always related to something that has to be done for, or received from, someone else. Love, in the objective/material paradigm, must be traded. While it is true that trading love increases experience of it, trading is not essential. Nothing needs to be done to experience love—it simply IS.

Take a moment to be still and to consider what it could mean if your basic nature, the very fibre and material of your body, mind, and spirit were made from and immersed in the energy of love. Consider what it would mean if this thing that we are seeking is actually what we are made of, not separate from us, not something that has to be searched for, sacrificed for or suffered for, not something that has to be taken or given, stolen or bought, forced or extracted, cajoled or manipulated. What if your nature, your being, your existence, is love? How might your way of seeing the world change if this were true?

Part of the difficulty of experiencing love is that it is not something that can be easily experienced with words, thoughts, or the conscious mind. Love is a foundational energy and is therefore very easily formed into whatever we choose to make with it. If the mind imagines fear, the love energy around us condenses, slows its vibrations, and restricts its flow in our bodies so that we can experience the fear that we have chosen. If we choose to hate or destroy, love energy becomes hate and destruction and this is what we experience. Like clay that can be moulded into any shape but still retain the quality of being clay, love is the action potential of the Field, taking the shape and aspect that is directed by the consciousness within the Field. We direct our own small part of this consciousness, and so we mould the energy into the likeness of our own mind state and then see the reflection of ourselves in what we have made.

If love can be anything, though, doesn't that rather muddy the waters and make it more difficult to understand? If everything is love, how can we account for hate, suffering, and violence? How do we know what to fight against and what to search for? How can we know what to do and how to act? How can we possibly sort out what love is and what it isn't if everything is love?

This is a very important point, and it is a way to get out of one's head and into one's heart. Stop making distinctions, stop making judgments, stop seeing one thing as good and another as bad or thinking that you can discern what love is and what love is not. The first step in recognizing love is knowing that love exists in all things, all actions, all people, and all thoughts. Stop judging, fixing, searching, and striving, and focus on the intention to just let things be as they are, let people be as they are, and see things as they are and *not as you want them to be.*

Love, like any foundational truth, is actually very simple. When the mind is quiet and the heart's wounds healed, love is the soft whisper that guides us in our joy.

Chapter 14
Loving yourself

There are two basic motivating forces: fear and love. When we are afraid, we pull back from life. When we are in love, we open to all that life has to offer with passion, excitement, and acceptance. We need to learn to love ourselves first, in all our glory and our imperfections. If we cannot love ourselves, we cannot fully open to our ability to love others or our potential to create. Evolution and all hopes for a better world rest in the fearlessness and open-hearted vision of people who embrace life.

John Lennon

We accept the love we think we deserve.

Stephen Chbosky

Probably the most important thing that one can do in one's life and the greatest gift that can be given to the world is to learn to love oneself. This sounds perhaps like an overly inclusive and strong statement, but I firmly believe it to be true.

To understand the importance of loving oneself, and how it can affect the people and world around us, it is important to have an understanding of what love means in this context.

As already explained, love can be thought of as the energy from which everything in the universe is made; it is also the flow of this energy as it moves from the source through the manifest universe and back again to the source. Although the terminology I have used here may not work for everyone, I think that every religion or human system of philosophy has a place for love and an understanding of some form of the idea of *agapé*—love that is given freely with no need for return or repayment. It is generally understood that love entails giving and that this giving should be free and without strings or requirements. However, it is less often understood that love is energy and that, like electricity, it flows in a circuit.

To say that electricity is similar to love, it should be noted, is a bit like saying that a leaf from a single tree in the Amazon represents all rainforests of the world. There are some properties of leaves that are similar everywhere, but the forests of the world are much more complex than the single leaf can illustrate.

Still, a leaf's worth of understanding is better than no understanding, and there are some properties of electricity that can be useful to help in understanding love. In order to be useful, electricity has to *flow*—it has to move from a source through a resistor of some sort (light filament, dishwasher motor, heater) and then back to *ground*—back to the source. It is the movement of the electricity that makes it useful and *manifest*. If it is not moving, it can be held in a battery as a potential, but it is only a potential. To become real in a way that we can see, feel, or experience, and to actualize the potential, the electricity has to be allowed to move.

In the same way, love is only a potential until it is allowed to move. In a practical sense, all of us are giving and receiving love constantly simply by the default condition of being alive. However, most of us greatly decrease the amount of love energy that is available to us by believing that we are less than we truly are and by believing that we are less good, worthy, or capable than we truly are. By decreasing the amount of energy that is available to ourselves, we also decrease the amount of energy that is available to give to others and decrease our ability to shine the light of love into the world. This is the reason that learning to love oneself is so important. Love of self is the first and most important step in loving anyone else, and it is only to the extent that we love ourselves that we are able to love others.

The Golden Rule states "Do to others as you would have them do to you".[40] Unfortunately, the Golden Rule often does not work very well because human beings almost invariably do unto others what they believe themselves to be worthy of. In my many conversations with children, I have been astounded by the lack of worthiness that most children feel, and this lack of deep worthiness is endemic with adults as well. This lack of worthiness is also a foundation for all kinds of bullying, abuse, vandalism, power struggles, and other forms of violence—both in schools and in the adult world.

Of course, there is a difference between what the conscious mind thinks and believes and what goes on in the deep and often dark waters of the unconscious. Many people, especially those who are most in need of self-esteem, consciously believe that they have high opinions of themselves. Although it is possible to bring our deeper beliefs about ourselves into the conscious mind, they generally live far below the surface of our awareness and direct our actions without our knowing. There is a big difference between having a strong ego and actually loving oneself.

Self-love can be confused to mean feeding the desires of the ego, which generally involves interaction with money, things, power, sex, and/or violence. In fact, it is quite easy to tell the difference between true self-love and ego love because true self-love does not require anything more than is already present—no matter what that happens to be. It can take place in a mansion with a billion dollar bank account or in a hovel without enough to eat. It can take place for an executive of a huge corporation with the power to influence world commerce, a president of a country with power to influence the laws and policies that govern millions, or for a person who lives on the street and is ignored by everyone. Though it is generally easier to find without the hampering distraction of money or power, money and power do not automatically mean that is impossible to love oneself.

Self-love can also be confused with putting one's own needs before the needs of others. In some cases this is necessary—as in the example of oxygen masks in an airplane. It is necessary for adults traveling with small children to put on their own masks before helping their children. This makes sense

---

40 Luke 6:31 (Holy Bible: New International Version)

because if the adult passes out from lack of oxygen he or she will be unable to do anything to help his or her children anyway. It is necessary to take care of oneself in order to be able to have anything positive to give to others. However, when taking care of oneself begins to mean taking from others or hurting others, it has begun to be turned inside out.

As we begin to increase our level of self-awareness, through the practice of meditation for example, it can become increasingly clear that our actions and perceptions are directly linked. Who we think we are is constantly reflected back to us by the way we perceive the people and events around us. The more hatred, violence, and judgment we feel inside, the more we see it outside of ourselves as well. The unconscious mind, however, is unable to distinguish between inside and outside and so it sees this outside violence and fear as internal violence and fear. This is, of course, frightening and uncomfortable, so the unconscious mind then tries to get rid of the fear by putting it outside again. This only makes more fear, and the cycle rapidly increases its intensity. Conversely, the more we refrain from harming others with our thoughts, words, or actions, the more we also refrain from harming ourselves. Seeing worthiness on the outside creates belief of worthiness on the inside, and this also creates an ever-increasing cycle—but in a much more pleasant and life giving direction.

If one is aware of what happens inside when one commits cruel, selfish, or harmful actions, the action itself becomes its own punishment. We cannot harm others without also harming ourselves. However, we can hide from this fact by pushing the awareness of our own pain into our unconscious minds. This generally results in chronic muscle tension, decreased sensitivity and less ability to experience joy or pleasure. It also distorts the flow of love energy in our bodies and restricts our ability to receive love—which is really our life force—from the universe.

This becomes a self-sustaining cycle. Decreased ability to receive love results in increased internal discomfort, decreased ability to feel pleasure and increased experience of need. Being unwilling to face these feelings, the conscious mind searches for more power, more money and more violence in order to fill the increasing sense of emptiness inside. A person in this state cannot stop for long without the emptiness enveloping them. They therefore are trapped in a growing spiral of destructiveness and pain as they literally attempt to take life from others in order to replace the life-energy that they have cut off by their own actions.

A common way to create loyalty in followers has, for centuries, been to force a person to commit an action so abhorrent that they could never forgive themselves. This has been, and probably still is being, practiced in Africa when young people are recruited for militias. These young people are forced to do things like kill their own parents, participate in torture, or participate in slaughter of innocent village people. Once they have done this, the horror of it becomes a wall of pain that makes it nearly impossible for them to examine their own minds and actions. They lose their ability to feel the pain of others because they have lost the ability to experience their own deep loss, pain, and feelings of guilt and horror. These people can then become truly cruel.

Although most of us do not experience this degree of separation from our ability to love ourselves, still most world cultures are not very good at supporting love of self. In one way or another, our ability to act as clear channels for the love that flows into and through us is diminished, bit by bit, as we age.

To get an idea of how your subconscious mind treats your internal self, try paying attention to the following things for a few days:

- Pay attention to the judgments that you have about other people. In traffic, in shopping lines, at home, at work—what do you hear yourself saying about people? Can you pick out a repeating theme? (Incompetence, stupidity, unworthiness, uselessness, lack of value, wish for harm, or violence, comparison…)

- If you have a spouse or partner, pay special attention to your judgments of him or her. These reflections will be especially close to the things in your shadow that you do not want to own. These are the things in yourself that you have labeled as bad, unworthy, unacceptable, or evil.

- Pay attention to the things you think to yourself when you make mistakes or you are not feeling good. Look for themes or repeated recordings in your mind.

- On a scale of 1 to 10, rate yourself in the following areas:

1. Physical appearance

2. Personal power

3. Popularity

4. Intelligence

5. Worthiness of love

Paying attention to these things can give you a good idea of the level of esteem you have for yourself and will give you a baseline to work from. Be careful not to use the results of this exercise as another way of getting down on yourself. Just note it without further judgment and then use it as a foundation for change. It is very likely that these exercises will point out some ways in which you can be more kind, loving, and compassionate with yourself.

Exercise for loving yourself

What if everything you feel, everything you are, everything you see, everything you can experience in any way is a product of the Field, activated by love energy? What if even every negative thought, every pain, every fear or illness or anger is made from love energy used in unhelpful ways? What if every cell in your body, every ache, pain, tension, neurosis, pleasure, and desire is simply a swirling sea of energy activated and made of love?

This is likely to seem very far-fetched and strange to imagine, but for a few moments allow yourself to suspend your disbelief, ignore your dissenting thoughts, and imagine that nothing exists that is not love.

Find a quiet and comfortable place to sit or lie down. Close your eyes, breathe deeply into your abdomen, and sink softly into the warm sea of love that surrounds you, penetrates you, IS you. Let your thoughts float by like clouds—give them no attention.

Know that you are already there, already whole, already everything that you need to be. Allow the awareness that you are already love to penetrate to the core of your being.

There is nothing left to do or to fix or to change.

There is nothing left to heal or to finish.

Just breathe. Relax.

Who you are is enough.

YOU are enough.

Be grateful.

Let Go.

Remember: The key to manifesting anything is to know that it is already yours. You don't have to feel like you are enough. It's already enough to know that *enough* is there in spite of what you may or may not feel. Say thank you to whatever you are experiencing. Let it be.

Chapter 15
Love's different levels in the body

Love consists in this, that two solitudes protect and touch and greet each other.

Rainer Maria Rilke

If you judge people, you have no time to love them.

Mother Teresa

As you release yourself from your mind's preconceptions and arguments, and as you begin to experience your body more fully, you will begin to find that love feels different according to the level, or chakra, from which you are experiencing it. Love responds to the frequency and intention of the consciousness that directs it. Just as clay takes the shape that the potter gives it, love takes the form and flavour of the intention that guides it.

At different times in our lives, we develop our understanding of different aspects of love. One is not necessarily better than another, and each has an important part to play—just as the music of each instrument in an orchestra plays a part that goes together to become a beautiful symphony. The base tones are lower vibrations and the treble tones are higher, but that does not make one better or more important than the other. Both are important in the music. In the same way, love can be experienced from lower and higher vibrational viewpoints. Each of these has positive and negative aspects and each of these is a part of the symphony of love. As we learn to understand

and experience each aspect more clearly, the strength and beauty of our own symphony also increases.

The Chakra system offers a helpful framework for conceptualizing different levels of love and how each is experienced and expressed. You don't have to believe in chakras for the ideas to be useful—they can also be thought of as psychological stages of development or parts of the structure of character. However, the energy system that chakras are a part of offers a much larger and more flexible understanding than what can be had with psychology alone. As you move into the awakened worldview, the energy perspective will be increasingly more meaningful for you.

There are 7 major chakras in the body, and many other smaller chakras as well. There is a great deal of literature available about the chakras, their meaning, and cultivation of these energy centers. We will examine them only briefly here—further reading is recommended if you wish to learn more.[41]

1. The Root Chakra

The first chakra is physically located behind the pubic bone in the area of the perineum and is associated with the adrenal glands and the "five F's" reaction—"fight, flight, freeze, fuck, or feed"—which also correspond to the brain stem and our most basic and primitive ways of responding to the outside world[42] . From the level of the first chakra, love is something that is experienced as a shared connection with others and the need for group survival. With respect to love, the first chakra is the center of group consciousness, connection with family, tribe or group, and connection with the physical world. *Need* is emphasized, and love from this level is often very needy,

---

41 As with most things these days, an internet search will yield a great deal of information about the Chakras. One book recommendation that combines western psychology with information about the chakra system is: *Eastern Body, Western Mind: Psychology and the Chakra System as a Path to Self,* by Anodea Judith (1996). Another good book, from a much different perspective is *Healing Chakra: Light to Awaken My Soul* by Ilchi Lee (2002).

42 As explained earlier, we can fight with or run from something, and if neither of those actions work then we can freeze like a deer in the headlights. If we don't have to do these things then it's safe so we can either eat it or try to reproduce with it. These are the basic functions of the reptilian brain, and also the basic functions of the deepest level of our own brains.

clinging and focused on lust, instinctual sex, and procreation. It is also about protection of family and *tribe*—the group that is identified as your own.

Unawakened love from the first chakra can be dull and brutish. Sex is animalistic and automatic, and loyalty to the group as well as animosity to anyone outside of the group is also automatic. Negative, or unconscious, first chakra love is extremely self-centered, self-protective, possessive, and protective of a chosen group. This kind of love is based on the judgment of *in* or *out* and this judgment can change rapidly. If a person is judged to be *in*, they will be protected at all costs. If *out*, violence is generally very near at hand.

When awakened, this chakra moves more into conscious awareness. The root chakra's strong identification with connection to a group expands to an understanding of the spiritual truth of *oneness* of all things and beings within the Field. As this chakra's power is accessed, it becomes a source of vibrancy and physical health and energy. This is the chakra of connection with earth, with the physical, with the body and with biology. As such, its awakened energies tune into love that is deeply connected to the earth, rooted in the physical, and able to act in harmony with nature.

The first chakra is the home of the Kundalini energy—the energy that is said to rise up the spine from the root chakra to the crown chakra when a person has a deep spiritual awakening. It is the source of vibrant physical energy, creativity, and the ability to feel secure and safe in the world. The root chakra is also particularly connected with the *6th* chakra, or third eye, and so awakening of the first chakra is also connected with the groundedness necessary for successful awakening of higher spiritual understanding and with psychic abilities.

Unawakened first chakra love is often seen in movies or stories about Greek heroes and in Biblical stories from the Old Testament. In these stories, "love" often means willingness to protect, to serve, and to stand with. Between men and women, love of this kind is generally about the physical act of sex and the survival based business aspects of betrothal—linking of families or groups and redefining the lines of who is *in* and who is *out*. This kind of love is expressed in words and actions having to do with service, protection, duty, loyalty, fealty and debt. It is also expressed in neediness, clinging, insecurity, and the feeling that one can't live without one's partner. V

With the collective guilt that is experienced by western cultures at this time, the fears of climate change and impending disaster, and the constant barrage of anxiety mongering by the media, insecurities in the first chakra are quite common. Added to this, there is also an increasing sense of disconnection from nature and from the source of our food and basic survival needs as cities grow and agriculture becomes relegated to factory farms. Taken together, all these factors tend to cause difficulties in developing the first chakra. Clingy, needy, and insecure love relationships, anxiety, adrenal overload, obesity and weight issues all have connections with this level.

The root chakra is the seat of physical and emotional strength, vitality and security, and is too often considered to be "low" or not worthy of attention. A strong foundation is needed for further development. As people awaken, the root chakra energies may transform from their instinctive, survival-based state to a deeper, more conscious awareness of connection, security, oneness, and safety.

An affirmation that can be helpful when faced with first chakra issues is *I am. I am safe.*

Nature is a wonderful teacher and healer, and each chakra has nature experiences that can help to remind us of its strength and vitality. For the first chakra, going barefoot in a natural setting at dawn and sunset can be strengthening, soothing, and revitalizing.

2. The Sacral Chakra

The second chakra is located above the genitals and near the navel. This chakra is primarily concerned with the sexual organs and the physical, sexual, and energetic functions of relationship and sexuality. It also expands the individual survival energy of the first chakra to a wider focus as it is concerned with survival of the species.

Love from this level is primarily sensual and sexual in nature. It is concerned with physical attractiveness, physical contact, pleasure, the sexual act, and the powerful biological urge to reproduce. It is also concerned with both the romantic idea of relationship and, at a generally more unconscious level, with the instinctual and functional level of relationship. Second chakra love is what is found in Harlequin romances, most "love" songs, and most of what our present culture deems as "romantic love".

A closed, or still sleeping second chakra, which is unfortunately very common at this time, creates repressed, distorted, and addicted behaviour. When out of balance, second chakra love is confused with addiction and with escape through pleasure. When this happens, the drive for personal pleasure can easily turn to substance abuse, relational violence, and relational abuse of all kinds. Alcohol, cocaine, heroin, crack, meth, marijuana, sugar, over-eating, smoking, gambling—all of these addictions are related to second chakra weakness.

The same needy emptiness and unbridled obsession with appetite and desire that is at the bottom of substance abuse is also a powerful aspect in physical, sexual, verbal and emotional abuse in relationships. Although relational abuse also involves power issues from the third chakra and control issues from other levels as well, it is based in first chakra insecurity and second chakra neediness. Victims and abusers will seek each other out, not understanding that they are simply opposite sides of the same coin. People who find themselves continuously in abusive relationships would do well to work on the second chakra before attempting to find a new mate.

An unbalanced second chakra also contributes to sexual dysfunction in both men and women and to physical problems with the prostate, bladder, uterus and other genital organs.

When awakened, the second chakra becomes a deep source of stability and personal power and is the well from which the emotion of joy flows. It promotes comfort with one's own emotions and the ability to share deep intimacy with another. Located at the body's center of gravity, it provides physical balance, dexterity and grace. It also balances the energies of instinct and desire and allows for conscious fathering or mothering as well as deep sharing and savouring of all sorts of sensual pleasures. Sexuality and sharing of the sexual act is unencumbered with repression or fear and also free from addiction and need so that love is a free giving and receiving of pleasure with another. This love forms strong pair bonds and strong family bonds and provides a firm and peaceful base on which to build the structure of community that can promote the survival of the species.

A second chakra affirmation is *I am enough. Everything is already OK.*

Nature experiences for the second chakra are moonlight and water, ocean, waves, floating, swimming, skinny dipping and dancing in the rain.

3. The Solar Plexus Chakra

This chakra is located between the navel and the sternum, in the area of the solar plexus. It is associated with will, individuation, self-confidence, worldly action, and power. It is also a center of relationship in that when we establish connections with other people, we exchange energy with them. In addition, this is the center responsible for digestion and transformation, taking in the energies from around it, and digesting and transforming them into experience that can then flow and be released. It is associated with the stomach, pancreas, and digestive organs.

The solar plexus chakra, when awakened, is a center of supportive and confident self-love that is connected to a higher sense of Self rather than just the small ego self. It provides the energy for passion in life, including passion in love, and is a source for strength, authority, personal grace and ease. It also is a center for humility and *power-with* rather than *power-over*. Strong function in this chakra provides a sense of self-worth and charisma and enables a person to move from the second chakra pair bond to the larger community with strength and effectiveness.

In its unbalanced or negative form, love at this level is centered on possessiveness and control. It requires a hierarchy, seeks to dominate and be in a power-over position, or to be victimized, controlled, and powerless. Shame and unworthiness are closely associated with this chakra, as are tyranny, cruelty, bullying, and the need to control others in any way.

Balanced and positive love from this level entails having a strong enough sense of self-worth and self-confidence being able to allow others to be themselves without the need to change them. It does not need to control or force itself on others and is able to enjoy contact with others without possessiveness. It radiates a strong sense of self, of confidence, and of security and is very attractive to others.

A third Chakra affirmation is *I deeply love and approve of who I am. There are no failures—I learn from everything I do.*

Third chakra nature experiences include activities involving *sunlight, sunflowers and summer.*

4. The Heart Chakra

This chakra is the most well-known of all of the chakras and is the place from which it is generally thought that love originates. The heart is in the center position of the seven main chakras and is the chakra of unification. There is a pattern moving up the chakras of focus on individual and then on collective aspects of concepts and functions. The first chakra's focus is individual survival, the second is on relationship and survival of the species, and the third is on individual self and empowerment. Continuing this pattern, the fourth chakra extends the solar plexus level empowerment of the individual self to empowerment and acceptance of all people, ideas, and things. The heart resolves paradox, unifies opposites, and allows for acceptance of people and things, just the way they are.

When unbalanced or closed, the heart can be overwhelmed with grief and can also be enmeshed in a kind of giving where seemingly "selfless" or kind actions are done with an expectation of return or with strings attached in some way. A wounded or closed heart can become angry and "spiky", pushing people away and not accepting nurturing or love from others. It can also become cynical, cold, and judgmental and in doing so become tangled in solar plexus power issues. A closed or un-awakened heart is often fearful, hateful, blaming, condemning, despairing, longing, or envious. It demands love from others but is afraid to look inside and realize that love must come first from within.

Awakened love from this level develops into unconditional and nonjudgmental love. This love is given without any strings attached, simply for the sake of giving it. This love can also be given to anyone, regardless of marital or family connections, race, opinions, or religion. Heart level love is the first level of transcendent love and allows for a love that is pure, not needy or attached, and not troubled with greed, possessiveness, or power issues. It is also a level where love is expressed from our own individual truth and authenticity, rather than as a reflection of cultural or religious expectations.

Awakened heart level love realizes that there must be self-love before there can authentic love for others. It flows naturally with its own light and warmth, warming and lighting the people around it. Heart love is open, flowing, generous, kind, compassionate, and freeing. This is the love that lets something, or someone, go and welcomes them back again if and when they wish to return or stay.

A heart affirmation that can be helpful is *I forgive myself. I am willing to love everything about myself.*

Nature experiences include being in natural settings at sunrise and sunset, the season of spring, and untouched natural settings.

5. The Throat Chakra

This chakra is located in the throat, between the head and heart, and links our ability to respond mentally and logically with our ability to react emotionally. This chakra is the center of creativity and verbal expression as well as all other forms of expression. It is also associated with hearing and being able to hear or listen to others.

When closed, imbalanced, or asleep, fifth chakra love becomes repression of self, lack of self-expression, judgmental repression of the rights of others, and disconnection between head and heart. Self-confidence and self-love are repressed and held down and we can lose sight of our own truth, tying ourselves to the truth of another, becoming lost in someone else's cause, sometimes to the point of fanaticism. We also become insecure about the truths we cling to and feel a need to defend them, push them on others and judge others as wrong. In its association with hearing, a closed fifth chakra results in not being able to hear others, not listening well, and not honoring the truth of others. It often results as well in a feeling of not being heard or listened to and of not being respected for one's own opinions and ideas.

The throat chakra has a strong connection with the sacral chakra and therefore plays a large role in relationship and sex. When closed, this chakra inhibits sexual expression, creative playfulness, and the deep authenticity that is necessary for awakened sex. In this case, sex tends to become repetitive, surface, boring, and unsatisfying; it is a meeting of bodies only, without an accompanying meeting of mind, heart, and spirit.

When awakened, this chakra combines the energies from all of the other chakras, synthesizing all these energies and giving them expression; it is therefore the center of expression of self. It is also at the beginning of the transcendent levels of energies and so connects the little self with the larger *Self*. Love from this level involves speaking the truth fully, clearly, and courageously as you see it. It also involves recognizing that "Truth" is not absolute and that there are many truths. It continues the recognition of non-duality begun at the heart level and begins to accept both pleasure and pain as being part of the same continuum. An awakened fifth chakra gives understanding that others can have their own opinions and beliefs without trying to change these beliefs, "win" an argument, or belittle another person's ideas. It is OK to both hear and be heard, to honor the ideas of others, and to be respected for one's own ideas.

At the level of the fifth chakra, love is not personal or attached and has very little connection with desire, physical pleasure, or reproductive imperative. Instead, love is about self-discipline, being able to follow one's own inner guidance, ecstatic self-expression, speaking and living one's own truth, and allowing others to live theirs. It is also about equality, lack of judgment, and having the freedom to live and express oneself in one's own unique way. These qualities, combined with an open second chakra, also allow for a sexual experience that becomes a deep and spiritual dance of self-expression, creativity, and profound authentic sharing of self with another.

Possible throat chakra affirmations are *Everything I do is an expression of love. I accept my own creativity and wholeness.*

Nature experiences include exposure to blue sky and reflections of the sky in water.

6. The "Third Eye" or Brow Chakra.

Moving up the line from the root chakra, each succeeding chakra adds a new aspect while also integrating the characteristics of the chakras before it. The third eye chakra is sometimes called the "command chakra" because its physical actions are on the pituitary and pineal glands, which are in turn in charge of regulating the rest of the endocrine system. It is also the seat of mental powers and is the highest center of command of all of the body's physical and mental systems. In addition, this chakra is thought to be the seat of psychic powers, providing the possibility of conscious connection with planes and realities that are at higher vibrational states than the physical.

Love at this level is completely different from the love found at any of the lower levels. The energies of this chakra function at the meeting place of the opposites that make up this physical universe and the level of manifestation of the material world from the subtle energies of the Field. The differences between male and female are less distinct, and such things as attachment, social connection, physical pleasure and continuation of the species are not of high concern.

Of course, all the chakras work together, and depending on the state of awakening of each of the chakras, the sixth chakra can also change. In the case of a relatively closed sixth chakra a person will tend to be very fixed on the physical reality and the five senses, unwilling to experience or believe in anything else, and will be very attached to the objective/material worldview. Most people in this situation, if they have made it this far in this book, will now be very close to throwing it out, or at least deciding that it is not for them. People in this situation will have difficulty experiencing the depth that is possible in relationships and their worlds will be severely limited by the scope of what they can believe in. In love, they will be rational but generally not yet able to experience the joy and connectedness of the meeting of souls or expansion into the subtle energies that can enhance intimacy and sexual experience.

In the case of a relatively awake third eye chakra, along with relatively open lower chakras, a person will have a much deeper and broader perspective of the universe and of the possibilities at their disposal. In love, they will be more intuitive and able to connect with a partner at a depth that goes far beyond the attachment and emotional ups and downs of the lower chakras. At this level, love is for all beings and is also detached from all beings. When applied to a personal relationship, it is a meeting of souls and a contact of energies at many levels. There is great freedom, deep respect, and a kind of constancy that goes far beyond the trials, tribulations, beliefs, and limitations of this world. Affirmations for third eye energies are *I live in the truth of my grace, beauty, intelligence and unlimited nature. I am responsible for the quality of love and happiness in my life.*

A third eye nature experience is exposure to stars and the night sky.

7. The Crown Chakra

Although there are other chakras located beyond the physical body, the crown chakra is the final physical point of connection with the energy of the Field as it is referred to in this book. It can also be thought of as the point of connection with unified consciousness, God consciousness, or ultimate being. At this level, understanding of the universe opens to a vastness that dwarfs even the worlds and universes accessed through the psychic senses of the sixth chakra. The crown chakra is the seat of unity and the source of the experience of oneness, connection to all things, and bliss.

Love at this level is not personal or attached in any way. From the viewpoint of the crown chakra intelligence, we are all equally brilliant and infinitely valuable individual points of light, part of the light and energy of the whole of creation. We are immortal beings, experiencing life and creating our own realities according to our vast previous experience and our desires. There is no death or life, separate and distinct from each other; they are both a part of the same continuum.

When this chakra is closed there is a sense of disconnection, fear, existential angst or lack of faith. Depression is common as is the opinion that there is nothing beyond this human life. Death is seen as a black hole into which all of us fall and there is nothing beyond this point.

An awakened crown chakra extends our universe immeasurably and connects us with the awareness that we are not alone, that we are not separate from the source of all that is. From the awareness level of the seventh chakra, there is no longer a need for attachment to physical love, as the impossibility of being truly separated from love is understood. There is no need for, or lack of, love; it comes directly from the source and does not depend on anything that can be obtained in the physical world. If the crown chakra awareness is fully awakened, the ups and downs, emotions, suffering and joy of the physical world become unimportant, and love is something that simply is, extended and enacted through all things and beings. Love at this level is universal, completely detached from judgment, and in no way tied to possessiveness or individuals. Everyone and everything is worthy, complete, and whole simply by the fact of being. Nothing else is needed.

Although it is possible to find exercises for practicing the awakening of this chakra, it is something that will happen in its own time and through trust and simply allowing more than through specific practice. The Crown chakra is at a level where practice ends and where the consciousness of the ego cannot go. People who have awakened this chakra report the experience of being able to use the mind at will, but being fully free of it as well. It has been described somewhat like "cloud" computing—letting go of the individual processor of a standalone computer and plugging into the data cloud that is accessible from everywhere. Time takes on a different meaning. Thoughts, words and actions happen as needed and in the moment of need without forethought or afterthought. One lives fully in the moment.

The Symphony of Love

Each person has the same basic "instruments", but every individual also plays his or her own unique symphony depending on the qualities and levels of flow in each chakra. This is part of what provides the vast and exciting differences in our world and also what makes relationships so educational and exciting. As we relate with others, we join our symphony with theirs and make new music.

The chakra system and all its associated concepts provides a helpful framework for understanding the complexity of love's symphony—individually and in relationship. This framework also helps to identify places where we could change our experience to make it more positive or more fulfilling. By honestly comparing our own way of expressing love with the chakra characteristics, it can be easier to understand where we may be creating unnecessary pain for ourselves or others and how we can improve or deepen our expression and experience of love.

Chapter 16
Awakened relationship

Don't rush into any kind of relationship. Work on yourself. Feel yourself, experience yourself and love yourself. Do this first and you will soon attract that special loving other.

Russ von Hoelscher

The purpose of a relationship is not to have another who might complete you, but to have another with whom you might share your completeness.

Neale Donald Walsch

...the only way a relationship will last is if you see your relationship as a place that you go to give, and not a place that you go to take.

Anthony Robbins

When I was a monk in a temple community in Thailand, the spiritual leader would often take a group of people from the temple traveling. I once asked about these trips, inquiring about what they did and saw. However, the response that I got surprised me. I was expecting to hear about interesting sights, scenery, activities, maybe about places where they had good food or met interesting people—the normal things that one thinks about when traveling. Instead, I got a short lecture on the proper purpose of travel.

Travel, I was told, should not be something that is done with the intention of getting something. It should not be an activity where we *do* this place or that place, go to *take in* the scenery, or to *take* anything at all. Instead, travel should be something that is done only if we feel we are able to take a sense of wholeness and blessing to the people and the energy or *spirit* of the place. *Don't go to take—go to give.*

Going to a place with the intention of giving requires a strong sense of confidence in a form that is not very common—in my experience at least. In order to believe that my presence in a place can provide a *blessing* in some way, I have to believe that I have something to give, that I am able to give, and that I am worthy of giving as well as receiving. I also have to understand the difference between the ego's idea of blessing and a way of blessing that is less cluttered by attachments, desires and insecurities.

For instance, if I go to a place with the feeling that I am superior, that I am giving the gift of my presence to this place in order to teach, reform, or change people, that is not a blessing in the sense that my teachers were thinking. In the same way, if I go to a place with the understanding that I am paying my way and I therefore have the right to expect a level of service, comfort, adventure—whatever it is that I expect—in return, that is also not what they were thinking.

Being able to give a *blessing* in the sense that they taught me is comparable to being a light. It doesn't matter if there is another light around or not. It doesn't matter if anyone notices the light or not. It doesn't matter if anyone uses the light or not. The light is simply there, and it gives its *blessing* by shining for anyone to see who wants to see it. This light does not expect anything, does not require anything, and does not have an intention to take from anyone or anything. The intention is to go, to shine as brightly as possible, to give light, and that is all.

To me, the idea that one does not take from a place when traveling but goes to give instead has far-reaching implications. What would it be like if everyone related to the world and each other in this way? How would the world be different if everyone had enough awareness of their own wholeness that they could make each action and choice come from the intention of giving and of blessing? If everyone felt and acted this way, we would live in a new and very different world—and this is exactly the point of the Awakening. It is possible to remember that we are whole and it is possible to consciously choose to be a light that shines this wholeness into the world.

When we go to a place and we are able to shine the light of our own wholeness, we give the blessing of a transformational vibration that can literally help to change the world. This is not a coercive thing and does not include expectation of change, superiority, or any of the regular "ego" desires and manipulations. Giving in this way is only about remembering who we are and shining this remembrance out for others so that they can more clearly see their own true reflections if they wish to do so.

If we visit this same place with an intention of taking, getting something, or needing something, we also change the world—but only by helping to maintain and strengthen the fear and insecurity that is already present. In this case, we tune into the channels of desire, attachment, fear, exploitation, and manipulation, and we add our own energy to these channels as well as strengthening these feelings for ourselves. This is not necessarily wrong or bad and is actually in alignment with the objective/material worldview. However, if you wish to live in a more awakened way or to help others to become more awake, it is not very helpful[43].

There are many similarities between travel and relationships. Both involve stepping into the unknown, encountering new customs and ways of doing things, experiencing new ways of connecting and sorting out differences. In the end, however, travel simply *is* relationship because everything that we do as humans involves relationship in one way or another. We relate with each other, with animals, with our world, with the objects that we own, and with ourselves. There is no part of anyone's life that can be devoid of relationship in one way or another.

---

43 There are often times and situations where we are not able to feel whole or to give. This is not something to feel guilty about or to beat oneself up about. It is, however, something to become aware of so that it can change more quickly and easily. There are times when a relationship needs to be released, a situation needs to be changed, or when we truly need to just allow ourselves to be nurtured and to receive this nurturing love. It is part of the adventure and challenge of life to know where we really are in each moment and choose our path based on this awareness, rather than trying to force things to be the way that we think they *should* be.

Intimate romantic relationship with a sexual partner is an idealized form of relationship that has not always been the norm. Other stories[44] of relationship have been more prevalent in the past. These stories include planned betrothals for alliances, power, or financial reasons, marriage for business, marriage for mutual support or physical survival, marriage as care-taking, and many other reasons for tying oneself to another. The idea of marriage and love coming together in the same package is a relatively new experiment—one which continues to have many growing pains as we move beyond the teenage idea of romantic love and into more mature ways of being with each other[45].

This adventure of reinventing love in intimate relationships is also very exciting however, and it is a part of the Awakening. As more people move away from the old stereotypes, sexual roles and expectations, and as our cultural understanding of intimate relationship matures, we stand on an exciting threshold of discovery. There are so many possibilities, and intimate relationships are the place where we can test our learning, open our hearts, find and accept our shadows, and learn to be in this world in more loving, gentle, kind, and life-affirming ways.

As we practice and realize new maturation within our relationships, we will also eventually come full circle and back to the primary awareness of the Awakening: *we are beings of energy and light, experiencing a human existence. What we see in this world is a reflection of what and who we believe ourselves to be.* Relationships of all sorts, but especially intimate relationships, are simply mirrors of who and what we think we are and of what we think the world is about. It is through our relationships that we come to know ourselves and also that we experience the adventures, playfulness and/or lessons that we choose for ourselves in this life. Although the many choices and difficulties

---

44 *Love is a Story* by Robert J. Sternberg (Oxford University Press, 1998) discusses the ways in which intimate relationships can be thought of as stories and discusses the kinds of stories that different people envision. It is a helpful book—and a helpful thing to know about your partner. It works best to find a partner who sees love with the same kind of "story" as you do.

45 For more about the history of Romantic love and how it is changing and maturing, see *About Love: Reinventing Love for Our Times* by Robert C. Solomon (Madison Books, 2001). Also, *Journey of the Heart: The Path of Conscious Love* by John Welwood (1990).

that arise in relationships can seem very complex, they are much easier to understand when viewed through this perspective.

Consider yet again: What if it is true that you are more than this physical mind and body? What if it is true that what you see and experience is a projection of what you believe and of who you believe yourself to be? (Something that is certainly true on a psychological level and up to you to believe or not on an energetic level). If these things are true, how would it change the way you see yourself, your partner, or your ideals and desires in relationship?

Regardless of the situation within a relationship, we are able—and obliged—to make choices. These choices can seem to be incredibly complex and daunting. However, the awakened perspective helps to simplify the choices and clarify what we are really doing. Although the way in which these choices are worded may change from person to person according to his or her understanding, here is a list of the choices that I find most helpful to remember when I am struggling in relationship:

- *I can choose to express wholeness* **or** *brokenness.*
- *I can choose to act from integrity* **or** *from blame and criticism.*
- *I can choose to give and receive* **or** *to manipulate and take*
- *I can choose to let go* **or** *to cling*

* * *

Express wholeness or brokenness?

You may be starting to notice that much of what is said in this book is repeated in different ways and that we are going in circles in some ways. If so, that's great! The truths of life are actually much simpler than we like to believe, and there is not really that much to know. Like the Buddha's flower sermon, discussed earlier, all that is needed for enlightenment can be said by holding up a single flower—if only we have the ability to understand.

The exercises and concepts in this book are all aimed at helping us to awaken within our relationships—intimate and otherwise. All the complexity, exercises, and skills are aimed at providing new ways of seeing ourselves so that we can relate to others in more wholesome, caring, and life-giving ways. Relationships of all sorts are where we get to test our skills and awareness and where we get to experience the results of our choices.

In an intimate relationship, all our beliefs about ourselves and about the world around us are played out on a very small stage, and it is on this stage that many of our most intense dramas occur. We can hide from ourselves out in the world, but it is much harder to hide from what we see behind the closed doors of our homes and the privacy of our personal relationships. Behind these doors, the façades are down, and we get to see our true beliefs about ourselves reflected in our opinions of our partners and family and in our reactions to the demands of intimacy.

The things that happen behind these closed doors can become hugely complex, difficult, violent, heartbreaking, and even terrifying. The complexity is so huge and the problems so endemic that thousands of books and millions of therapists are not enough to make them better. However, the complexity and the problems are based on a misunderstanding. They are based on the misunderstanding that we are less than we really are, that we are small, needy, selfish, dependent, fragile, and in many ways, *broken*. This is the deep subconscious belief best fostered by our present way of living and by the objective/material worldview—both its scientific and religious components. The simplicity of wholeness is almost completely overlooked.

In their book <u>2012 Awakening</u> Sri Ram Kaa and Kira Raa suggest that we should

> *"Redefine relationship as the soul-centered ecstasy of joyously celebrating the truth. ...All relationship begins in the ecstatic knowingness of your authenticity, of your wholeness."*[46]

"Wholeness", in this case, can be thought of as a deep sense of knowing that you are whole, complete, and OK just as you are. This state of knowing

---

46 Kaa and Raa (2008)

and being does not depend on your state of health, how your body looks, what you own, how popular you are, or how intelligent you are. It does not depend on who you know, how much power you have, or who you can influence. It is simply an awareness and internal belief that in this moment *I am worthy, I am OK, I am whole.*

This does not mean that you will not change or that there is no room for improvement. It does not mean that you don't need to pay attention to ideas or criticisms from others. It does mean, however, that you understand in a very deep and grounded way that it is OK to be you and that you can honor and accept whatever IS for you in this moment. This belief starts with something very simple: a choice. As you choose, so eventually you will experience.

From the perspective of energy and the Field, intention comes before manifestation. What you believe yourself to be is what eventually is expressed. Therefore, if you choose to believe that you are whole, eventually this is what you will experience.

Wholeness is not dependent on what is happening or on what you are feeling. If I know that I am whole, I understand that good or bad feelings are temporary, that I am changing and renewing in every moment, and that this will also change. If I believe that I am broken, I also perceive my experience as proof of that brokenness. "I am broken, I am bad, and I am unworthy". To the extent that this is part of my deep belief system, I will create aspects of this badness in all of my relationships—particularly my closest relationships.

In the same way, if I believe myself to be whole and OK, this will also become a part of my way of relating to others. Although the mind can rebel and lose itself in all of the complexities of "how" to do this, the choice is still quite simple. Believe in my own wholeness and worthiness or believe myself to be broken and unworthy. The choice has to come first. Once I have chosen with commitment, the information that I need for the "how" will begin to come to me.

When I make a choice for wholeness, I change much more than how I view myself. If I am whole, my partner is also whole, and if I am worthy my partner is also worthy. As such, she is worthy of my respect, my care, and my love, and I am worthy of hers. I can give these things because they are part of me; I can receive them for the same reason. I am worthy of love because I AM love.

This viewpoint is also a strong reminder of boundaries. I will respect myself enough to take care of myself and not tolerate conditions that are not respectful. I can choose to tell my partner what I need, to stand up for myself, and not allow myself to be a victim. I can choose to leave a relationship if my partner does not wish to live in a respectful way. I cannot force my own opinions or desires on my partner, but I am worthy of the strength and courage to love and respect myself.

Whatever the situation in which I find myself, I will be better equipped to deal with it if I start from a belief in my own wholeness and worthiness. Making this choice sets the foundation for fulfilling relationships and also for the other relational choices.

Another aspect of wholeness comes when we receive the opinions of others. I am sometimes asked to speak to classes about bullying, and one of the demonstrations that I use involves a tissue. In the demonstration I will casually pull a tissue from my pocket, blow my nose, and then offer the dirty tissue to the students. Surprisingly, some students actually volunteer to take the tissue, while others express their opinions with "pooh" or "yuck" kinds of noises.

The point of this demonstration is that we are constantly being offered gifts by other people. Many of these "gifts", like the tissue, contain all kinds of yucky stuff that the other person is trying to get rid of. What we generally forget is that we don't have to accept the gift that is offered. However, many of us, like the students who wanted to take the tissue, actually feel that we need to take this "stuff" that others thrust our way, and we make all kinds of extra suffering for ourselves because of it.

In the school yard, the "gift" that is given is generally something like being called an insulting name, being excluded from a group or activity, or being harassed in one way or another. It is harder to deal with physical harassment, but for things such as name calling kids can learn that they don't have to accept the "tissue". Instead of accepting the insult and feeling the need to defend themselves, children can choose to remember that the insult does not belong to them, let it go, and focus on positive thoughts about themselves.

A person who feels confident and whole is not bothered by insults or slights for very long because there is nothing for the insults to stick to. "I'm sorry you have a problem, but I'm OK. This is not mine. I like who I am. I can let it go". From this perspective, the insult that was offered truly is a gift because it has helped to remind me to pay attention to my own wholeness and to practice letting go. I can say "thank you" and move on.

This scenario holds true in the adult world as well. There are many situations every day, especially in intimate relationships, where we have the choice of taking something personally and being upset by it or of letting it go and not accepting the "gift". In many of the relational dramas that occur, the other person does not even know that they have done something that their partner finds offensive. A small incident is misinterpreted, and a small emotional fire starts when one partner takes offense; the fire grows as angry communication, puts the other partner on the defensive, and pretty soon there's a roaring bonfire of relational angst. Dramas like these are based on a basic belief in lack of wholeness that results in a perception of being wronged, anger, attack, and escalation of hostility. They can be eliminated simply by believing in one's own wholeness and not taking offense.

"Tissues" can be offered to, or thrust upon, others at many levels. The most difficult level to deal with, generally, is the physical level. When someone attacks us physically, it is generally time to get outside help. Students need to tell a teacher, and adults need to tell the police or find a way to ensure their physical safety. Physical abuse is a huge problem and not one to take lightly. If your partner is abusing you physically, you need to get help, and if this does not work, you need to leave. Period. Anything less than this is not being respectful of who you are or of your partner. Both of you need to get out of the victim/perpetrator cycle.

On a verbal level, "tissues" can simply be not accepted. Use of the Ho'oponopono prayer, focus on wholeness, and the practice of not taking offence can put out most "fires" before they even start. Sometimes, however, there are situations that are repeated or that hit us in places or ways that we just can't let pass. In these situations it can be helpful to use some of the exercises from the chapter on healing the past, to journal about the feelings, and/or to talk to a trusted friend or counsellor.

Since the verbal level is all about communication, using healthy communication techniques is important. If you still feel offended or hurt after doing your own work with an issue, and you need to tell your partner about it, it works best to use communication that shows that you accept your own feelings and that you can stay within your own boundary.

The simplest way to do this is to use the communication formula "When you (name what the person did)", "I felt (name what you felt)", "and I would like (say what you want)". Once you have stated *what happened, your feelings* and *what you want,* it is up to the other person if he or she will give you what you want or not. Your job here is to state your feelings and desires clearly— not to manipulate or change your partner. If your partner is unwilling to support you in what you need, you have a choice of letting it go, or of taking steps toward solving your problem on your own. Positive communication allows you to take responsibility for your own needs, rather than depending on your partner to meet them for you.

If positive communication is a problem for you and/or your partner, it is a good idea to learn more about it. A Google search for "I statements" will pull up a lot of very helpful information. If this is not enough then it can be very helpful to work with a professional to learn this skill. Being able to speak to people in a non-confrontational way can bring huge decreases in the amount of drama and trauma in your life!

Sometimes verbal "tissues" can become so prevalent and obnoxious that they become chronic verbal abuse. If this is the case, it is important for you and your partner to get help. Verbal abuse can be damaging in ways that are sometimes deeper than physical abuse and can undermine your ability to recognize your own wholeness. If your partner is willing to participate, learning to change communication habits can help to deepen a relationship and heal rifts. If not, it is time to seriously consider leaving the relationship.

"Tissues" can also be offered on an energetic level. This is generally much more subtle, but it is happening all the time. If you have ever experienced a feeling of being kicked in the stomach by someone's words, you have felt one of the less subtle energy "tissues". However, they are generally not this obvious. Energy tissues can feel like a sucking or draining feeling from some people, a feeling of confusion or loss of confidence around certain people, or all kinds of physical tensions, discomforts, or anxieties.

If you become aware of energetic "tissues" being offered to you by others, you can choose to not accept them in the same way that you can choose to not accept verbal tissues. (Energy "tissues" always accompany verbal or physical "tissues" anyway, but they can also happen without the verbal or physical component). Once you become aware of what is happening, you can use the Ho'oponopono prayer to clear your connection with this energy and give forgiveness to yourself and the other person.

Repeat the prayer until you feel the energy changing, even slightly. Take a few deep breaths and choose to remember your own wholeness, breathing in the awareness that you are a being of light and energy, whole and complete. This is not an emergency, you are safe. Feel the ground through your feet and breathe out any anxieties or anger that you feel. Allow yourself to have space inside and open yourself to the light that shines effortlessly through you from the source. As the source light shines out, the "tissue" becomes unimportant. Let it simply dissolve into the light.

An interesting exercise that can help to release energy "tissues" is the Catholic practice of crossing one's self. This may not be comfortable for you due to its religious connotations. However, the action actually works directly with your energy field and helps to release energy that has become stuck, regardless of any connections with religious beliefs. If you want to experiment with this, here is how to do it:

- With your right hand held about an inch in front of you, start at the top of your forehead and sweep your hand down the center of your body to the base of your chest

- Come straight back up to shoulder height and then over to the left shoulder

- Sweep straight across your chest to your right shoulder

- Come back to center and straight back up to your forehead

- With hand cupped and palm pointed down, sweep quickly down the front of your body and continue your arm in an arc away and to your side, as if brushing away a cloud of dust

- Repeat if desired.

You can also ask for help with energy "tissues". It can be helpful to ask help from whatever source is comfortable for you. Jesus, Krishna, Rama, Buddha, Allah, Archangel Michael, Mother Mary, your Higher Self, Universal collective awareness, Creator of all that is—it doesn't really matter who you ask. Just know that help is available, and it will come when you ask for it[47].

If you would like to learn to feel these energy "tissues" more clearly and more often you can simply set an intention to become more aware of them and start paying attention. You may be surprised what you discover. It can also be helpful to take classes—there are many energy awareness classes offered in most cities. Energy courses such as *Reiki, Healing Touch,* and *Theta Therapy* are good places to start.

Although the discussion of who is right, who is wrong, and who has hurt whom can become a seemingly insurmountable problem, the first step toward resolving the conflict is to remember your own wholeness and to act from it. The mind will be filled with "what if's" and will attempt to become confused or to find complexities that make it seem impossible to escape

Don't listen to your mind's arguments. Don't allow your mind to make more complexity.

Choose wholeness instead of brokenness.

This is not a crisis.

You are OK and you are whole.

Now look at the problem again, and use your skills to act creatively instead of re-acting out of old patterns.

---

47 You don't need to take my word for this. Put away your skepticism and try it, if you choose, and see what happens. (But be honest with yourself!). Also, you don't need to believe in other dimensions or beings for this to be helpful. It can also be seen as a psychological technique where you are giving a suggestion to your subconscious. Either way, the effect is the same.

Keep choosing and observe the results of your choices.

Act from integrity or from blame and criticism?

If the first choice—to act out of wholeness rather than brokenness—is fully understood, none of the other choices are actually needed. A person who feels whole will never blame another person anyway, and most problems can be resolved simply by returning to a place of wholeness inside. However, we are all still human, and it takes time and practice to develop a strong sense of wholeness and confidence—even though it initially can be a "fake it 'til you make it" situation. While we are practicing, it is helpful to use blame and criticism as a marker or road sign indicating that we've stepped off the path of wholeness and entered into dangerous territory.

Blame and criticism are toxic to any relationship—intimate or not. Blame is a misunderstanding based on an idea of smallness and powerlessness, and it is well supported by the objective/material worldview. However, as people become aware of its toxic effects and on the reality of the mirror effect, it becomes obvious that blame has no place in an awakened relationship.

Blame almost always comes out verbally as "you" statements. "You did this, you did that, you hurt me, you forgot, you don't love me, you're an asshole..." Whenever I hear myself saying "you" a lot, I know that I have some work to do. I am not taking ownership of my own feelings, I am outside my boundary, and I am communicating in a way that is sure to create and/ or escalate conflict. In addition, I am being disrespectful of myself and of whichever "you" I am upset with at the moment because I am stepping out of my own integrity.

Integrity, remember, is about structural strength. It is the strength of character that we have and the resources that we are able to access inside, and it can be practiced using the four agreements from Don Miguel Ruiz's book (and my addition):

- Be Impeccable with your word

- Don't take anything personally

- Don't make assumptions

- Always do your best

and: "Do what you think is right, even (and especially) when it is difficult".

Blame undermines integrity and responsibility because it results from a projection of my uncomfortable feelings onto someone else. If my feelings are "your" fault, I have given you my problem, I have given you responsibility for my feelings, and I have given you my power in the situation as well. Now everything is on your shoulders. I don't have any power to change things myself, so my attention is on manipulating or forcing you to do the changing. None of this is strengthening to character, self, or relationship.

On an energy level, blame sends out hooks and barbs like harpoons attached to strings. These hooks attempt to attach to another person's energy field so that we can inject our upset energy directly into their space. These same strings or "cords" as they are often referred to in energy work, also allow us to take some of the other person's energy. The real goal of blame is to produce guilt, and we know when this is accomplished because the other person seems to deflate and feel bad while we begin to feel better. When this happens we literally take some of their energy away from them. Along with helping to steal energy from another person, guilt also gives us an ability to manipulate or force the other person to do what we want them to do. Now we have cords attached and can literally "pull the strings" to make the other person behave as we think they should.

This is all a rather underhanded and insidious way of getting cooperation from someone and generally results in resentment and bad feelings. It also results in both parties feeling less worthy, less capable, and less whole. How can I feel whole if I give away the ownership of my own feelings, give away my power, and then use my own weakness as a way of manipulating someone else and stealing their energy? In one of the strange paradoxes of human behaviour, this strategy forces me to remain weak because I believe that this is the only way I can get what I want from other people. My weakness is what appears to make me strong.

Interestingly enough, this "weakness" can be expressed in two different ways. One way of expressing the internal weakness caused by blame is to be a victim. Habitual or chronic victims are visibly weaker or visibly injured by someone else and can then use this injury (unconsciously of course) as a way of getting help, support, and energy from others—and for instilling guilt if possible in the person who injured them.

On the other side of this are the "perpetrators" or bullies. These people express their weakness through intimidation and abuse. In the school yard, "victims" can often later become bullies, and bullies sometimes become victims. They are simply mirror images of each other, both playing different sides of the same game and both striving for the same thing—escape from weakness through blame, guilt, and/or control of another person's energy.

In relationships this dance is played out constantly as well—sometimes in very subtle ways and sometimes in very overt, abusive, and dangerous ways. If you have been living with abuse for a long time, if you feel that you are stuck, or if you feel afraid for your safety, it is essential to get outside help. Asking for help is NOT a sign of weakness. It is a sign that you have found your courage and stepped back into your integrity.

Most situations are hopefully not this serious, however. If you realize that you are playing the part of the bully or the victim or you catch yourself blaming your partner it is important not to go into guilt about it. To go into guilt about what you are doing is simply to continue to play the game you have been playing already.

Instead of repeating the blame/guilt pattern, it can be very helpful to use the exercises and ideas from the chapter on healing the past. If you don't have time to do this, you can at least take a few deep breaths, use the Ho'oponopono prayer, and do your best to touch into your wholeness. Remembering that one of the benefits and purposes of relationship is to give you the opportunity to grow in your own integrity and strength, use this situation to practice. As best you can, speak from your wholeness and communicate what is bothering you using the word "you" as little as possible. Use the "I statement" formula "When you..., I felt..., I would like..." to help you.

Going through the steps above will give you the information and the security you need to be able to take ownership of your feelings and to communicate these feelings to your partner in a respectful way. It is important to remember that communication does not mean getting what you want. If you want something from your partner, it is your problem—not his or hers. Your job is to communicate clearly and then to take responsibility for yourself. If your partner is unwilling to comply, you have the choice of letting go of the desire or of finding other ways that you can fill the need for yourself. By taking responsibility for your own feelings and desires, you are saying "no" to manipulation of your partner and "yes" to taking care of yourself. You are also using your own creativity to solve your own problems and empowering both yourself and your partner.

Couples who blame each other are like two bricks tied together and dumped in the water. They compete to see who can pull whom down fastest. Couples who learn to act from their own integrity are more like balloons— each one lifts the other higher. Choosing to act from integrity or from blame is like this in every situation—blame is a brick tied around your neck and the necks of everyone around you. Integrity is a balloon that gently lifts you and everyone with whom you come into contact.

Which choice do you want to make in your relationships?

Choose to give and receive or to manipulate and take?

At one point while I was staying at in Thailand, I wanted to ask my teacher about the difference between giving and receiving. Usually he was quite good about answering questions, but this time when I went up to sit near him, he continued talking to other people and ignored me for quite a while. As I sat near him, I fell into a kind of reverie and noticed that I was feeling my heart more acutely. I began to feel a flowing sensation and a kind of joyful warmth. This sensation connected with the question in my mind, and I began to realize that giving and receiving are actually two parts of the same action—at least on the energetic level. In fact, there is no difference at all, as both are part of the flow of infinite energy that is life. Giving and receiving are just the two poles of the circuit, like positive and negative electrodes in an electrical circuit, which allow the flow to happen. The best and most satisfying flow happens when energy can be both freely given and freely received. All of this happened as a felt understanding in my heart—words to explain it came a bit more slowly. As my mind was formulating words to explain to myself what I had just experienced, the teacher finally looked my way and smiled. "So what was your question?" he said.

Giving and receiving in relationship can be a smooth and empowering flow, or it can be a battleground of control and rebellion, and this battleground is often the central theme in relationships.

Another story I think has some connections here comes from my experience as a school counsellor when I met a young boy. He was only ten years old but had an ability to observe himself and what was happening around him and come out with what were sometimes quite profound understandings. He and his younger brother were constantly fighting and bickering, which was one of the reasons he was in counselling. His father also had addictions issues, the boy had been witness to many fights, extreme anger, and other things that go with this. However, his family life had become more stable, and he and his brother were learning to get along better. One day he told me that he had noticed himself being mean to his brother and that his brother wasn't reacting like he used to. "I kind of miss it," he said. "It's like I know I ought to change, but I want him to get mad. It gets kind of boring sometimes when he doesn't react like he used to."

This boy had realized something that happens constantly in relationships—we get used to behaving in a certain way with each other and to the excitement and drama of it, and then if it changes to a more peaceful or loving way of being, we will often unconsciously—or even deliberately—sabotage things so that we can feel the old way again. It feels uncomfortable being closer or more loving. It feels unfamiliar, and it demands that we use our creativity more. It also forces us to change our images of who we are and who our partners are, which can be both frightening and difficult.

Making these changes, however, also frees up energy that can be used in much more positive ways. This can happen in intimate relationships as well, when couples are used to fighting and to creating drama around issues rather than finding ways to resolve them peacefully.

In the arena of giving, there is often a battleground that can include anything from who cooks, does the dishes or takes out the garbage, to who initiates love making, who gives gifts when or who seems to take more and who feels like he/she is always giving. The list is endless, really, and the tally of slights and wrongs and times when *I* didn't get what *I* needed or when *I* gave more than *you* can get very long. Sometimes it feels like this list is written in blood and chained to a relationship like the iron balls that used to be chained to prisoners' feet.

If left to the analytical mind, finding one's way out of this morass of control and pain can become an extremely complex and nearly impossible task. However, if the problem is given over to the heart, it becomes simpler.

The need for control and power is centered in the lower three chakras—survival at the base chakra, connection, relationship and sexuality at the navel chakra, and control and sense of ego self at the solar plexus chakra.

If I am insecure about basic survival needs from the base chakra, it does not matter how much I have or how much I am given, I will not be able to give freely and easily or to receive without neediness, greed, or a sense of ungrateful entitlement. On the other hand, if I am secure in my sense of trust in whatever greater force or being in which I choose to trust, I can have nothing at all and still be able to give freely and easily.

From the level of the second chakra, if I am insecure about my worth and worthiness, if I am insecure about who I am in relationship to others and I feel unworthy, ashamed, or without intrinsic value, it will be difficult for me to receive love from another. I will be needy and empty and have difficulty really giving as well. Instead of true giving, I will easily be caught in attached giving until I feel drained and resentful, always hoping that finally my partner will give back and meet my unstated desires. When I finally get what I want, I will have difficulty believing it is really there or jump quickly into fears of losing it.

From the level of the solar plexus chakra, insecurities revolve around my ability to express who I am and to use my power in the world. Insecurity at this level means that I have to control my partner in order to feel like I am real, whole, or worthy. I believe that if I don't take care of everything it won't get done or it won't get done well enough. Sometimes I convince myself that my partner is not smart enough or capable enough to do anything right. I have to be on top of everything and tell him what to do like another child or dominate her so that she doesn't leave or threaten my role as the "boss" in the household. (Of course, any of these roles can easily be assumed by either men or women, and there are infinite variations on these themes).

In any of these situations, the flow of giving and receiving is interrupted and the love energy that is actually unlimited and always present is treated as if it is limited and in short supply. The other person becomes an object to be controlled, cajoled and manipulated in order to meet the needs generated by my insecurities.

As discussed earlier, the way out of this mess is to step away from trying to analyze it or even to fix it and instead focus on generating a sense of wholeness in your heart. The heart can also hold insecurities of course, but choose to focus on the wholeness that is there instead. Starting on the inside by nurturing and caring for your own beautiful heart, you will eventually find that you have less need to control, manipulate, or take from others.

Generating this sense of wholeness is a process that shouldn't be expected to happen overnight. However, even starting out on the path of realizing and remembering your own wholeness can have effects quite quickly. The exercises and concepts in this book will help you. Once we have embarked upon and committed to the expression of wholeness, the Universe itself (God or the Field or however you wish to name it) seems to step in and supply the information, opportunities and teachers as they are needed. Trust in the process and, it will unfold for you.

In the unfolding, observe your choices with your partner and learn to see when you are manipulating, taking, controlling, or expecting. These are very helpful markers that can act like road signs on the highway, indicating that you can turn off and try a new route. Each one is an exit sign, giving you an opportunity to take a different road and to practice giving and receiving from your wholeness instead.

Notice your disgust when your partner fails to do what you wanted once again and catch yourself. Think of your boundary and use it to separate what feelings, needs and desires belong to you from those that belong to your partner. What do you really want? How much of you is in your partner's circle, expecting, manipulating, controlling, or needing? How can you take this energy and control back into your own space where you can use it more effectively?

The answers to these questions are not easy, especially when we have been so indoctrinated by a system of thought in which everything is the fault of someone else. However, as you begin to practice the tools of boundary, containment, communication, forgiveness, and self-empowerment, you will begin to find that all your relationships become far more rewarding and that you will feel more empowered, strong, free, and happy. Again, there are choices—do you want to keep doing what you are doing and getting what you are getting because it is easier and more familiar, or do you want to be happier, more free, and more empowered?

If the answer is the latter—you want to feel more free, happy and empowered and you want a relationship that is deep, loving, and fulfilling, you will not arrive at your goal by taking, demanding, controlling, or expecting.

My wife, Joy, taught me a great deal about the importance of giving without expectation of return and without strings of control or judgment attached to the giving. She had a way of letting me know with a soft touch, a look, or just in her presence that she loved me without conditions. This did not mean that she gave up her sense of self or gave up her own boundaries. However, she had a very good understanding of feminine energy and power, and she did not have a need to compete with me. Her power and mine were different but equal, so they complemented and supported each other rather than competing and tearing each other down. On an energetic level she gave me energy from her heart freely and shared herself with me with honesty and integrity.

When she became ill and we were told she had only a few months to live, she still gave of herself and her energy freely. Although she was often in pain, she didn't allow the pain or the fear to pull her into negative thoughts or irritability. Instead, she maintained and even increased the giving from her heart so that everyone who came in contact with her felt the power of her love touching them.

People asked me at times if I felt exhausted or needed a break from caring for her, especially toward the end when the nights were so long and her pain was so strong. I have to say that had she been a different person I probably would have, as I am certainly not a hero in any way. However, the quality of her giving was such that I did not want to be anywhere else, and I didn't feel tired in my role of supporting and caring for her. We were able to practice giving and receiving in the way I experienced when sitting near my teacher where the action of receiving became a part of the action of giving and vice versa. Joy empowered herself with love and gave it freely. I was able to receive and to complete the circuit so that she could also receive from me. Even in the darkest times, this circuit of giving/receiving sustained us both.

Joy's example is one that will certainly stay with me for the rest of my life, and perhaps beyond. There are so many excuses that we can have for withholding love, for placing conditions on our love, for being too weak or unworthy, wounded or hurt to give our love. However, Joy faced steadily increasing pain, the specter of death and loss, hospitalization, surgery, and the steady loss of her body as it dwindled to skin and bone. Through all of this, she managed to keep giving from her heart and to make me and those who visited her feel that we were loved.

Joy is my example of love and giving, even in extreme situations. She took charge of her own state of mind and chose to see love despite the huge presence of pain and possibility of fear. She made her state of mind her priority, and she died the way she lived—with love and grace.

When I—and if you choose, when you—face an issue in relationship to a partner, or to any person or situation, I think that Joy's example is one that helps to simplify the choices. Will you give love without expectations, or will you attempt to demand and control in order to stay safe? Will you believe in yourself and your own depth and power so that you can give to others, or will you believe in your weakness and vulnerability so that you must defend and compete?

These choices determine what you will find in your relationships with others and especially with your intimate partner. What choice do you want to make?

Let go, or cling?

On every level and in every way, our mind/body system is in a constant state of change. We know this, science confirms this, Eastern religions have always said this—but still, it is hard to accept and experience. Instead, we cling to the idea that there are things in our life that are constant. The mind is set up to recognize, name, and categorize things, to make images of them, and then to add data to the image each time we encounter it again.

A child sees a cup for the first time, for instance, and learns the word "cup". Now the sound and the image of the object are paired. As the child grows, more cups are encountered, and the mind builds a category for "cups" and their meanings and associations. This same child also sees how his mother and father relate to each other and begins to build images and associations with the ideas of "mother" and "father" as well as "husband" and "wife". These words also gather new images and associations as the child watches television, meets other families, and matures enough to begin having relationships of his own.

In all these cases, the action of the mind is to record, recognize, and categorize. Once the mind has named and categorized an object, it ceases really to see it anymore. Instead of seeing the object as it is, the mind sees the object along with all its past experiences and judgments of the object. A cup is lumped in with all other cups and compared—is it a beautiful cup or a useful cup or an ugly cup or a fancy cup? How does it compare to other cups?

This job of recognition, categorization, comparison, and judgment goes on all the time in the mind, and this is unfortunately not a helpful thing for relationships. Because of this built-in habit, I form an opinion about my partner and make an image of her in my mind. This image is partly about her, but even more it is about my own experiences, memories, and filters that sort out what I am able to perceive and what I want to see. I build my image and then I cling to it. "This is who I married. I know her," I think.

As time goes on, this image often becomes tarnished. I start to see things I don't like and add them to the image. I get bored because she is just the same old "wife", and I get angry because she isn't what I want. My image becomes very important to me, and I keep adding all the hurts and pains and things that she does wrong. Sex becomes dull and repetitive because I'm just repeating patterns with my image of who I married. Eventually, my image gets so heavily painted that I can't see the real person at all anymore—all I can see is the image of my desires and disappointments. At this point, many couples split up and go off looking for someone new so they can start the process of image making all over again.

The irony of this is that every instant every person is changing and every second there is a new person being made from the form of the old. Every person in existence is also a one in billions individual, the only one to ever exist and the only one exactly the same that ever will exist. Each and every person on this planet is an amazing and incredible work of art and miracles just by virtue of the fact that he or she exists. If we have the ability to even begin to see this in another person then we also can begin to see the miracle of our own existence in the mirror of our partner.

Boredom in relationship is a result of not understanding change, and it is a result of building images of the people we purport to love, rather than striving to see them for the amazing beings they truly are—new each moment. The choice of letting go or clinging is the choice between creating a relationship that moves toward stasis, dullness, duty, boredom, and uninteresting sex or allowing a relationship that is constantly changing, evolving, exciting, and free. The choice to fight change and cling to images feels safer, has few surprises, and doesn't take any creativity. However, couples who let go into change and renewal are never bored, stay younger and healthier, have more fun, and tend to have a much more exciting sex life as well.

Of course, it is easier to start a relationship with conscious attention to letting go of habits and images than to wait twenty years and then try to let go of all of them. However, it is possible to start at any time—after all, everyone is always changing. With this in mind, here are a few exercises to help you to practice letting go with your partner:

1. Make a habit of waking up each morning and reminding yourself that the woman or man beside you is not the same woman or man you went to bed with. You do not know how much change has happened through the night. You truly do not know all of who this person is. He or she is a wonderful mystery. Remind yourself of this as often as you can.

2. Practice seeing your partner as a treasure. The time you have with this person can never be repeated, never be returned, and this is a tiny moment in the scope of all of space and time. You do not know how long you will have with this person. Perhaps years. Perhaps minutes. Remember this, and take time to just watch or be with your partner without judgment, as if you were looking at him or her for the first time. Breathe into your wholeness, let go of grudges that you hold and hurts from the past. That past is gone. What can you see in the fullness and magic of this moment?

3. Take nothing for granted—just as you would if you were dating for the first time. Look for the automatic assumptions that you have about your partner, the role that he or she has in the relationship, the jobs that you each have, etc. Let go of expectations that these things will stay the same.

4. Change some things. Make a game of doing something unexpected now and then. (Be careful here to do things that can involve your partner though. The idea is to learn to appreciate each other more, not harass, scare, worry, or get away from each other)

5. Think of your partner as "Thou" instead of "you".

6. Sit with your partner and each mark your boundary circles using yarn or rope. Sit in your circles at a distance that

feels comfortable to both of you—not too close and not too far away. Decide who will go first (person A) and second (person B).

Take three deep breaths, breathing into your sense of wholeness.

Take three more deep breaths, breathing into your heart and feeling love for your partner.

Person A then starts by saying: "I release and free you from any energetic expectations from the root chakra, and I lovingly cut the cords of these expectations. Please forgive me for any harm or pain that I have caused you at any time and in any way at this level." Person B focuses on sending love to person A and replies "I forgive you". Person A then imagines any energetic expectations—visualized like cords or ropes—being lovingly cut and released. It can help to visualize a beautiful rose between the newly cut ends of the cords as a symbol of love and protection.

Continue in this way through the second chakra, near the navel, the third chakra at the solar plexus, the fourth chakra at the heart, the fifth chakra in the throat, the sixth on the forehead between the eyes, and the seventh at the top of the head.

Repeat the exercise with Person B now cutting the cords and asking for forgiveness and person A sending love and forgiveness.[48]

* * *

A warning about practicing conscious relationship is that you will get to know your partner better than you have before, and you will learn more

---

48 *The Lover Within* (Henderson, 1987) is a good reference for energy based relationship practices, as is *The Intimate Couple* (Rosenberg, Kitaen-Ross, 1996).

about who he or she thinks he or she is at this time. You may not like this very much. You may find that the images you have built are completely wrong and that your partner is someone else entirely than you expected, or even wanted.

Part of being free and able to respond to the moment is that there are no formulas to say what to do in this situation or that situation. There is only the moment. Perhaps you will find that you don't like this person at all and it is time to let go of the relationship.

Perhaps you will find that you don't like this person, but it is because you are uncomfortable with the reflection, and you know you have work to do to change yourself. This gives you an opportunity to grow and change.

Perhaps you will find that a relationship that was growing stale is revitalized and the person you are with is the lover you have always dreamed of.

Whatever you find, you have moved into a relationship that is more authentic, less insulated, and less dull. As stated before, "All relationship begins in the ecstatic knowingness of your authenticity, of your wholeness"[49]. By letting go into change, you have freed your partner from the images, assumptions, and expectations that held him or her in shackles and freed yourself as well. For some, this will be a wonderful and even ecstatic release. For others, it may at first seem painful and difficult. Either way, it is a step in a direction of expansion, freedom, intimate truth, respect, and growth—and this is a good thing!

Expanding possibilities

No matter who or where you are, you are in relationship at all times. You may be single and alone, surrounded by family and friends, or even a monk in a solitary cave, but there is still no way to avoid relationship in this life. At the very least—and also the very most—there is the relationship that we have with ourselves. From this relationship comes the pattern for all others,

---

49 Sri Ram Kaa and Kira Raa, 2012 *Awakening* (2008).

including the way we interact with animals, objects, and the world as well as with other people.

Since relationship is about the way we interact with the people, animals, and objects around us, it is completely dependent on what we believe those people, animals, and objects to be. The definitions that we give them determine their worth, and worthiness, and this in turn determines how we act and interact with them.

From the objective/material viewpoint, as has been discussed often in this book, the fundamental secular assumptions about the nature of people, animals, and objects is that we are made of little particles that can be separated and taken apart. We live in a universe that is ultimately random but which follows predictable laws. We are simply the sum of our parts; we are separate and divided from each other, and we are the product of a process of selection that chooses those of us who are strongest and most fit and discards the rest as surplus. We live a little while, compete for mates and try to get what we want in a world where the main fact of life is that there is not enough for everyone and the strongest, smartest and most beautiful will get most of everything. Then we die.

There are, of course, many religions with widely differing beliefs, and many of them do not agree with the objective/material way of seeing the world. However, the predominant belief systems over the past several thousand years have included a large degree of control along with their spirituality. Sex and the body have been denigrated and vilified, shame and guilt have become a foundation of who we believe ourselves to be, and God has been confined to what seem to be very human levels of intelligence and emotional development. Though the essence of these religions points to greater truth, the dogma has limited us to a viewpoint where we are shameful, sinful creatures, struggling to repress the evil within us in order to live up to the expectations of a God who preaches love but burns us in Hell if we don't do what we are told.

From one side, then, we are told that we are random, insignificant, and possessed of animal instincts for competition, mating, and survival. From the other, we learn that we are sinful, possessed of shameful desires and a terrible weakness for violence and debauchery of all sorts. These are the foundations on which we build our pictures of ourselves and others, and these are the viewpoints that shape how we relate to ourselves, our world, our intimate partners, our children—everyone and everything with which we come into contact. Is it any wonder, then, that there is so much violence in the world?

The Awakening offers an expanded viewpoint of the universe and within it this planet and all the life that is on it. This expanded viewpoint combines science and religion into a new synthesis of ideas in which the physical nature of reality is a Field of infinite probability. This Field is expressed as an inter-connection of waveforms that manifest as objects, animals, plants, people, planets and stars. The definition of what it means to be human expands so that we can see ourselves as, at minimum, beings of light and energy existing in a physical form that is connected to, and a part of, all that is. It also opens the possibility that this "beingness" that we are is far larger, greater, and more beautiful than we have ever imagined before.

Imagine if all people on the planet understood and fully felt this expanded viewpoint as the reality of who they are. Imagine if *you* understood and fully felt this expanded viewpoint as the reality of who *you* are. How might it change the way you see yourself? Your intimate partner? Your children, friends, co-workers? The animals and plants and objects around you?

How might it change the way you relate with your world if you knew that everything you do, think, and say is a part of the co-creation of the reality around you and that you are a gift to this world. How might it change your way of seeing others if you understood fully that there is nothing that is more important than your state of mind and that each person in your life is also a shimmering being of light and energy, co-creating this reality?

This is not a utopian dream, impossible vision, or spaced-out loss of touch with reality. This is an awareness that has been known to sages for millennia but which is just now coming into the awareness of large numbers of people worldwide. Many people are already living in this worldview, and many, many more are now taking their first steps into redefining what it means to be in relationship—with themselves, with others, and with the world around them. This redefinition of relationships is essential to us now as we waver between the old way of understanding reality and the expanded vision that moves beyond Newton and the worldview which his discoveries helped to create.

How do you choose to see yourself and others and on what foundation do you wish to rest your relationships? Listen well to your heart, and let it guide you. There is so much beauty that awaits you if you do.

Chapter 17
Awakened Sex

The pleasure of living and the pleasure of the orgasm are identical.
Extreme orgasm anxiety forms the basis of the general fear of life.

Wilhelm Reich

At the heart of pornography is sexuality haunted by its own disappearance.

Jean Baudrillard

Sex is a spiritual experience.

Deepak Chopra

There seems to be a general belief, highly promulgated by the media, that sex is an end to which every man and woman must aspire. It is the highest pleasure available; it is a sign of social acceptance and success; it is the cure for the ailments of fear and loneliness; it is a necessary right of manhood; it is a measure of worth for both men and women; it provides excitement and colour to life—and the list goes on.

The messages that we get about sex from the objective/material perspective are, however, somewhat confusing. On one hand, sex is a central facet of marketing, media, and life intentions, while on another hand it is shameful, embarrassing, dirty, and bad. And on yet another hand (belonging to someone else I suppose) sex is primarily a biological function with the impersonal purpose of continuation of the species.[50]

All these ways of looking at sex have some truth. Sex can be seen as a great way to sell products, as a restricted and taboo object of craving and shameful desire, or as an instinctive biological drive common to all animals. All these ways of seeing sex, however, filter and limit our experience and control the way that we see and relate with our sexual partner(s) as well as all other humans around us.

Sex as a commodity produces assumptions of worth that turn people into objects. Sex as a shameful behaviour creates a convoluted confusion of internal repression, shame, desire, and often deviant behaviour, as internal drives wage war with opposing beliefs deep in the psyche. Sex as a biological and evolutionary imperative reduces our notions of "love" to impersonal biological programs and reduces our sense of individual worth to just a statistical breeding member carrying out our pre-programmed duty of carrying on the species.

Each of these viewpoints is a partial truth that carries a number of assumptions about the meaning of being human, the origin and purpose of human behaviour, and the meaning and purpose of being alive in the first place. In the arena of sex, assumptions based on these viewpoints have a tendency to deaden and kill the experience of union, communion, healing, trust, love, and pleasure that can and should be the foundation on which sexual relationship is based.

Western culture and its cultural heritage have demonized sex for millennia, and this demonization has woven itself into our belief systems with a frightening tenacity. Before looking at some principles for better sexual relationships, therefore, it is helpful to first look at some of the deep rooted misunderstandings that get in the way of a more awakened experience of sex.

Because assumptions about sexuality are so deeply rooted in our beliefs of who we are, it can be quite challenging to have them refuted or pronounced

---

50 For some great information on the weird, wonderful and remarkably variable sex habits of insects and animals, and a good grounding in the evolutionary biology of sex as well, *Dr. Tatiana's Sex Advice to All Creation* (2002) is an excellent and entertaining read.

as being bad or even the softer "unhelpful". Most of us still identify with and in some ways cherish these beliefs, even if they have a tendency to increase dysfunction in our relationships. If you experience discomfort while reading the next section of this chapter, just note the discomfort and allow it to become a question. What is it about this sexual assumption that I cherish? How do I allow it to define who I am? Do I really want to keep it?

There are no wrong answers here. You are free to keep any of these beliefs for as long as you wish. Freedom requires an ability to choose, however. If reading this chapter has opened an awareness of choice for you, it has already given you greater freedom.

With this in mind, the following are some generally unhelpful assumptions about sex that are derived from or connected to the objective/material worldview and which cause problems for many people as they search for sexual meaning and fulfillment.

* * *

Unhelpful Sexual Assumptions from the objective/material worldview

Sex is a commodity

As we have discussed elsewhere in this book, the objective/material worldview tends to see humans as objects which fulfill rolls and functions. Of these functions, one of the most important is that of sex since this is what enables the continuation of the species and the passage forward of genetic information. Without sex, there would be no humans in a hundred years (give or take a few) and so natural selection has made procuring a mate and engaging in sexual intercourse one of the most basic and unquestionable instinctive priorities of all animals.

Humans are not different from animals in this regard. However, we use our amazing minds to raise our sexual instincts to much greater heights of complexity than most animals. Sex, in the human world, is a commodity for

Todd L. Blattner

which we strive generally with greater vigor than for money, beauty, property, or power. Evolutionary biology tells us that money, beauty, property, and social power are all part of the great game of competition for a mate. There are other purposes, of course, but a principle reason for playing the game is so that mates can be procured and the species can be continued. From the evolutionary viewpoint, we are all just animals fulfilling our instinctual drives to stay alive, spread our genes, and continue our line. Sex, therefore, is a highly prized commodity, but the individual men and women are interchangeable and disposable.

The popular media, of course, adds a great deal of glitz and gloss to the rather bleak outlook of evolutionary biology. The media, as already mentioned, paints a rather different picture of sex—a picture where it is something to be craved and sought after, associated with all that is good in life, and also associated with all that it is possible to achieve in life. However, the media still, by and large, works with sex objects rather than people. Women are portrayed as objects more than men, although this is rapidly changing. In either case sex is seen as a valued and limited resource, a product to be bought and sold and competed for like any other product. It is very difficult to see the deep inner beauty and worth of a person when seeing through these viewpoints, and it is therefore also difficult to experience authentic and meaningful sexual union with another that goes beyond physical or emotional need.

When sex is a commodity, it becomes something that is both artificially scarce and valuable. The sexual industry produces billions of dollars each year and touches everyone in one way or another. As a commodity, sex is something to be bought and sold, or taken, or stolen if necessary. Pornography, prostitution, and rape, along with all the other more subtle forms of exploitation are at least partially a result of this view of sex as a limited resource and people as objects.

Partner as object

Individuals, in the objective/material worldview are only statistically important and function as objects carrying specific attributes. As long as enough humans survive to keep a breeding population going, it doesn't matter very much who the survivors are. This is a partial truth which helps to create the mistaken impression that we are disposable objects. Marketing and the consumer culture carry this idea further, and the objective/material interpretation of Darwin's competition for survival rounds out the picture.

Any way we look at it, the objective/material worldview supports the premise that people are like any other material object or resource. They can be loved and appreciated, certainly, but when push comes to shove, "my" needs are what are important to me, and I will do what I can to get those needs met. In our worldview, if a tree is in the way, you cut it down. If you need a resource from the earth, you take it. If you have garbage to dump, you dump it. If a business can be taken over, you take it over. If a person has something you need, well, there are social protocols, but one way or the other, generally you take that too.

This viewpoint of others as less important or more disposable than oneself carries over into sexual relationships. Sex is an opportunity for an extremely deep and intimate meeting of body and soul in the human form. This depth of sharing is something that our present culture and way of seeing the world does not prepare us for. Instead, sex is generally entered into from a viewpoint of shallow goal fulfillment.

When we see our partner as an object, we focus on orgasm, performance, and fantasy. The focus on orgasm puts a specific end point in mind and turns the sexual encounter into a rush for a particular finish line rather than a journey in which the pleasures of each moment are savoured. Focus on orgasm also makes performance into a huge issue and adds pressure and tension to a situation where relaxation and confidence are most important. It is difficult to relax and enjoy the journey when you are constantly trying to get somewhere else.

Sex is Shameful and dirty

The belief that sex is shameful and dirty is one that causes tremendous harm and wages havoc in our world. The sexual drive is one of the deepest drives in our nature, and it is a drive that spans the gap between physical and spiritual. It exists on all levels and can be a vehicle for expression of deep union in a given moment. To say that it is shameful and dirty is to say that the body as a whole is shameful and dirty, and even beyond this, it is also an affirmation of original sin and the shame of *being* in the first place. If I must be formed by sexual union between my parents and this union is shameful, what does this say about who I am? What is the result of being a member of a species where sex is both the only way to continue the species and an act of shame? What is the result of a child growing with the teaching that his or her sexual parts are shameful and dirty and that sexual thoughts are bad, of the devil, and full of shame?

The only possible result of this is that the child is forced to lose contact with his or her wholeness. Instead, he or she learns to judge the body and the body parts, to objectify the body and to repress its feelings and needs. This judgment and dualistic viewpoint of good and bad is then projected into the world and becomes the filter for how everything else is seen. The internal shame is intolerable and so it is pushed out into the world to be seen in the actions of others.

It is not a coincidence that rapists are among the most despised of all criminals. They are the external expression of the sexual shame and anger that is endemic in our culture. Their choices cannot be condoned, and their actions cannot be tolerated, but they are also victims. Individually, they are often victims of abuse in their own past. Collectively, they are victims of the projection of our culture's sexual illness—an illness that is turned not only against human victims but also against the earth itself as we press our needs forcefully against ecosystems that have not invited us and which are badly harmed by our actions.

The sexual drive is so powerful that it is feared. Most religions, at least most religions based on a male-oriented and patriarchal viewpoint, have sought to subjugate and control the sexual drive. Earlier matriarchal or pagan religions were more sexually open and thought of sex as a part of the creation principle in which we all could partake. For these religions, sex was often a ceremonial rite and a sacred act. When the male religions took over, however, Adam and Eve covered their shameful parts with fig leaves, and the human race undertook a long and painful period of attempting to repress, control, and vilify the sexual urge.

In the Awakening, we are moving toward finding a balance between male and female energies and reclaiming our sexual wholeness. The great power of sex does make it dangerous. It is easy to become addicted and lost within the various levels of drive that can be attached to sex—pleasure, need, power, and unconscious instinct. This danger and power must be approached with respect, awareness, personal strength, and courage, as sexual energy is derived from an energy that is more powerful than simply the physical and much larger than an individual. Like Nature, and like the quantum properties of the Field itself, sexual energy is not something that can be overcome or fully controlled. However, it can be channeled and directed, and this requires moving the sexual energies up from the lower chakras into the heart and higher centers where they are more refined and more centered in responsible awareness. Channeling and directing sexual energy is an art that requires both self-love and self-discipline.

Shame, however, is not a substitute for self-discipline. Shame is a control mechanism of the lowest order, used by those who wish to control others through domination and degradation. Shame is a weapon of mass destruction, and it wages this destruction in the bedrooms of our world, spiraling out into our lives and touching every aspect of how we see ourselves and each other. When sexual shame and repression become extreme, they are acted out as rape, sexual violence, sexual hatred, and the many sexually "deviant" behaviours that are rampant in our world in this time.

If there is only one precious gift that could be given to a child, it would be to love the wholeness of the body and the self without shame and to see others in this way. Courage, self-control, and integrity cannot come from shame and repression. They can only come from the practice of deep love and openness to all our levels of being and through acceptance of the wholeness of who and what we are.

Fantasy

Fantasy is another issue that can cause problems in relationship. Fantasy is a way of not being present with what is really happening right now. This is a deadening factor in sexual intimacy because the act of sex is, or at least can be, about being fully alive and being connected with another person on many levels—physical, mental, emotional, and spiritual. It is not possible to be deeply connected with another person and deeply present in one's own experience while also being in a fantasy vision that you have made up and projected into the situation.

Sexual fantasy is an exciting expectation of an imaginary future that creates an image of desire and projects this image on top of whatever is actually happening. Sexual fantasy is also an aspect of the assumptions that sex is a scarce commodity and that people are objects. Fantasy relies on images and scenarios where another person is available to fulfill "my" needs, requirements, and images. On both a psychological and energetic level, these projected images can be very real—often more real to the person imagining them than the physical reality that is around him or her.

Fantasies can never truly be fulfilled, but it is the need and the craving for fulfillment that is actually desired—not the person who takes on the role of partner for a given time. A stripper at a nightclub undulating on the stage can stir up a lot of excitement in the men around her. For most of those men, waking up with her in the light of morning after the alcohol has worn off is not nearly as enticing.

Fantasy is not necessarily bad or harmful, but it is generally on an opposite pole, far away from a more true and shared experience of deep love and communion in sexual relationship. Fantasy is a substitute for communion, when people are unable to be present enough, open enough, or vulnerable enough to trust and deeply be with another person. This deep *being with* does not need imagination, special settings, special scenery or locations, or any of the things normally associated with romance. It can use these things—they are not harmful in themselves—but they are also not necessary.

Ironically, some sex therapists actually suggest that fantasy can play an important role in sex and teach clients to imagine they are with a fantasy partner or in a fantasy situation, while they are with their real partner, as a way of building excitement. This can help, at times, but it is important to keep in mind what you are trying to accomplish. If the goal is to have an orgasm, fantasy can sometimes be useful. It is possible that this use of fantasy can also work as a kind of psychological bridge back to finding enjoyment with a partner—and this is the hope of therapists who suggest it.

I find, however, that fantasy is on an opposite pole from awakened sexual communion. Like the lights and glitz in a stripper bar, it seems to add excitement and mystery but when the lights come on, reality can be quite harsh. Sexual communion looks directly at what is real with such great integrity and presence that the magic and mystery of being alive needs no further embellishments. Fantasy tends to be faster and easier than awakening to sexual wholeness and authenticity, but it falls far short in depth, fulfillment, and longevity.

In addition, fantasy fully promotes and endorses the assumptions of "other as object" and "sex as commodity" as well as completely removing a person from the present moment. Any one of these things is a killer to intimacy. Together they are not only intimacy killers but a recipe for a worldview in which rape, misuse of each other and resources, violence, and meeting of "my" needs at all costs is accepted as the norm. This is a worldview, in short, pretty much like the one in which we presently live.

Pornography

Some kinds of pornography take fantasy to extremes and can become addictions that are very difficult to escape. Addiction to pornography is an eventual killer for real sex, as it is fuel for a desire that is imaginary and insatiable. No partner or situation can live up to the fantasy, and the addicted person is doomed to live with a burning dissatisfaction and continuous craving. The addicted person believes that fulfillment of the desire resides in an "object" that is "out there" somewhere. Fulfillment must be given by, or taken from, someone else—someone who meets a particular imaginary image. Unfortunately, this image is so hugely composite and so completely out of touch with the reality of what makes sex wonderful that it cannot survive in reality. The image always shatters with sufficient contact, and the search for a better "object" continues. The addiction is really to craving itself—to the feeling of almost getting what is sought after. Actually getting it seldom matches the projected desires and never lasts.

Awakened sexuality requires a big step of understanding as well as trust, which is difficult for many people to accept. It requires being more open, more real, more trusting in the moment, more creative, more tender, and most of all, more truthful. As you practice seeing your partner as a person, as a deep, powerful and mysterious being, one of a kind in all time, sharing this moment with you, you will also begin to see more deeply into the depths of your Self and achieve an intimacy far greater and longer lasting than any fantasy could ever bring.

Beware, however! This kind of intimacy is not for the faint of heart. It will also stir the depths of your shadow and bring much from the darkness into the light. The great mantra for intimacy as well as for remembering that your partner is not an object to fulfill your needs is *I am responsible for my own feelings, needs and desires. I will not blame!*

Sex is a way of proving manhood and masculinity

Like other misconceptions, the belief that sex is a proof of masculinity does carry some partial truth. Sex generally does bolster one's feelings of self (self with a small "s"), whether one is male or female. It is an affirmation of connection and also a deep evolutionary success marker that produces a hormonal reward. When we have sex, we fulfill a biological prerogative and nature rewards us so we'll want to do it again.

However, for many men this need for bolstering of self becomes excessive. In this case, sex becomes the proof of "my" masculinity and therefore takes on a critical role in determining who I am. If I believe that my masculinity can be proven by a physical act, I am starting out with a diminished understanding of masculinity, and of self, in the first place. Sex, and perhaps more importantly all of the macho imagery and swaggering that can go with it, becomes the rickety set of poles and supports that is holding up my idea of self. As long as I can find a sex object out there to exploit, I can keep my sense of self. If I become incapable of performing or of getting a partner, I'm nothing.

These are quite high stakes, and there is little room left in the equation for intimacy or sharing. Everything must be based on performance—getting in, getting the job done, and getting out with as much noise, flash, drama, and perhaps paraphernalia as possible. Here, the focus is on the action but not the person and on the performance, not the relationship. As such, it objectifies everyone involved, makes real intimacy impossible, and creates a high tension situation where dysfunction is likely. This is sex for boys who don't yet know how to be men, whatever their age may be. It is sad because believing in a need for proof of manhood creates the circle that keeps a man from realizing his own maturity. Stop trying to prove that you are a man, and you will be many miles closer to actually being one.

Although some women may be doing a bit of gloating at this point, women aren't off the hook on this one either. It is more common for men to try to prove themselves through conquering sex objects, but some women do it too. Women also often use the virility of their men as an indication of their own desirability. Attracting and holding a virile mate also scores evolutionary—and therefore social—points. "He made love to me three times last night" is a more ego-building thing for a woman to say than "he rolled over and snored loudly".

Sex proves that I am wanted

A more common female approach to low self-esteem in sex is to use it as proof of being wanted and needed. Just as in the male approach, where masculinity needs to be continually propped up by sexual exploits, women often need to prop up their sense of being needed, and therefore worthwhile, with sex. Many women repeatedly put themselves in situations where they are likely to be victimized by approaching sex from an energetic and emotional base of needing to be wanted.

Healing and healthy relationships involve people who want each other, and there is nothing wrong with wanting to be wanted. However, it does become a problem when the wanting becomes a desperation or neediness that has to be fulfilled from the outside. Healthy sexual relationships happen when both partners have at least the beginnings of self-esteem and an understanding that they are sharing their wholeness with another, rather than needing to be completed and filled by the other.

Of course, men can also need to be wanted and can take on this role in a sexual relationship. Either way, sex for the purpose of feeling wanted generally becomes boring and repetitive at some point, and the partner who is needed becomes dissatisfied. As tension builds between the needy partner and the reluctant partner, a dynamic is established where the needy partner is seen as being less and less desirable and wanted by the reluctant partner. This strengthens the fears of the needy partner, who tries harder to be wanted, and the negative spiral goes around and around.

As with other relational issues, the practices in this book can help to move out of this negative spiral. Partners who believe themselves to be whole, responsible for their own needs, complete, and worthy will either build a stronger and more satisfying relationship with each other or realize that it is time to release each other and do so with caring and integrity. The key is to stop trying to fix or change your partner and to do the work to find your own wholeness first. As Victor Frankl, a concentration camp survivor, author, and therapist, states "When we are no longer able to change a situation, we are challenged to change ourselves." When you can come from your own wholeness, the dynamic of your relationship will change, and you will know each next step to take as the time comes to take it.

Sex is a purpose for living

From the objective/material perspective, this is especially true for men, since their evolutionary job is pretty much done after ejaculation happens. Sure, they get to hang around and be providers, but this often isn't a lot of fun. Women have a longer term purpose in nurturing their children, so they can let go of sex more easily, focusing on their role as nurturers. For men though, sex can be subconsciously confused with a purpose for being. From an evolutionary point of view, if you're not able to sow those wild oats pretty heavily, you're not doing a good job of fulfilling your biological destiny. If you can't "get it up," you've pretty much lost everything of importance, and you're going to have to do a lot more fighting, bragging, and otherwise bluffing to make up for it.

The human mind has amazing abilities to twist things up, and so this basic drive for sex and wild oat sowing as purpose can become sexual addiction, internet porn addiction, drive to commit rape, and all sorts of behaviours that are generally labeled as aberrant, deviant, or degenerate. It can also become sex that is done as an act of conquest, power, violence, and/or as a way of proving that I still "have it". Youth, vigor, potency, power, social acceptance, self-worth, purpose—it's all tied together in our social understanding of sex and the consequences of "not getting any" are therefore high indeed.

Sex is about performance

This is a myth that is very closely related to the beliefs that sex is a way to prove manhood or womanhood or that one is needed or wanted. The need to perform in sex is generally based in insecurity as well as fantasy. It is a belief that I am not good enough just being myself, so I have to show how good I am with the use of special techniques, showing how long I can last or how well I can please my partner. Both women and men know, though it is generally not explicitly considered, that if I can make my partner addicted to me, they won't leave, and/or they will do what I want them to do. Therefore, performing well is an important part of sexual/relational strategy.

Physical performance, for a man, centers around the ability to have an erection and to keep it long enough during intercourse to bring his partner to orgasm. Concern about physical performance puts a great deal of pressure on a sexual encounter and therefore tends to remove spontaneity and intimacy. It changes the focus of the encounter from an "I and Thou" time of being with a beloved partner to a more impersonal and pressured attempt to impress and manipulate an object external to myself (the man or woman that I am with) so that he or she will like me and help me to build up my image of who I am.

Women can also have physical difficulties with sex ranging from the inability to have an orgasm (which is actually quite common) to pain during intercourse. These issues can have physical causes, just as the inability to have an erection can have a physical cause. However, just as they are for men, these issues are very commonly connected to psychological and energetic causes as well—often related to sexual abuse and/or restrictive beliefs about sexuality and the body.

There are so many possible causes for physical inability to "perform" for both men and women that it would be irresponsible for me to say that all these issues can be related to psychological and energetic causes. However, I believe that a large number of men and women who have problems in these areas would be better served by doing the work of looking at their beliefs and anxieties as well as the energetic restrictions and contractions that they feel around sexual issues than by using only the traditional medical approach to treatment with medication.

An example of this is a client I worked with who was having difficulties with impotence. He had investigated medical reasons for this and had not found any, though he was continuing to investigate that avenue. However, he and his wife of many years had separated several years earlier and his life had become quite stressful and difficult. He had a large amount of guilt about his separation as well as belief systems from early childhood that helped to accentuate his feelings of guilt and unworthiness when he was with women, including a deep gender prejudice against his own sex.

Gender prejudice is actually very common and can be against either men or women—passed on by the beliefs of the earliest care giver, which is generally the mother. "Men aren't to be trusted, men leave, men are violent, men are brutes"; "Women are sluts, women are controlling, women can't be trusted, women should be subservient to men," etc. If you carry a prejudice that is against your own sex, you will tend toward guilt about who you are on a deep level. If you have a prejudice against the opposite sex, you are more likely to distrust the opposite sex, and this can come out as actions ranging from violence to subtle devaluation in the way you treat your partner.[51] It can also come out as sexual dysfunction, especially when it is a prejudice directed against one's own sex.

This man's therapy involved many facets: He began to take action to give himself more personal time and decrease his stress, he realized the gender prejudice he held and began to work on forgiving himself and accepting the positive aspects of his own masculinity, and he worked with his guilt and finding internal forgiveness. In addition, he practiced removing the performance anxiety when he was with his new partner and focusing on the love and intimacy that could be shared by being together using massage, "skin

---

51 Gender prejudice is actually a huge issue that runs deeply in most people's lives and which wreaks subtle havoc in our relationships. For more information about gender prejudice, it is suggested that you contact a therapist who is trained to lead you through discovery of your own prejudice and how to work with it. Ask a prospective therapist if he/she understands the idea of gender prejudice and how it affects relationships. You can also find people specifically trained in this concept, and in the mind/body approach to therapy through the Integrative Body Psychotherapy website at www.ibponline.com. You can also find information about gender prejudice in Jack Rosenberg's books, referenced in the reference pages at the back of this book.

time"—just being naked together—sensual touch, and energetic intimacy. It took time and lots of personal work and growth, but this man recovered from his impotency problem and found that it had actually been only the symptom of many much larger issues. Once he had cleared up these other issues, the symptom went away.

Sexual performance problems, then, can act as a symptom of problems from many different systems. If sexual performance is recognized as an indication of problems in other areas, it can be a path to tremendous healing and a catalyst for personal growth. Another choice is to ignore the deeper psychological and energetic aspects of physical sexual dysfunction. In this case, they will remain buried and continue to cause unresolved problems in many areas of one's life.

It is important to remember the premise of this book, which is that the universe in which we live is much bigger, more mysterious and more subtle than we have been led to believe by the objective/material worldview. In the awakened worldview, sexual energy is an aspect of the creative force that lies at the heart of this physical universe of opposites. In the human body, sex can bring us into communion with this creative universal energy. If we understand ourselves to be a flowing fountain of energy, balancing between the equal and opposite creative poles of the masculine and feminine then it is only natural to also understand that personal balance and removal of blockage to this flow leads to health and well-being. If we remain in the objective/material worldview and see ourselves as biological machines operating on purely classical chemical and physical laws, then it makes sense to take a pill and screw like crazy while we can.

As always, it is up to us to choose if we want to use a physical symptom as a catalyst for awakening into new ways of freeing ourselves from past restrictions, or to maintain the entrenched belief systems of the objective/material way of seeing the world.

Sex is about technique

This is another myth that is capitalized upon by media and advertising in many ways. It is rare to find at least one magazine in the checkout isle of a grocery store, for example, that doesn't have a cover headline for "50 sex techniques that will keep your man wanting more" or "Secret sex techniques to revitalize your sex life," etc.

It is true that techniques can be useful. Learning to use massage, learning how to have more control (for men) with when or if they orgasm, learning how to touch each other and communicating what you like and don't like—all these things can be helpful. It can also be very useful to learn about Taoist sexual energetic practice, sexual tantra, and the use of energy to enhance intimacy in sexual practice. However, these are also disciplines that require quite a lot of personal development, commitment, and restraint.

The point here is that while technique can be useful and helpful, it is extremely important to remember to keep the goal of sexual practice pointed at realizing and growing the intimacy of an "I, Thou" relationship with another human being. All the technique in the world is of little help if used between people who don't love each other. They may achieve great orgasms, or not, but they will miss the point of what sex is and can do, and they will put the focus on achieving a momentary pleasure rather than an ongoing development in depth and love.

The art of sex is to be able to incorporate technique and be open to learning new things, but also to understand that the techniques are not the focus, the goal, or the end point. Even orgasm is not the goal or end point; if it is, the other person becomes an object again—a means to reaching an end just like any other object in our lives. The challenge in awakened sex is to constantly recognize the divine aspect of our beloved.

Even if you believe in only the physical world, the person you are with is far more of a miracle and mystery than science can begin to explain at this point. If you choose to incorporate understandings from the Awakening, this person is also an aspect of the unlimited "Field", an aspect of "God" or "Goddess", a mystery that extends beyond this physical space and time and into many dimensions and realities. Look beyond the images and assumptions that you have about this person and look instead for the great changing mystery of this never returning moment and the dancing light that is your partner. If you can see the awesome mystery and beauty of your partner, you will also deepen your experience of the mystery and beauty within you.

Principles for better sex

Sex can be hugely complicated. It is a physical/mental/spiritual joining with another person that goes far beyond what most of us consider when we are actually engaged in the action. On the physical level, it is a biological activity, mediated by hormones and instincts, deeply engrained and embedded with an instinctual drive to procreate and carry on the human species. The psychological level incorporates all this and adds many new layers including territory, power, self-worth, self-image, past trauma, and the working out of relational issues from our parents and other important early relationships.

On the energetic level, sex is an actual merging of energetic selves where we transfer a part of our vibratory essence to another person and receive the vibratory essence of another into our own being. It is a deep merging and one that both enriches us with the beauty of another and also stirs up the depths of our shadow as unresolved issues in our partner resonate with parts of ourselves that have been locked away. When we ignore or objectify any part of ourselves or our partners, it reduces what sex can achieve while also intensifying the problems that it can stir up.

Sex has been used for millennia as a path to enlightenment because it is so connected to all of who we are and because the joining of two beings is a step in the direction of the great joining and return of all beings into the "Oneness"—that which is beyond this space and time.

It is important to remember, however, that from the Awakened viewpoint, paths are not really necessary. It is more useful to consider oneself to be already whole, already complete within the "Oneness" than it is to consider oneself as incomplete and on a journey to become better. When we act from the belief in "already OK, already complete," things around us automatically begin to reflect wholeness back to us. We perceive the reflections, our belief in wholeness is strengthened, and the positive spiral continues. This is equally true in our sex lives, and it simplifies things considerably.

Having said this, the mind generally abhors simplicity and will probably get stuck in circles of trying to "get somewhere". If this is the case, the following principles can give it something to work with while it is learning to accept the deep awareness that the path is not required.

Sex is about Relationships

First and foremost, sex is the ultimate physical expression of relationship. It, therefore, is enhanced when any relationship skill is enhanced. As you practice any and/or all the skills and insights discussed in this book—or any other source that you decide to use—you are ultimately also working on your sex life. Increase your awareness of who you are and your skillfulness in relating to others, and it will pay dividends in your bedroom as well.

Relax, release, and be alert

Physical orgasm requires a delicate balance between two aspects of the nervous system that are both directed by the unconscious mind. These two systems are the sympathetic and parasympathetic parts of what is called the autonomic nervous system. The sympathetic part is responsible for excitement, arousal, and contraction. The parasympathetic part is responsible for relaxation, release, and expansion. When these two systems are balanced, there is a very pleasurable relaxed alertness that allows the mind and body to function at high levels. It also strikes a balance between relaxation and tension that helps to build a physical, mental, and energetic charge in the body. This charge is built by carefully walking the line between release (discharge) and tension, which holds onto the charge. It is building this charge that creates the pleasurable sensations as the charge increases, reaches a climax, and then finally discharges in orgasm.

Difficulties with orgasms are often associated with the way in this charge pattern happens in individuals. Premature ejaculation, for example, happens when a person is unable to build a charge very high or to hold a charge. Generally this is a result of too much excitement and/or fear from the sympathetic response without enough relaxation from the parasympathetic side. This of course is connected to other psychological, emotional, and energetic patterns and issues that are unique to each individual. However, understanding the idea of balance between excitement/relaxation and charge/discharge can be a helpful step toward improving one's sex life, and improving many other areas of life as well[52].

Be Present

Presence is another huge topic and one that is related to all of what is written in this book and to the Awakening. Essentially, presence is the ability to be right here, right now, and to experience this moment as fully as possible. It means an absence of running away into a state of mental distraction that detracts from the here and now experience.

Distraction has a multitude of forms, most of which manifest as either being "split off" or "cut off" from experience. All of us experience both these conditions to some extent in different situations, but most people tend toward more of one than the other.

Being split off entails a psychological/energetic habit of being detached from one's body experience. It involves mentally and energetically leaving when things become challenging, too close, or too threatening. Many people live in this state more or less all the time and simply increase or decrease their degree of detachment according to how threatened they feel. Intimacy is, paradoxically, very threatening and frightening, as it requires opening into a deeper honesty and self-realization than many of us are used to. The sexual act is therefore one that can be frightening on a deep and unconscious or preconscious level, something which in turn upsets the sympathetic/ parasympathetic balance, affects the charging pattern, and affects how sex is experienced.

Splitting off is a coping pattern developed in childhood, often in reaction to traumatic situations that the child can't avoid in any other way. Meditation, yoga, massage, body/mind practices in any form, and body/ mind oriented therapies can help to soften these patterns and begin to bring a feeling of safety that encompasses a wider variety of life situations. This sense of safety can also both enhance, and be enhanced by, the practice of "I,

---

52 This is another area where an IBP (www.ibponline.com) therapist, or some other mind/ body therapist can help. Jack Rosenberg's books, especially The Intimate Couple also contain more information about this topic.

Thou" sexuality—sexual relations consisting of mutual respect, love, tenderness, and creation of safety where performance is not the principle focus.

"Cutting off" has a similar result to splitting off but happens in a different way. When one cuts off, one becomes less present by numbing out and not being able to feel emotional and physical sensations as clearly. Where split-off bodies tend to have a somewhat relaxed and possibly dreamy or "spacy" appearance, cut-off bodies tend to be muscular, tight, and rigid.

Both "split off" and "cut off" reactions are defenses against situations that were experienced as being overwhelming, frightening and/or out of control as a child. These situations caused the child to find a way to escape and leave his/her own full presence or ability to be in touch with his or her own experience in the here and now. It is difficult to live in the world without acquiring some degree of defensive loss of presence, and there are very few people who are truly and fully *present*. However, sexual intimacy is a place where presence can be learned, practiced, and expanded.

As you practice "I, Thou" respect, creating safety, removing expectation, and seeing the mystery of your partner, it will also help to expand your ability to be present. Being present will expand your ability to be safe, respectful, and loving, so you will create a circle of growth that can enhance your life and your partner's life for as long as you are together—and beyond.

Be in your wholeness

Presence is actually an aspect of wholeness, but wholeness is larger and, paradoxically, simpler. This is because wholeness is something that needs to be experienced wordlessly from the heart, not analytically from the brain. Wholeness is based largely on belief or faith, and as mentioned in the introduction to this section, belief in wholeness can be all that is required—as long as it is honest. Wholeness doesn't mean we can ignore our neuroses, faults, and unhealthy behaviours. It just opens the door to allow them to fade away as we stop putting our energy and belief into them.

Choose to believe that you are worthy. Choose to believe that you are whole. Notice your brain's confusion, rejection, and refusal to understand these ideas. You don't need to pay attention to the brain's complaints that it doesn't understand. The truth is that your heart does understand wholeness, and you are already whole—no matter who you are or what you have done or what you have or what you look like. Let your mind scream "NO! I AM NOT WHOLE. THIS IS A LIE!" if it must, but choose to ignore its sniveling. Breathe deeply. Direct your attention and your breath to your heart. Relax into the knowingness that you are already whole, complete, enough, held, and loved.

All the practices and concepts in this book are aimed at this same simple understanding: You are whole, you are OK, you are worthy, you are complete. This is something that is your natural state. Let go of you who *think* you are and who you truly are will naturally be present. In this natural state, there is no need to try to be whole, to try to be worthy, to try to be complete or loving or kind. All of this arises from who you are, if you can release everything that you believe yourself to be.

Bring your natural wholeness with you into your sexual intimacy as you touch your partner and your partner touches you. Bring your natural wholeness with you when you join your bodies with open eyes. As you choose to release your images and thoughts of both yourself and your partner, the natural spontaneity and joy of who you truly are will have more space to make the moments magical.

Energy Dance

When a couple dances together in ballroom style dance, there is a dynamic that is very sexual and a practice that can be very useful in the bedroom as well. In dance, it is usually accepted that the male partner leads and initiates and the female partner chooses and follows. In same sex couples, these roles can be switched more easily, but often same sex couples tend to have one partner who takes on the "following/choosing" role and one who takes on the "initiating/leading" role. In any case, the dance is a situation where charge is built between two opposites who fit and work together. They are equal, but different.

In the dance, the man initiates a step or a spin, and the woman follows, or not, as she chooses. The couple is able to move in unison and to flow with the music because they trust each other, they sense and read each other's bodies and movements, and they give each other consent to play a particular role at a particular time. Sexual energy builds between passionate partners precisely because they are willing to play the male/female roles that are both equal and opposite, and this builds an energetic charge that is exciting and pleasurable.

There is a depth, strength, wisdom, and power of being a woman that goes beyond my ability to describe, and it saddens me that more women do not realize the power and beauty that they own by simply being female.

In the same way, there is a deep self-assurance, gentleness, strength, and courage as well as a wildness and playfulness that is a part of being male. This is also often missed, as males become caught in the stereotypes of power, machismo, or violence.

In the energy dance of sexuality, the depths of the female principle chooses, invites, welcomes, and holds the male principle, and the male in turn enters, supports, and renews the female. We can, however, be both to each other, changing from leading to following, from receiving to giving, initiating to accepting as we feel the energy change inside. Being open to this flow and following the rise and fall of the energies as they move in our bodies becomes a beautiful, artful, and creative dance.

Sex is an energy dance where flexibility and creativity of mind, body, and spirit allow couples to explore the balance and exchange of love that flows between them. It is a giving and receiving where leadership is passed fluidly back and forth and where both partners are respectful of the power, depth, and wholeness of the masculine and feminine principles.

In the martial art of Aikido, one learns to think of energy as a dance that happens in circles. It is all about a flow of give and take and balance, happening in circles of motion around a center which is both the physical center of balance of the body and the emotional/mental/spiritual balance of alert relaxation discussed earlier. In this dance, there is not attack and defense so much as there is energy which has intention and flow. One person begins the energy and intention, it is met by the other, and in the meeting it is redirected. New balance forms, centers change their relationships to each other, and new action is initiated.

In sex, the principle of dance follows these ideas of flow and balance between partners that creates a situation of infinite creativity and variation.

Partners who are able to understand the principle of energy dance find that they do not fall into repetitiveness or boredom. Each time of togetherness is a new creation, just as each moment of togetherness is an independent and new moment.

To use this principle, partners consciously embody the wholeness of who they are, enacting the male and female aspects of the creative principle and surrendering to the dance of energy that flows from receiving to giving, initiating to accepting, and back again. This is a timeless, creative, passionate and joyful dance. Let go, and surrender to it!

Containment, commitment, and responsibility

These three principles work together and are the forces that balance the playful ecstatic release of sexuality. Awakened sex requires that each partner accept and work with his or her own emotional issues without blaming or projecting them on the other person. Containment is the use of boundaries as discussed earlier as well as the emotional tools of working with anger and strong emotions and the other tools for living skillfully.

As I have said before, awakened sex is an expression of many levels of whom and what you are, so as you learn and apply tools for skillful living, these tools begin to enhance and grow the depth of communion that you can achieve with a partner. This kind of depth requires a strong feeling of safety that can only come from the knowledge of both your own full and complete commitment and that of your partner.

The commitment that is made does not necessarily have to be one of being together forever, however. Rather, the commitment is to complete honesty with yourself and with your partner and to forgiveness and acceptance. It is a commitment to working with your own issues as they come up, communicating with honesty and not trying to change your partner. It is also a commitment to presence—the kind of presence that says "I see you, I hear you, and I appreciate you. I will face my fears. I will strive to know and live my truth. I am committed to wholeness."

At a ten day silent meditation retreat that I attended, I met a man who had also been practicing Vipassana for several years. On the eleventh day, when we could talk, we were discussing relationship. He said he found it interesting that he would begin to get frustrated with his wife and see all kinds of problems that he thought she needed to fix or change. Then *he* would go to a retreat, and when he got back, *she* would be better! This is an excellent example of the practice of containment, commitment, and responsibility because it shows how the problems that he saw in his wife were projections of his own unrest. By containing rather than blaming, and by responsibly doing his own work rather than trying to change her, he was able to get over his frustration and also make the relationship work better.

Let Go

The physical experience of orgasm is about release of control. It is an explosion of energy that runs through the body, bypassing the conscious mind and opening doors into the unconscious and spiritual spaces that lie beneath or beyond the mind. It can be a momentary escape from the ego, a relief from judgment, and a release of energetic blockages. If sufficient charge is built in the body in the act of lovemaking, and if the body/mind system is able to relax sufficiently and let go of control, the release of the charge flows through the nervous system like a surge of water purging and cleaning a network of channels. It helps to relax the body and mind, release mental tension, and purge away energetic blockages that have built up. On a physical level, it also releases hormones and endorphins that help to enhance one's ability to feel love, increase desire for pair-bonding, and produce a feeling of well-being in the body[53].

This ability to relax and let go of control in order to experience a full body orgasm was actually considered to be an indication of returning mental/physical health and a sign of a successful cure by Wilhelm Reich, a psychotherapist, researcher of sex and energy, and contemporary of Freud. His book The Function of the Orgasm[54] gives a very detailed physical and energetic description of what the orgasm is, how it works, and why it is important. Although the four hundred plus pages of this book contain very useful

---

53 Of course, these results are often decreased or eliminated altogether by previous psychological and/or physical injury or trauma. If one is not able to let go of control—and there many reasons that this may be—then much of the benefit and pleasure of orgasm is lost.

54 *The Function of The Orgasm* (New edition edition), Wilhelm Reich (1989). Also by Wilhelm Reich, *Character Analysis* (3rd edition, 1984), first published in 1933.

information, the simplest summary would be to say that orgasm assists and facilitates the physical/emotional/energetic action of letting go.

Letting go, in all ways, is a central practice of the Awakening. In awakened sexuality, letting go involves releasing oneself and one's partner from judgments, fears, grudges, past anger, disappointments, and negative feelings. It also involves opening oneself to deepening levels of vulnerability, openness, abandon, and ecstasy. This requires understanding and clearing one's own boundaries, taking charge of one's own feelings, and taking responsibility for one's own needs. When both partners are willing to do this, it is possible to build a feeling of safety in the relationship that contributes to further opening and letting go.

Release of control requires willingness and intention, and it also requires the acceptance, patience, and safety that allow us to face fears and pain that cause the need for control in the first place. In reality, there is very little we can control in life. However, in an attempt to feel safe, we try to assert our will on others and on ourselves. In sex, this can result in power struggles over when sex happens, if sex happens, and how sex happens. It can also result in dysfunction in the way that one builds, holds, or releases the charge of sexual energy in the mind/body/energy system. Need for control spawns rules, lack of spontaneity, certain "right" and "wrong" ways to do things, creation of inflexible rituals, and other practices that both restrict and constrict sexual experience.

We all have a need for control to one degree or another. Awakened sexuality provides a powerful opportunity to build safety, connection, and acceptance with another human being and to learn to relax into this safety. Each time we relax further, however, it touches deeper places and can bring out fears and insecurities that were previously hidden deep inside. Without understanding, these fears and/or uncomfortable feelings are blamed on our partner, and the need for control will increase.

If, however, we recognize that these uncomfortable feelings have been released precisely because we have entered a new degree of safety, vulnerability, and openness with our partner, we can take responsibility for the feelings, thank them for coming into the light, and let them go.

As in all other areas of life, all choices in sex come down to only one real choice. We can choose love or we can choose fear. Both are always present and available. Fear screams the loudest and is always more demanding. Fear takes us outside ourselves and throws blame at whomever it can—generally the person who is nearest and dearest to us. Fear denies, restricts, contracts and controls, and fear feels desperate, insecure, and threatened.

Love is soft and quiet and full of integrity. It is skillful enough to communicate what it wants and needs and strong enough to understand that it cannot force another to provide them. Love is comfortable and secure, confident in itself, and able to flex and change as needed. Love expands, releases, accepts, supports, and nourishes. Love lets go.

Practice letting go, and all that it entails in love and safety, intimacy and respect, integrity and freedom. It will not fail to deepen and enhance your experience of sexual fulfillment as well.

* * *

The quotations at the beginning of this chapter introduced three concepts about sex, each of which carries a message for awakening. Wilhelm Reich suggests that the pleasure of life is the same as that of the orgasm—or can be. This is a radical idea (admittedly many of Reich's ideas were radical) but one that is well worth consideration. What could it be like to experience life with the kind of ecstatic abandon and freedom that can be experienced in an orgasm? What could it be like to experience life as an affirmation of creativity, of respect, union, and communion as can be practiced and experienced in the sexual act? What if much of the restriction and fear we feel when faced with intimacy and relationship is the same restriction and fear we feel when faced with saying "YES" to life?

As we succumb to our fear, we also succumb to our restrictions and smallness. Pornography, as suggested by Jean Baudrillard, is one of the ways that sexuality is lost to a substitute that promises more and delivers less. There are many of these substitutes, both for sex and for the vibrant sense of being alive that is a possibility for each of us. These are the choices with which we are faced as we step into the Awakening. How can we learn to discern between that which is truly life-giving and that which is a deceptive substitute? How can we learn courageously to say "Yes" to intimacy with another, and intimacy with life itself, instead of substituting the dulling influences that are offered in such abundance by our culture? How can we let go and fall into the safety of communion with a loved partner or communion with the world and our own lives rather than contracting with fear into our protective defenses? How can we experience the sexual nature and ecstasy of relationship, and how can we expand that experience into larger circles in the way we experience our lives?

These are questions that each of us has to answer for ourselves, as the answers are individual and specific. It takes courage to ask them, courage to look honestly at one's life, and courage consciously to choose. As Deepak Chopra suggests in the third quotation, "Sex is a spiritual experience". In truth, it is a physical, emotional, energetic and spiritual experience, but it is in aiming at the highest principles that we can begin to have the courage to let go of who we believe ourselves to be and in doing so uncover who we truly are. Practicing sex as a spiritual experience and practicing life as a spiritual experience are one and the same thing. This is an awakened practice, one that does not deny or repress or revile the physical but one that maintains awareness of the expansiveness of our being and the potential we embody.

Awakened sex is synonymous with awakened life. Sex is an expression of life, an expression of who you are, an expression of your expansiveness as well as an expression of your defenses and repression. Sex is a symptom of life, with as many meanings and intentions behind that statement as you care to give it. How does the way you *do* sex mirror how you *do* life? This is a question that can open many doors and lead you deeply into the Awakening.

Chapter 18
Where do we go from here?

When once it is a fact that there is no movement in any direction of improving, changing, or evolving into anything different or better, then what is there is something extraordinary.

U.G. Krishnamurti[55]

The World is merely an illusion, albeit a very persistent one.

Albert Einstein

You are already enough. Everything is already enough. Be what you already are.

Luang Por Posee

We have come a long way from the opening ideas in this book proposing that the world may not be what we thought it was. We have passed through some of the history of our present worldview, examined the concept of the Field, and examined ways that science is questioning and stretching the old paradigms. We have also looked at the idea of awakening into a new way of seeing the world and how this idea can apply to such things as dealing with strong emotions, forgiveness and love. A big question, however, is—so what? So maybe this new paradigm makes a difference in how I can see the world or get along with other people, but really that's nothing incredibly

---

55 U.G. Krishnamurti has been called the "anti-guru". His works are all freely available at http://www.ugkrishnamurti.net/

new. Techniques for managing emotions, the notion that we should love each other, and the idea that forgiveness is a good plan have been around for thousands of years, and nothing's really changed because of it. How does this *Awakening* propose to make a difference? What's the point, and where does it go? How are these new ideas any better than what we had before, and why bother to change anyway?

These are very important questions. There are so many books, gurus, teachers, paths and religions, all saying that they have the way or that they know something about the meaning and *truth* of the world. It can become very discouraging, frustrating, maddening, and sometimes even frightening to try to make one's way through all this and to decide on what is *true*, looking from the inside out.

In the world governed by Newton's laws and by the old paradigm, there seems to be at least the possibility of certainty, stability, and dependability. A measuring stick, for instance, can get the same result ten thousand times when used to measure the same object. In the same way, in the old ways of practicing religion, there is dogma and tradition that offers certainty of belief. To step away from science or to allow old traditions or religions to change is to invite the fear of uncertainty.

However, we live in a time where it is nearly impossible to pretend that things will remain the same. The rate of change in our lives is hundreds of times greater than it was for our grandfathers, perhaps thousands of times greater than it was for our grandfathers' grandfathers. There is so much change, so much activity, that it is nearly impossible not to begin to feel an uneasy questioning of the things that previously made us feel safe or secure. In astronomy, the universe keeps getting bigger and stranger and our little planet shrinks accordingly. In physics, the solidity of the world around us— and even of our own bodies, has been shown to be an illusion, and the predictability of natural laws has become the mystery of quantum uncertainty. In biology and medicine, our bodies (or the bodies of animals and plants that we modify) are becoming almost as malleable as machines as we replace or regrow parts and recombine DNA. In the world around us, we see ice caps melting and storm intensities building. In governments and countries, we see economic struggles and social unrest; in families we see unprecedented numbers of single parents and people who are isolated islands, plugged into games, the internet, TV, alcohol, or drugs. All around us, there are signs of instability—signs of change, and these signs of change cause instability in religion as well as science.

Riding the waves of this instability is becoming more challenging, and as the waves grow larger and the current of change runs faster, it tugs, worries, and threatens at the threads connecting us to everything to which we cling. Governments, jobs, families, friends, institutions, religions, ideas—they are all in the current, all subject to the changing waves and uncertainty of our time. As these things and ideas to which we cling and with which we identify begin to crumble, morph, or re-invent themselves, we are forced to look at ourselves and do the same thing, and this, finally, is the reason that a new paradigm is necessary.

But what, really, is this new paradigm? How can it be understood when there is nothing solid about it. What can be believed if every truth is only a partial understanding, if every idea is simply a concept to be used and then set aside? How can we manage if there are no absolutes—anywhere?

The purpose of this book has been to point to some concepts that gently direct a skeptic's mind toward a new way of seeing the world. In many ways, it is the story of my own journey, following the path of my resistance to change and my reluctance to admit that the world is less predictable and solid than I found comfortable. It is also the story of moving from complexity toward simplicity because the old paradigm is based on the mind, and the mind delights in complexity. In order to convince a mind to change, it has to have concepts and ideas to deal with, and the complexity of thoughts is not generally satisfied with simple answers.

Now, however, if you have read this far, it is likely that your mind is more open to the possibility that the world may be different from what you believed. That's all that is needed—the willingness to accept that what you know may be wrong. From there, things become simpler. This is because in the new paradigm, there are no ideas that are important. There are no concepts that have any real meaning. There are no beliefs that are solid. The world around us is simply a projection in the Field, an illusion of life and death and suffering and joy that feels so real that we are not able to step aside from it and see the lights playing on the screen. Instead of understanding the illusion, we build up more and more complexity in our minds, thinking that we *are* our thoughts and our bodies and becoming stuck in the chattering of our brains and the angst of our emotions.

None of these things are *real* in the sense that none of them are permanent or solid. All the complexity that we see and become is nothing but a temporary playground of illusion and dreams, and the only thing that can really be done is to let go. Even this can't really be *done*. It is something that happens by itself when we forget to hold on for a moment.

Of all the words in this book, the only two words that really mean anything are *LET GO*. All of it is necessary, in its own way. For most people, it takes time to understand just how profound these words are, how necessary, and how freeing. It also takes a great deal of courage once we begin to realize the extent and depth of our attachments to the ideas, people, images, and comforts around us. To *let go* at first seems like a sacrifice, an unwanted and terrible thing, a huge and terrifying loss of identity, security, and control.

However, letting go is the real purpose of all of the exercises and ideas in this book. To forgive is to let go, to love is to release into the flow of loving energy—which is to let go, to be grateful is to let go of pride and entitlement and open to the flow of life—which is to let go, to be kind is to let go of judgment, to awaken in any way is to let go of attachment to the illusions we have created and see the truth of change around us. To heal is to let go of ideas of illness, injury, judgment, and lack. To relax is to let go, to be silent or still is to let go.

To understand this idea—to understand that there is really nothing to learn, nothing to do, nothing to fix, nothing to change about oneself in order to be at peace in the world can be amazingly freeing. It can also be terrifying when one is not ready, and this is why it is necessary to have many books, many words, and many practices. It doesn't really matter which book, which words, or which practice, but it does help to understand that ultimately there is nothing to be done. Not even letting go.

There is a story in Richard Bach's book *Illusions*[56] about a little creature that lived clinging to the rocks at the bottom of a river. This little creature watched the current flowing by and longed to let go and float with it, but all the other creatures warned that terrible things would happen if it let go. Letting go would cause it to be smashed against the rocks by the current, and how could it survive without the security of the stone to cling to? Even so, the little creature let go and, as it had been warned, was at once smashed into the rocks by the current. Soon, however, it was lifted up and floated with the stream down the river. It passed other colonies of clinging creatures and they said "look—one like us who flies and is free. A savior!"

Letting go is like this. The fear and uncertainty of releasing our hold on old beliefs, old ways of seeing the world, and old habits is too strong, so we fight to maintain the images we have made of the world. As Richard Bach says later in the same book "Fight for your limitations, and sure enough, they're yours". Most of us stay clinging to our rocks, not even seeing a possibility of any other choice. However, moving from the old paradigm to the new is really a simple decision. Do you want to fight for your limitations, or do you want to step out into an excitingly mysterious world and follow new questions to more fulfilling answers?

Expansion into the new paradigm opens doors to universes of possibilities. Literally. The possibilities are so huge that it can be very confusing and easy to feel lost—and there are no maps or absolutes to guide the way. In fact, attempting to use maps, concepts of absolute truths, or any fixed idea at all will always become a hindrance at some point along the way.

There is an old Zen saying, "If you see the Buddha on the road, kill him." This is not, of course, supposed to be taken literally and is not about killing anyone. It is, however, all about the necessity of finding your own truth inside you. Teachers are necessary and helpful. They can point the way, help you through difficult spots, and speed up the journey greatly. However, there is always a point where you will need to be able to listen to your own inner voice, trust your own inner wisdom, and follow your own path. There is always a point where you will need to leave your teachers and go your own

---

56 Bach (1977)

way—perhaps eventually to find new teachers, perhaps to find that you no longer need teachers at all.

This book is only an introduction to a journey that is so vast that it dwarfs galaxies. Who you are is so much bigger than what you can possibly imagine right now. I, who am writing this book, have been given only glimpses, and even this is enough to know that the world we believe we live in and the thoughts and ideas that we generally think of as *me* are only tiny parodies of what I really am. There are no limits...

With this in mind, I would like to leave you with a few principles that can help you if you choose to step beyond what you currently know. These principles are like the proverbial finger pointing at the moon. They help to give a direction, but they are not the direction, let alone the destination. Eventually, you will develop your own principles and guidelines for your own journey. And, eventually you will outgrow even these ideas. Sooner or later, you will outgrow the need for a journey at all.

In the meantime, however, here are a few ideas that can help to guide you as you step out beyond the territory of the known and start to investigate the vast and exciting mystery in which we exist:

i am not my thoughts and feelings

You are not your thoughts, you are not your beliefs, you are not the opinions over which you struggle and fight. You are not your desires. You are not your feelings. You are not your pain or your suffering or your joy. Do not confuse these things with your *Self*.

Do not get confused between the little *i* and the eternal essence of life of which you are a part. As you expand into the Awakening, these ideas will at first seem ludicrous, then desirable but unreachable, then possible but far away. Slowly—or in some cases quickly—your world will expand. It is possible to live in a state of expansion that is beyond your thoughts, your desires, your feelings, and your little self. Be open to this possibility.

Don't ditch your religion

If you are currently a member of a religion—any religion—moving into the new paradigm does not mean renouncing or leaving the faith that you already have. In fact, it is better to stay with your own faith, as it will give you more balance and discernment as you move forward into new ideas. Throwing the proverbial baby out with the bathwater is not necessary.

What is necessary is a willingness to stretch, expand, and loosen the beliefs you hold. Look for the essential keys of your faith, and work to let go of all the rest. Look for the ways your faith agrees with other religions and other faiths, and let go of the rest. Bit by bit, piece by piece, simplify your faith to distill its essence. Peel away the layers of your belief, constantly finding new ways to let go, new ways to expand, new ways to open to and embrace the great mystery which is the heart of all religions. Step into the mystery and open your mind to let the spirit of your belief teach you directly.

You can awaken inside your own beliefs and use your beliefs to power further awakening. Set yourself free as you let your religion help you to let go.

Don't give your power away

If you look, you will find teachers, paths, and practices everywhere. Most of these claim to be the best or the only way. Almost all of them want your money or your time or your support. Many are a sham and a fake, some can help but not very much. Some will try to take your soul even if they don't take your money.

There is no list or guide to tell you what is true for you, who you can trust, and who you would be best to stay away from. In the awakened relationship, teachers and gurus are guides but not dictators, helpers but not lords, mentors but not gods, coaches but not owners. There is a fine balance between trusting your little self to a path and a teacher or giving away your power and choice. It can be helpful to trust and to follow—but an awakened relationship is not about power. If you find a teacher who takes from you more than is given, who diminishes you, claims to be more than or better than you or who tries to take your power in any way, run! This is not someone to trust.

It is helpful to let the little self diminish, but it is not helpful to be disconnected from the source—conceptualized in this book as *The Field*. Allow teachers to help you to diminish the little self and ego, but do not let anyone come between you and your own connection with the divinity that you already are.

Relax and expand: Know that you are already all that you need to be

Fear and all negative feelings result in some form of contraction. Physically they contract muscles; mentally they contract and tighten belief systems and increase the strength of clinging and holding. Energetically, they also cause contraction, decreasing the amount of energy available, the space that your field fills, and the amount of life force that runs through your body.

The other way to react to whatever is going on is to expand into it. Expansion includes the positive emotions, especially gratitude and love. Expansion also generally involves relaxation because relaxed muscles and a relaxed mind allow for the lack of resistance that is needed to be able to expand. Expansion does not mean physically to grow bigger, but it does mean to become more relaxed and comfortable in your body, more flexible in your mind and thought systems, and more aware and free in your energy systems.

As a general principle for moving into the Awakening, it is better to relax and expand than to try, strive, push, or contract. Awakened action is very different than old paradigm action because it comes out of ease and flow rather than out of tension and force. Therefore, allow yourself to move towards greater ease, greater flexibility in mind and in body, and learn new skills so that you do not have to resort to force. This is not something you have to try to make happen or try to force yourself into. It is not something to do through will power, wanting, pushing, or striving. Simply know that you are already relaxed, already "OK", already all you want and need to be, and allow yourself to ignore and release everything else.

Breathe, This is not a crisis, I am OK, Relax, Let it go. Re-mind your mind: say these things to yourself often.

Say "Yes" to life, and then say "Thank you"

This has become a cliché to a certain extent, but it is still a useful principle to remember. *Yes* is an expansion word that invites growth, experience, change, and plenty. It is a *flow* word that allows things to come and go with ease. It is a courageous word that does not mourn what is gone but accepts what is present. *Yes* is a free word that opens doors, strikes chains, and releases bonds. Yes is an opening.

Thank you, as discussed earlier, is an essential concept in the Awakening. If *yes* is an opening, *thank you* is a gate that guards the opening. Without gratitude, the gate swings closed, and very little is allowed to pass. *Yes* opens a space for something new to happen, but without gratitude, it quickly becomes stagnant. Gratitude creates movement, opens to flow, and invites plenty.

Progress is not measured by peak experiences, only by letting go.

In the fullness of the Field, there is no need for progress because in the state of existence beyond time and duality, everything is OK as it is. However, in this universe there is generally a desire to know if we are moving ahead or getting somewhere. Many people become confused by the experience of highs that transport them into peaks of ecstasy, visions of other worlds, or special powers and abilities. These things can become quite addicting—but they are not a measure of spiritual progress. They are more like window shopping—looking through the shop windows and being excited by the wonderful wares on display. Window shopping can be fun and even educational, but once you've passed the window, you may never return. There are so many windows that a million lifetimes would not be enough to look through them all, and still in the end there would be nothing but the desire for more windows. This is an endless search.

Enlightenment, therefore, is not measured by what you experience. Rather, if it is measured by anything, it is measured by how easily you can let go of your experience. As you develop in your remembering of the flexibility, adaptability, non-judgment, and non-attachment that are your birth-right, the experience of "enlightenment" floats softly closer. We are not separate from the ecstatic blissful oneness of all that IS—but we believe ourselves to be. Peak experiences remind us of tiny pieces of the oneness and these reminders can be helpful. However, letting go releases the bonds that hold us in our delusion and opens the doors to realization that right here and right now are all we ever need.

Just stop. Return to the point of stillness: You are OK, just as you are. The world is OK, just as it is. Relax. Release. There is no need to fix anyone or anything. You are already enough. Everything is already enough. Let go.

From complexity to simplicity

There is a story in which a questioner went to the Buddha and said "I want to be happy, how can I do this". The Buddha replied "First cut out the "I" because that is ego clinging. Then cut out the "want to be" because that is greed. All that is left is "happy".

In another famous story from Buddhism (already mentioned in this book), the Buddha gave a special sermon to his most accomplished monks. His entire sermon was simply to hold up a small flower. The monks who understood were able to feel and experience the depth, beauty, and mystery of the flower and its connection to all that is. Millions of words can attempt to explain the complexity of this understanding—but it takes a mind that is ready for simplicity actually to understand and experience it.

As a principle, move toward simplicity in everything you do. Simplicity in food, simplicity in housing, simplicity in livelihood, simplicity in relationship, simplicity in living.

There is nothing for the mind to understand. Let Go. Say Thank You. You are already enough.

Look inside, follow your own questions

Finally, move toward your own inner knowing. When you follow your own connection and guidance, anyone and anything can be your teacher. Let go of answers, but look for bigger questions and follow them to simpler experience.

You are already enough. This needs to be repeated because the mind does not understand it—but you are not your mind, and you will eventually remember. You are already enough.

Live as if you understand this, and eventually you will remember that you always have.

Pointing fingers at the moon

If you are starting out as skeptical about these ideas as I was, it may take you a while to begin to feel more comfortable with them. Stay away from this end of the book for a while and just allow your mind to become comfortable with the possibility of the Field.

The principles in this book for moving into the Awakening are simply ideas, and ideas are simply pointing fingers at the moon. The finger is not the moon. The finger cannot even touch the moon. All that it can do is direct attention in a particular direction.

This is the function of all the ideas you have found here. They are simply fingers, pointing not at the moon but at the incredible potential and capacity that is inherent in this human existence.

It is my great hope that some of these pointers will speak to you and that in some way this book can help you to remember a little bit more the greatness, the mystery, the power, and the humility of who you are.

May you live gently and give kindness to yourself. May you open yourself to the adventure of not knowing and the courage of not understanding. May you walk in this world in peace and simplicity, and one moment (perhaps this one) as you are thinking of other things, may you softly fall awake into the timeless being that has always already been yours.

With love,
Todd

Bibliography

Adam. (2007). *The Path of the Dreamhealer: A Quantum World of Energy Healing*. Toronto, Ont. Canada: Penguin Books.

Bach, R. (1970). *Jonathan Livingston Seagull: a Story*. New York: MacMillan Company.

Bach, R. (1977). *Illusions*. New York: Dell Publishing Co., Inc.

Beck, D., & Cowan, C. (1996). *Spiral Dynamics: Mastering Values, Leadership and Change*. Malden, MA. USA.: Blackwell Publishing.

Braden, G. (2011). *Deep Truth*. Carlsbad, California: Hayhouse Inc.

Bradshaw, J. (1988). *Healing The Shame That Binds You*. Kansas City, KS: HCI Publications.

Brahm, A. (2005). *Who Odered this Truckload of Dung? Inspiring Stories for Welcoming Life's Difficulties*. Sommerville, MA, USA: Wisdom Publication.

Callanan, M., & Kelley, P. (1993). *Final Gifts: Understanding the Special Awareness, Needs, and Communications of the Dying*. New York: Bantom.

Chilton Pearce, J. (2002). *The Biology of Transcendence*. Rochester, Vermont. USA: Park Street Press.

Chopra, D. (1990). *Quantum Healing: Exploring the Frontiers of Mind/Body Medicine*. New York: Bantam.

Chopra, D., Ford, D., & Williamson, M. (2010). *The Shadow Effect*. New York: Harper Collins. Retrieved July 5, 2011, from http://theshadoweffect.com/

Coloroso, B. (1994). *Kids Are Worth It! : Giving Your Child The Gift Of Inner Discipline*. New York: Harper Collins.

Conze, E. (Translation). (n.d.). The Heart Sutra. Retrieved August 23, 2011, from http://kr.buddhism.org/zen/sutras/conze.htm

Dyer, W. (2007). *Change Your Thoughts—Change Your Life: Living the Wisdom of the Tao*. Carlsbad, CA: Hayhouse Inc.

Eden, D. (2008). *Energy Medicine*. Toronto, Ont.: Penguin.

Elert, G. (2009). The Physics Fact Book: An Encyclopedia of Scientific Essays. Retrieved November 13, 2010, from http://hypertextbook.com/facts/

Feinstein, D., Eden, D., & Craig, G. (2005). *The Promise of Energy Psychology: Revolutionary Tools for Dramatic Personal Change*. London, England: Penguin Books.

Fleischman, P. (1999). *Karma and Chaos*. Seattle, Wa. USA: Vipassana Research Publications.

Fremantle, F., & Trungpa, C. (1975). *The Tibetan Book of the Dead: The Great Liberation through Hearing in the Bardo*. Boulder, CO. USA: Shambhala.

Gibran, K. (1923). *The Prophet*. New York: Alfred A Knopf, Inc.

Gilbert, E. (2006). *Eat, Pray, Love*. London, England: Penguin Books.

Gilbert, R. M. (1992). *Extraordinary Relationships: A New Way of Thinking About Human Interactions*. New York: John Wiley and Sons, Inc.

Goenka, S. N. (n.d.). Vipassana Meditation. Retrieved July 7, 2011, from www.dhamma.org

Gottman, J. M. (1999). *The Seven Principles for Making Marriage Work*. New York: Random House Inc.

Haisch, B. (2006). *The God Theory*. San Francisco, CA: Weiser Books.

Hanh, T. N. (1998). *The Heart of the Buddha's Teaching: Transforming Suffering into Peace, Joy, and Liberation*. Berkeley, CA: Broadway Books.

Hanh, T. N. (2003). *Creating True Peace*. New York: Free Press.

Harper Neeld, E. (2003). *Seven Choices: Finding Daylight after Loss Shatters Your World*. Austin, TX. USA: Warner Books.

Henderson, J. (1987). *The Lover Within: Opening to Energy in Sexual Practice*. New York: Station Hill Press Inc.

Herbert, F. (1965). *Dune*. Randor, Pennsylvania: Chilton Book Company.

Households and the Environment: Energy Use. (2007).*Statistics Canada*. Retrieved July 5, 2011, from http://www.statcan.gc.ca/pub/11-526-s/2010001/t004-eng.htm

Integrative Body Psychotherapy. (2011).*IBP Online*. Retrieved February 7, 2011, from http://www.ibponline.org/

Jaksch, M. (2002). *Learn To Love: a Practical Guide to Fulfilling Relationships*. San Francisco, CA: Chronicle Books.

James, T. (n.d.). Lost Secretes of Ancient Hawaiian Huna.

Jeffrey, S. (Ed.). (2011). *Dissolving the Ego, Realizing the Self: Contemplations from the Teachings of David R. Hawkins*. Carlsbad, CA: Hayhouse Inc.

Judith, A. (1996). *Eastern Body Western Mind: Pyschology and the Chakra System as a Path to the Self*. Berkeley, CA: Celestial Arts Publishing.

Judson, O. (2002). *Dr. Tatiana's Sex Advice to All Creation: The Definitive Guide to the Evolutionary Biology of Sex*. New York: Henry Holt & Co. LLC.

Kaa, S. R., & Raa, K. (2008). *2012 Awakening: Choosing Spiritual Enlightenment over Armageddon*. Berkeley, CA: Ulysses Press.

Kabat-Zinn, J. (1990). *Full Catastrophe Living: Using the Wisdom of Your Body and Mind to Face Stress, Pain, and Illness*. New York: Bantam Dell.

Keirsey, D. (n.d.). Existence Itself: Towards the Phenomenology of Massive Dissipative/Replicative Structures. Retrieved July 25, 2012, from http://edgeoforder.org/pofdisstruct.html

Kornfield, J. (1993). *A Path With Heart: A Guide Through the Perils and Promises of Spiritual Life*. New York: Bantam Books.

Krishnamurti, J. (1964). *Think on These Things*. New York: Harper& Row.

Lama, D. (2005). *The Universe in a Single Atom*. New York: Morgan Road Books.

Lee, I. (2002). *Healing Chakra: Light to Awaken My Soul*. Las Vegas: Healing Society Inc. Retrieved from www.healingsociety.org

Lee, I. (2005). *Human Technology: A Toolkit for Authentic Living*. Sedona AZ, USA: Healing Society Inc.

Lee, I., & Jones, J. P. D. (n.d.). *In Full Bloom: A Brain Education Guide for Successful Aging*. Sedona AZ, USA: Best Life Media.

Lozoff, B. (1985). *We're All Doing Time: A Guide for Getting Free*. Durham, NC: Human Kindness Foundation.

Mcdonald, J.H. (1996) *Tao Te Ching*, by Lao Tzu - a complete online text. Retreived from: www.wright-house.com/religions/taoism/tao-te-ching.html

McTaggert, L. (2007). *The Intention Experiment*. New York: Simon and Schuster.

McTaggert, L. (2008). *The Field: The Quest for the Secret Force of the Universe*. London: Harper Collins.

Moody, R. A. J. M. D. (1975). *Life After Life*. New York: Bantam Books.

Moore, T. (1998). *The Soul of Sex: Cultivating Life as an Act of Love*. New York: Harper Collins.

Newton, M. (1994). *Journey of Souls: Case Studies of Life Between Lives*. St. Paul, MN: Llewellyn.

Newton, M. (2000). *Destiny of Souls: New Case Studies of Life Between Lives*. St. Paul, MN: Llewellyn.

Newton, M. (2004). *Life Between Lives: Hypnotherapy for Spiritual Regression*. St. Paul, MN: Llewellyn.

Newton, M. (2009). *Memories of the Afterlife: Life Between Lives Stories of Personal Transformation*. Woodbury, MN: Llewellyn Publications.

Oxford Dictionaries Online. (n.d.). Retrieved from http://oxforddictionaries.com/

Pert, C. (1997). *Molecules of Emotion: The Science of Mind-Body Medicine.* New York: Touchstone.

Prabhavananda, S., Isherwood, C., & Huxley, A. (1987). *Bhagavad Ghita: The Song of God.* Hollywood, California: Vedanta Press.

Radin, D. (1997). *The Conscious Universe: The Scientific Truth of Psychic Phenomena.* New York: Harper Collins.

Radin, D. (2006). *Entangled Minds: Extrasensory Experiences in a Quantum Reality.* New York: Pocket Books.

Roberts, G. (2003). *Shantaram.* New York: St. Martins Griffon.

Rosenberg, J., & Kitaen-Morse, B. (1996). *The Intimate Couple: Reaching New Levels of Sexual Excitement Through Body Awakening and Relationship Renewal.* Atlanta, Georgia: Turner Publishing.

Rosenberg, J., Rand, M., & Asay, D. (1989). *Body, Self, and Soul: Sustaining Integration.* Humanics Ltd.

Ruiz, D. M. (2001). *The Four Agreements: A Practical Guide to Personal Freedom (A Toltec Wisdom Book).* San Rafael, California: Amber Allen Publishing.

Silberman, S. (2009, August). Placebos Are Getting More Effective. Drugmakers Are Desperate to Know Why. *Wired.* Retrieved from http://www.wired.com/medtech/drugs/magazine/17-09/ ff_placebo_effect?currentPage=all

Solomon, R. C. (2001). *About Love: Reinventing Romance for Our Times.* Lanham, Maryland: Madison Books.

Sternberg, R. J. (1998). *Love is a Story.* New York: Oxford University Press.

Syrus, P. (1862). *The moral sayings of Publius Syrus: A Roman slave. From the Latin.* University of Michigan Library.

The Holy Bible: King James Version. (n.d.). Hendrikson Publishers.

The Princess Bride. (1987). Internet Movie Database. Retrieved February 7, 2011, from http://www.imdb.com/title/tt0093779/

Tiller, W. A. (2005). *Some Science Adventures with Real Magic*. Walnut Creek, CA: Pavior Publishing.

Tolle, E. (1999). *The Power of Now*. Vancouver BC, Canada: Namaste Publishing.

Tolle, E. (2005). *A New Earth: Awakening To Your Life's Purpose*. New York: Penguin Books.

Vipassana Meditation: As Taught By S.N. Goenka in the tradition of Sayagyi U Ba Khin. (2011). Retrieved February 7, 2011, from http://www.dhamma.org/

Vitale, J. (2007). *Zero Limits: The Secret Hawaiian System for Wealth, Health, Peace, and More*. Hoboken, New Jersey: Wiley.

Wellwood, J. (1990). *Journey of the Heart: The Path of Conscious Love*. New York: Harper Collins.

Wilber, K. (1980). *The Atman Project: A Transpersonal View of Human Development* (p. 240). Boston, MA: Shambhala.

Wilber, K. (2000). *Integral Psychology* (p. 303). Boston, MA: Shambhala.

Wilber, K. (2001). *No Boundary: Eastern and Western Approaches to Personal Growth* (p. 149). Boston, MA: Shambhala.

Wittgenstein, L. (1921). *Tractatus Logico-Philosophicus*. London: Routledge.

Yogananda, P. (1973). *Autobiography of a Yogi*. Los Angeles, Ca.: Self Realization Fellowship.

5 INFLUENCES/ENVIRONMENT - CAN BE INHERITED
    FROM PARENT
  UNIVERSE - NOT PRIMARILY ATOMS - BUT A VAST
  INFORMATION FIELD ANIMATED BY AN
  ACTION POTENTIAL CALLED ENERGY.
        POTENTIAL FOR:
                MOVEMENT
                ACTION
                COMMUNICATION

    ASIAN - "LIFE FORCE ENERGY"

6 OUT GROWING, THE OBJECTIVE/MATERIAL
    WORLD VIEW
155 FEELINGS OF CONTRACTION

P 167-168 Teach kids integrity
173 - Anger management
185 - Emotions can be compared
        to the strings of a guitar.
      A huge variation of experience
        in these emotions.

187 - Rumi (love)
189 - St Germain/violet flame
190 Archangel Michael
191 Laughing Yoga

200 Breathing
    202 Sydney Harris
216 Driving insanity of anger
225 Alcohol or drugs greatly enhance the mob
    effect
230 Simplify your life
256 Central shift - Awakening
293 Blame has no place in an Awakened
    relationship

X 303 Every instant every person's
        changing - A new person
      from the old.
X 304 The time you have with this
      person can never be
      repeated or returned.
307 Survival of the fittest ①
    Religion ②
308 INFINITE PROBABILITY